síbö́d

Buhok ka Adlaw (**Hair of the Sun**) embroidered by Rowena Caballero

MARIA CHRISTINE MUYCO

Ideology and Expressivity
in Binanog Dance,
Music, and Folkways
of the Panay Bukidnon

ATENEO DE MANILA
UNIVERSITY PRESS

ATENEO DE MANILA UNIVERSITY PRESS
Bellarmine Hall, Katipunan Avenue
Loyola Heights, Quezon City
PO Box 154, 1099 Manila, Philippines
PHONE +63(2)426-59-84 / FAX +63(2)426-59-09
EMAIL unipress@admu.edu.ph
WEBSITE www.ateneopress.org

Book design by Ali Figueroa
Cover design concept by Maria Chona Muyco-Nazareno

Embroidery on front cover:
Buhok ka Adlaw (Hair of the Sun) by Rowena Caballero
and *Ga-Binanog* (Dancing the Binanog, or Hawk-Eagle Dance)
by Conchita Gilbaliga

THE NATIONAL LIBRARY OF THE PHILIPPINES CIP DATA

Recommended entry:

    Muyco, Maria Christine.
       Síbod : ideology and expressivity in Binanog
    dance, music, and folkways of the Panay Bukidnon /
    Maria Christine Muyco. — Quezon City : Ateneo
    de Manila University Press, c2016.

       xvi, 244 pp. ; 22.86 cm.

       ISBN 978-971-550-742-4

       1. Dance — Panay, Bukidnon (Philippines).
    2. Music — Panay, Bukidnon (Philippines). 3. Panay,
    Bukidnon (Philippines) — Social life and customs.
    4. Ethnic groups — Panay, Bukidnon (Philippines).
    I. Title.

       394.3   GV1743   2016   P520150188

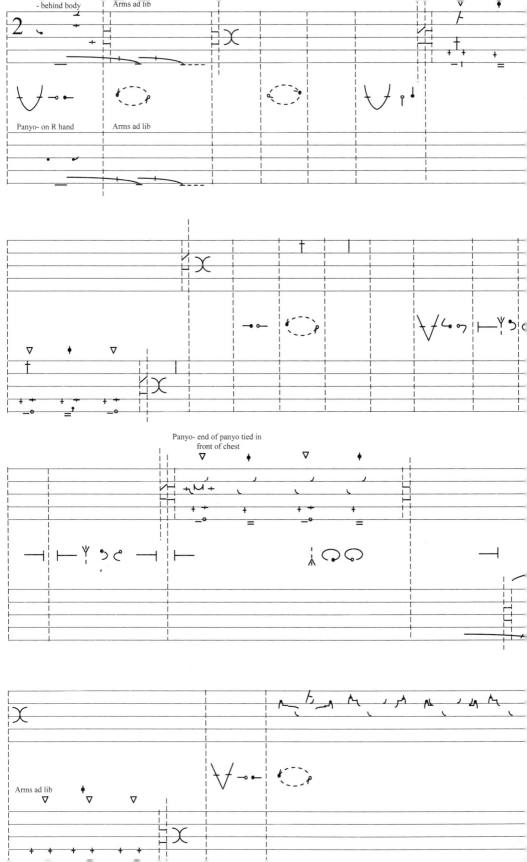

Contents

Figures

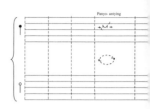

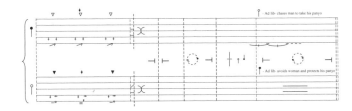

Preface

IN THE PANAY HIGHLANDS OF CENTRAL PHILIPPINES LIVE AN INDIGENOUS people called the Panay Bukidnon. Although some members live far apart from each other, the distance does not seem to matter when they gather for a *patawili,* a tradition of helping out in farm work alternated with dancing and playing musical instruments. It was at one of these get-togethers that I first heard the word *síbod* in the celebratory expression *"Ga-síbod dai-a!"* amidst music-making and dancing. The ecstatic energy among the crowd, as well as the musicians and dancers, elevated this event to a different plane of consciousness. Everyone was floating in revelry because everything was working well!

After the denouement of this excitement, I had the chance to reflect on what I witnessed and experienced. I was already in the second year of my research, yet I felt that I had not fully grasped the essence of binanog. With this experience, I was motivated to extend my explorations from the structural aspects of their music and dance to the wider gamut of their cultural life and its underpinnings. Uttered with much gusto, the word síbod posed a challenge of understanding a local knowledge deeper than the goal of performance.

This moment of transcendence also made me shift my focus from Western-oriented perspectives to that of the natives, in order to realize the specific context of what I was experiencing. This did not undermine my background knowledge of the Western perspectives, as this shift equipped me later in broadening my ontological dialogue between local and Western perspectives.

My exploration of síbod primarily extends a body of scholarship that deals with the Panay Bukidnon life, land, and culture. For instance, Felipe Landa Jocano (1968) writes about their social organization, kinship, culture, and demography in his book *Sulod Society: A Study in the Kinship System and Social Organization of a Mountain People of Central Panay.*[1] He also explored their epic-chants, particularly *Labaw Donggon* (1984). In line with the same interest, anthropologist Alicia Magos devoted long periods of time to research on Panay's epics and culture. Of late, she has recorded ten epics and had these translated from the chanter's language (*Binukidnon* or archaic Visayan) to

Kinaray-a, to *Hiligaynon*, to *Tagalog*, and then to *English*.[2] A summary and analysis of these epics appear in her article "The sugidanon of Central Panay" (1995). She also looked into their boat-building tradition (1999) and the cultural phenomenon of their kept maidens, called *binukot* (1995).

The focus on *binanog*[3] as a dance tradition of the Panay Bukidnon came later. Cecilia Suarez and Lourdes Famucol provided descriptive accounts of the binanog as a cultural form. Their collaborative report was essayed in the "Panay Bukidnon binanog dance: Tradition & transformation" (unpublished, written 2003).[4] Physical education professor at the University of the Philippines Heidi Tolentino (2005) writes about the transformation of binanog dance among Central Panay's highland people. In particular, she discussed the Panay Bukidnon's declining practice of the binanog, among other related expressive traditions. Change or transformation, as she said, is inevitable, but advocates of "indigeneity" (mountain folks or lowlanders) should teach the young ones the original music and dance (11).

From studies about the binanog as a descriptive form, I build on this cultural expression to dig deeper into the people's thought process and fathom their motivation in music-playing or dancing. Thus, I introduce síbod as a significant Panay Bukidnon ideology constituted in the structural and practice-oriented correlates of their bodily expressions. I found some of its correlates in several interesting studies: Kaeppler (1993) employs ethnoscientific structuralism to understand the dance of the Tongan, a Polynesian people, and its relationship to society in terms of "homology," that is, ". . . seeing consistencies between the related factors and the underlying structures that they express" (98); Mirano (1989) explicates the concept of *laro* (play) from her study about the *subli*, a traditional music-dance form practiced in Bauan, Batangas (Southwestern Luzon, Philippines) where "play" equals "pray" in the intertwined expressivity of song, music, dance, and praise. On the other hand, de Leon, Jr. (1990) relates to the synchronization of music and dance, as man has physical, psychic, sensuous, emotional, mental, spiritual levels whose ". . . survival and sense of fulfillment depends on the successful integration of these levels" (319).

Síbod is an experience of flow, which translates as *tayuyon* among the Panay Bukidnon, a state of having achieved mastery in different levels of structural and creative interplays. With a successful síbod in binanog, people gain another level of heightened experience in music and dance expression. This motivates people to bring in broader pursuits, such as communality, into their individual values. I see this related to *loob* (inner self) that Ileto (1989) explores in the poetics and performance of *pasyon,* a Filipino song genre. This expressivity is a driving force behind a political ideology that Filipinos employed for conducting revolution against their colonizers during the late 1880s to the mid-1990s. Though I do not exactly deal with revolts (or the present-day insurgencies), I discuss the mechanics by which síbod becomes a tool for managing socio-political relationships with and against forces that influence the Panay Bukidnon way of life.

The primary objective of this book is to contribute the ideology of síbod to the conversations of and about music and dance, and to the wider terrains of cultural studies. As one of its contexts is the binanog practice, this ideology becomes a driving force toward performance and excellence. Second, as the Panay Bukidnons' sense of self and worldview are altered by migration, communication, transportation, and exchange of people and goods—it is vital to comprehend their construction of principles behind playing music and dancing as well as developing the means to analyze how such principles reflect their practical dealings with each other in their community and with various external organizational bodies. In the years to come, it will be interesting to see how the balance between local and global exchanges is maintained with such occurrences. I see the work I have done in immersive research where fundamental values that drive expressive performance, and advocacy, are relevant as templates for broader actions involving indigenous peoples. These actions should always be grounded on the people's elemental ways and guided by their indigenous knowledge.

I consider my use of mixed methodologies and references from local and Western scholarship as a beneficial offspring of my exposures to multidisciplinary fields. My undergraduate and master's degrees were in Music Composition, but I took a Ph.D. in Philippine Studies with concentration in Anthropology, Ethnomusicology, Art and Dance Studies. Between my coursework in Philippine Studies, I received an Alternate Study Grant (also called the Sandwich Grant) from the University of the Philippines to study ethnomusicology and dance theories for a year at the University of California, Los Angeles (UCLA). These experiences were helpful as I weaved in my analysis of music, dance, and other culturally integrated forms in binanog.

To represent sound and motion, I employ the "Conceptual transcription, a graphic-acoustic definition . . ." (Ellingson 1992, 111) that draws its understanding from a local worldview, experiential learning, and exemplifying musical expressions, instead of just starting to discover the embodiments of cultural expressions. This is not singly a prescriptive or a descriptive form of transcription, because it locates itself in larger aspects of sound-making. With dance representations, I include linguistic guides, line drawings, numerical footwork, descriptions, and space illustrations related to síbod. In the Appendix of this book, I present the Benesh Movement Notation;[5] Yvonne Torres, a choreographer and dance transcriber, took the task of writing the binanog movements' intricacies via the Benesh notation. I am aware that this is a Western method that was originally used to record ballet movements; however, I thought this may give the formalist or dance academicians the details they need for whatever purpose its symbols and intricacies may serve. In another dance transcription, I utilize line drawings to illustrate the Panay Bukidnon dancers' use of space as well as options for direction based on my observations of them and my experience of the dance.

The copyright of this book is not exclusive to me as the author. I share this with the Panay Bukidnon community as represented by Lucia Caballero, an important figure in my study of the binanog music-dance tradition. All proceeds from the yearly royalty will go to the community trust fund, which primarily will support the maintenance of their School of Living Tradition (SLT) found in different parts of the Panay highlands. Whatever is extra from the funds will be channeled to their workshop activities to continue teaching their young ones about their expressive traditions.

I am indebted to the Panay Bukidnon community for unselfishly helping me fill in the gaps of ethnographic research in the Visayan highlands; to the University of the Philippines professors Elena Mirano (my research advisor), Alicia Magos, Prospero Covar, Zeus Salazar, believers of the "emic" perspectives; and to Steve Villaruz, the dance visionary. I also express gratitude to University of California, Los Angeles (UCLA) professors Jacqueline Djedje, Anthony Seeger (my research supervisor), and Susan Foster, a true scholar of the body in the mind; to professional and personal guide Demetrius Levi; to my family, and beyond all thanks, to the good Lord.

Síbod

Ga-Binanog
(Dancing the Binanog, or Hawk-Eagle Dance)
embroidered by Conchita Gilbaliga

CHAPTER 1

Encountering *Síbod*

LILY MENDOZA'S *BETWEEN THE HOMELAND AND THE DIASPORA: THE POLITICS of Theorizing Filipino and Filipino American Identities* (2002) focuses on Filipino ideologies. Her discourse mentions Nida and Taber's "dynamic equivalence" (1969), which attends to the specificities of context and analysis regarding the ways that similar cultural signs might be signifying and functioning differently in various contexts and usages. Using storytelling as one of Mendoza's approaches to narrativizing/conceptualizing, she involves herself with the translating experience of her research participants and, in the process of translating, notes how she is transformed by this experience as well. Similarly, I use a narrative method for building context to better understand a local ideology, and to establish a more consistent culturally grounded mode of communicating an idea, known to Panay Bukidnons as *sugid* (to tell). This is an act of explaining an event, commonly done through ordinary conversations or through traditional expressions such as epic chanting, ritual oral text, singing, myth telling, and other narratives.

Sugid, as an oral tradition, is a practical device in knowledge transmission. Writing is not a common practice for the Panay Bukidnons. Instead, they draw from their experiences and insights to explain seemingly incomprehensible matters. Sugid is a form of contextualization related to Nketia's view (1990, 75) as "a descriptive tool or background narrative used to search for relationships in culture." What the Panay Bukidnons would reveal via their sugid comprises their local knowledge (Enriquez 1990). Trimillos (1972, 17) refers to this as an "indigenous bias . . . a point of departure for social and musical analysis." It is interesting to note that sugid is the root word of *sugidanon*, the Panay Bukidnons' term for epic-chanting and the chant itself. The *binanog* (hawk-eagle music and dance tradition) is part of the many events in the sugidanon.

The Panay Bukidnons voluntarily *badbad* (explain) after a sugid when they sense that their listeners do not clearly fathom the meanings inscribed in their narratives. Badbad brings out the details that are relevant in the under-standing of poetic language, or metaphors embedded in oral lore. Badbad uses beautiful imagery in the same way that entangled pieces of thread are delicately drawn out and coherently woven together one by one. Untangling each piece makes the cluster of threads clearer, revealing each strand's smooth flow, making it useful once again for one's handiwork. Understanding this metaphor is relevant in translating the deep idioms of their vocal and body expressions into comprehensible threads of meaning.

Thus, sugid is not simply to narrate; it involves metaphorical and value-laden spoken text that may require a local worldview to clarify its meanings. Reynaldo Alejandro (1985) writes about the use of bird imagery in dances, providing the example of the binanog danced by the Manobo tribe in Agu-san Province. The dance imitates a bird's movements and is traditionally performed during the full moon. One dancer portrays the hawk as it swoops down on a village, while another dancer protects the people and chases the hawk away. The chase leads to the bird's death. This literature brings to mind a Panay Bukidnon myth that this book will analyze in relation to binanog as practiced in Panay and the people's communal values. The use of myth is also relevant in Manolete Mora's article (1987), "The Sounding Pantheon of Nature: T'boli Instrumental Music in the Making of an Ancestral Symbol." He exam-ines and interprets the making of the Boi Henwu's[1] symbol within the context of the Lake Sebu creation myth as a way to understand T'Boli music.

The Panay Bukidnon's myth about the banog (hawk-eagle) came to me one night after supper in my host's house. I asked Concepcion "Miningkol" Diaz about the binanog and how it was related to the patawili (gathering). I expected a direct explanation, but was instead given a whole night of story-telling, accompanied by much drinking of tubá (coconut wine), wherein my host relayed the tale interspersed with sips of wine. She also supplemented her sugid with demonstrations of her prolific dancing skill, joined by gong and drum music.

This story became our postdinner and presleeping activity that eventually led to discussions about the banog's commanding power, the animal world in the Panay Bukidnons's perspectives, and interrelationships that exist among the involved creatures. This also spurred everyone to dance the binanog the night that this tale was told:

FIGURE 1. The *banog* as illustrated by Menchie Diaz.

Sang tyempu nga nagpatawili ang banog, pinama-ug nya ang tanan nga kasapatan. Karon, kay iban nga kasapatan nag-buluntaryu, nagpagma-ug ang balabaw; tapos ku-un ya sa kasapatan kung padulhugun nila urang, di kaagi sa mataas nga bukid.

When the hawk-eagle called for a patawili, it called for all the animals. So when different animals volunteered to accept the invitation, so did the rat; then the hawk-eagle told the animals that if they bring the prawn to the gathering, the prawn could not pass through the highland or mountain.

Ti naghambal ya banog sa balabaw. Kuon ya balabaw na sya ang magpana-ug ka bala-i nyang urangun. Ti, tana nagpanaw nang amu dang adlaw; ma-abut tanan nga kasapatan hay, masaut ya banog, kay magpatawili. Ti, nag-isturyahanay ya balabaw kag urang, "Diya kita ya maagi para sa tawili, sa saut." Naghambal ya balabaw nga, "Ti para madali kita ka-abut to, manglaktud lang kita sa bakulud. Masaylu kita sa pihak kay dya man lang sa pihak ang Patawili." Ku-un ni urang, "Indi ko kasarang kay mataas." Ti mana ya balabaw, "Marapit man lang, maharun man diya na lang kita agi. "Ah," ti mana ni orang, "Ambot sa imo, basta pagustu kung diin timo maagi."

And so the hawk-eagle talked to the rat. The rat volunteered to help the prawn depart from its home, as the prawn was the rat's mother-in-law. And so that day, the rat left. All the animals arrived and the hawk-eagle danced, since it was the one who called for the gathering. And so, the rat and the prawn conversed with each other, "Let us pass here (pointing to the direction) going to the gathering, the dance show." The rat said, "Well, to hasten our arrival there, we'll take a shortcut on the hill. Let us move to the other side (of the mountain) as that side is where the gathering is." The prawn replied, "I won't be able to go that high. "Well," said the rat, "it is just near and it's shady, let's just go pass that place." "Ah," said the prawn, "it's up to you, you freely decide where to go."

Ti, panglaktud ya urang sa bakulud. Wala ya gin-suba sa sapa, gin bilin ya ka banog nga ginsuba, wara ya tana gin-suba ti amu naglaktud ya urang, ti kalulu-uy lang urang kay di tana kasarang kay mainit dun, nagpulula ya panit nya, napatay.

So the prawn took a shorter way through the hill. The rat did not allow the prawn to pass through the river contrary to the instruction of the hawk-eagle. The prawn instead took a shorter way. Poor prawn because as it could not take the heat, its skin turned red/burnt and so it died.

*Ti karun, nagtingala ya banog nga wara ya ka tambung
ang urang; nagbalibad ya balabaw nga basi may
kasablagan siguru.*

And so the hawk-eagle wondered why the prawn was
not able to attend; the rat reasoned, perhaps there was
a problem.

*Ti, nag-umpisa ya kunu ukasyun, dasun nagsa-ut ya
kunu banog. Nagtiririk gid ya kunu banog nagpalakpak
ya kunu pakpak kag naghuni na nalipay gid nga nag-
saut. Ti, sa subra ya kuno tara-taririk, nagasarurut
ya kunu banog nga paibabaw. Man, nagkadlaw ya
balabaw. Ti, anu tu pagkadlaw niya, nakita ya banog
sunguk ka orang sa ba-ba nya.*

Thus, the occasion started and the hawk-eagle danced.
It circled around, its wings clapped and it chirped,
as it was happy to dance. So with its overt whirling
around, it was able to hastily flee upwards. And so the
rat laughed. But as it laughed, the hawk-eagle saw the
antennae of the prawn inside its mouth.

*"Gin-aku a mu ya gali ang urang a mu tu wara ka-
abut! Para leksyun mu, para itumbas sa imung sala sa
pagkaun mu kay urang, patyun ka man naman kag
saraga-un sa kasapatan para matandaan na i-adi sila
sanda pwidi ka himu day-a, nga ga-liib sila parihu
nga sapat. Ti, a mu ti nga ginpa-ihaw ka banog ang
balabaw."*

You ate the prawn. That's why the prawn was not
able to get here! For you to learn your lesson, to
admonish your sin of eating the prawn, I would kill you
and distribute your body parts among animals as a
reminder that they should not do such a thing, as they
are all the same animals. So, the hawk-eagle ordered
the rat to be roasted.

Ti, nagbuluntaryu naman ang bukaw nga isaga naman kalawasun ka balabaw, ka gin pamartida kada isa. Ti mana ka bukaw, aku lang ya madul-ung ka saga sa sari-sari nga kasapatan: may amu`, may babuy sa talunun, may usa . . .

This time the owl volunteered to roast the body parts of the rat and apportioned these among animals. The owl said, "I would be the one to bring the shares to different animals: to the monkey, the pig in the wild, the deer . . .

A, wara man man gindala ka bukaw sa tanan. Ginlupad tayug-tayug sa mataas nga kahuy ka Lawa-an kay tuya dun tana gintuktukan. Tapus, naghambal ya banog nga "Wara man sa gihapun gintuman atu." Kag ginsugu nya ang ikaduha (nga sapat). Nagsumpa ya banog nga: "Ikaw bukaw, makita ta lang ikaw, saga-un ta man ikaw kag ipamartida ang lawas kag aku mismu matuktuk ka ulu, traidur ka, bilug ka mata, butlug 'ka!"

Ah, the owl did not distribute the apportioned food to all the animals. It flew up, up to the heights of the *lawa-an* tree and there, it pecked on the food. Thereafter, the hawk-eagle spoke: "The instruction was still not followed." It commanded another animal to take its orders. The hawk-eagle cursed the owl: "You owl, only if I would see you, I would also put you into fire and divide your body; I myself would be the one to peck on your head, you traitor, you round-eyed, bulge-eyed owl!"

Ti, amu kasaysayan ya ka bukaw nga-a sa gab-i sya ga gwa, kay hadluk sya sa banog.

So, that is the story of the owl—why it only comes out at nighttime; this is so because it is afraid of the hawk-eagle.

Our narrator, Miningkol, gave a badbad of the story. She explained that the banog's flight refers to its dance. When the animals gathered in a patawili, the banog positioned itself in the center of the group and showed various abilities. It flew with grace—the action plus the manner of the act is perceived as dance. There is also an expression of music when the banog's wings clapped and its mouth chirped.

Miningkol's badbad portrays the banog's creative abilities as markers of its potency and power. There is not only a centripetal direction involved where everyone is directed towards a center as occupied by the banog; there is also centrifugality as the banog distributes responsibilities to its fellow creatures. Both of these directions level the playing field of those in the patawili. The banog occupies an equal space with other animals of their community as it joined the gathering and motivated the sharing of food in order to reinforce a sense of community.

The social relationship of animals is parallel with the system of interactions in the Panay society. In the actual practice of patawili, people get together and bring family members to help someone plant or harvest crops. This social system encapsulates volunteerism or having one's will to decide on participation. The factor of social exchange also encourages one's presence and service in a patawili.

In 2004, I witnessed a patawili in Barangay Badas (Tapaz, Capiz). A couple sought help for a *kaingin* (slash and burn) to prepare their land for planting. People came and worked. The couple served food at noontime. During this break, people played their own drums and gongs. Upon hearing the initial rhythm played, some people stood and danced while others clapped or excitedly voiced out rhythmic vocables. Because of the excitement brought about by sharing food, music, dance, and other activities, there was no sign of fatigue from doing the farmwork. Everyone enjoyed this bonding activity.

Sharing is underscored in the story as something done or distributed in equal terms. Because the desired equanimity was not followed by the *balabaw* (rat) and the *bukaw* (owl) in the story, the banog had to punish them. The violation of its orders to bring particular members into the gathering also disrupted the full attendance of some animals. This dismayed the banog. The celebration of dance and music-making does not come to a full circle with members absent.

There are multiple layers of meanings in the story that reflect the binanog. On the surface, it seems that the binanog is only about acting like the banog, as the term suggests: the infix *na* (to act) between the syllables: *ba* and *nog* in binanog. Going deeper, one realizes the patawili's presence in the dance as other types of birds and creatures are associated in the banog's dance steps. The gathering of people when this dance is initiated, and their vocalizations that heighten the excitement of the dance and music-making, bring about collectivity and cooperative participation that are reflective of the patawili story.

The Panay Bukidnon elders noted that they have many ways of approaching this dance: the more birds a dancer portrays, the richer the dancers' style and mastery. Suping Gilbaliga, a respected elder and binanog dancer in Barangay Nayawan (Tapaz, Capiz), mentioned the *punay* (pompadour green pigeon), *uwak* (large-billed crow), *tikling* (barred rail), *bukaw* (Philippine owl), *balud* (spotted imperial pigeon), *kabog* (Philippine giant fruit bat), and other winged creatures in binanog.[2] Dance movements such as the *simbalud* take after the balud. *Sim*, simbalud's prefix, means *like*. There is also the *pinunay* (like a dove). The infix *in* refers to motions similar to a punay's.

Thus, the binanog incorporates multiple associations with other types of birds (see Appendix 5). These notions of similitudes with other birds belie a more complicated way of understanding the word and idea of the binanog. Here, the infix *in* is closer to *about* rather than *like* the banog. The binanog is a mimetic act. On another level it is a form of idealization that embodies the banog's commitment toward communality as it represents the balud, tikling, punay, and other birds in its movements. This communality of birds and other animals, in a larger sense, encapsulates the whole essence of the binanog that celebrates the presence of everyone in a patawili. Thus, I regard the banog in the story and as projected in the binanog, as a Bird of birds.[3] It is above every one of its kind, and yet, part of its kind. Its supremacy lies in embracing the qualities of other birds and animals.

The banog's story does not end here. Next, I will discuss the binanog and the people's imaging of the banog in connection to the story told. This discussion will cite some metaphorical or poetic forms of justification for the interruption of the music and dance that will clarify some communal issues, including the rendering of an effective performance. This narrative will interkinetically link birds and people in a local ideology that is related to music-making and dancing.

GA SÍBOD DAI-A!

The community of Panay Bukidnons nestles in various parts of the Panay Highlands in Western Visayas, one of the Philippines' major archipelagoes.

FIGURE 2. Panay Island in the Philippines.

It occupies the center of the country, sandwiched between the Luzon and Mindanao archipelagoes. Panay's lowland areas are famed as the home of the Spanish-influenced *zarzuela* (musical theatre), Ilonggo folk songs and dances, active *rondalla* ensembles (plucked/strummed string instruments), and various 20th and 21st century festivals conceived of and sponsored by government tourism agencies. There is the *Tultugan* (features bamboo-based music; bamboo as socio-economic tool) in Maasin, Iloilo; the *Ati-Atihan* in Kalibo,

Aklan and *Dinagyang* in Iloilo City—both events that embody and appropriate from the Panay Island's *Ati*, dark-skinned natives who embraced the Catholic faith and venerate the *Santo Niño* (the child Jesus); and the Binanog Festival in Lambunao, Iloilo. The latter differs from the binanog at the heart of my research. Even as its name and basic movements have been co-opted by festival organizers, the actual dancing is an amalgam created by dancers and choreographers who come from different parts of the region. Some Panay Bukidnons conduct workshops in preparation for this festival, yet the actual dancing during the festival is a form of competition and public display (i.e., street dancing), divorced from the ritual meanings that natives place at the center of their dance practice.

FIGURE 3. The Panay highland.

During my immersion in the Panay Bukidnon community in 2001, I moved from one *barangay*[4] (village) to another. A group of barangays is organized into municipalities. Examples are Calinog and Lambunao in the province of Iloilo and Tapaz in Capiz. Before reaching the boundary of Capiz, I went through Calinog, which is Iloilo's last municipality going north; from there I head deeper into the highlands.[5] Mountain ranges occupy Panay's western-

most portion, while its central and northern areas have gentle sloping reliefs;
flat lands, or plains, are found on its eastern and southern parts.

Including mountains, hills, irrigable ricelands, and water peripheries,
Tapaz' total land area is 511.4 square kilometers, with a population of 44,085
distributed among the fifty-eight barangays.

As I travelled, I witnessed rituals, festivities, and other communal gatherings in these areas. At times, I would stay in one barangay for three weeks,
then move to another barangay for almost a month. I would return to the
first place when there would be another ritual. Another reason for my mobility was the insurgency problem in some of these areas. As I was avoiding
encounters between military and communist insurgents, it was necessary that
I moved now and then to safer areas as advised by barangay leaders. As the
people considered all these barangays as a single Panay Bukidnon community,
I lived in this community for a year.

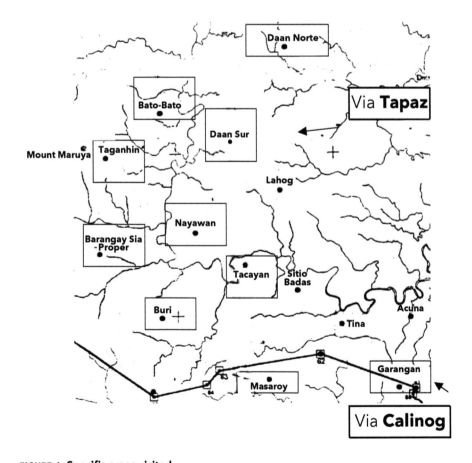

FIGURE 4. Specific areas visited.

When I stayed in Barangay Tacayan (Tapaz, Capiz), people gathered even though their houses were distant from each other. As word about me spread like fire, they curiously came to the house I was lodged in. Some were shy and walked past me, but some introduced themselves directly. When they all warmed up to my presence, they started to invite each other to play the *agung* (bossed gong) and *tambur* (cylindrical drum). With music filling the air, some feet started to tap the rhythm. My hospitable host, Mr. Rodolfo Diaz, told me that they were starting the binanog. Eventually, a pair of dancers glided their way to the center of the receiving room and danced.

The people gathered around the dancers. I was amazed to observe that they did not spectate passively, but rather, had become ambient formators who helped build excitement in the moment's atmosphere. Some of them took pieces of wood and tapped them on the floor, some enjoined the music by contributing vocables blending with the gong and drum rhythm, and others clapped and commented aloud about the dancers. Though everything in this spectacle of robust gong-and-drum playing, dancing, and crowd chanting seemed to work, a dancer cried, "*Wara dai-a ga-síbod!*" She looked straight at the musicians, indignant and disappointed. The gong and drum players exchanged words and tried to beat the music's rhythm again, but the dancer sat down. Those spoken words—Wara dai-a ga-síbod—meant the activity was not in síbod. The people suggested another player to replace the one who seemed to be causing the problem. The dancer still did not want to resume her dance any longer.

This activity's abrupt termination had me confused, so I inquired about the outcry. I was told it meant, "The music does not synchronize!" This points out that the music did not cohere with the dancer's dance. Upon further inquiry, I discovered this word had more meanings than that stated by the dancer. Strongly expressed, there were emotional and personal associations connected to the statement aside from its ideational value. The stoppage in the flow of music-making and dancing due to síbod's absence brought some questions to my mind. Why did failed síbod cause an individual to feel lost? Why was motion disrupted by the utterance?

The next day, the Panay Bukidnons went back to their daily chores, gathering again in the afternoon to resume the binanog. This time, the activity was continuous, with a buildup of excitement. I heard an ecstatic comment from the crowd: "*Ga-síbod dai-a!*" (Síbod is working!). It publicly approved a perceived perfect situation when different aspects in the binanog worked well. The dancers were vibrant as their bodies moved to the rhythmic beats continuously played by the musicians. All the musical instruments resonated and blended with each other. Word of the crowd's announced admiration spread. Passersby who saw the energetic crowd consequently brought in more people from the community's other areas to come and join in the cheering for the perfect moment.

The phrases "Wara man dai a ga-síbod" and "Ga-síbod dai-a" were punctuations that significantly put the binanog participants on the spot. It undeniably did the same to me. These phrases marked a contrast to or an intervention into the prevailing drone of sound and motion all going on at the same time—the drone of the performers, the crowd, and in a relative sense, mine. During those instances, I felt submerged in the habits and patterns of my work; in a way, the humdrum of those habits was my inner drone. The absence and presence of something articulated as síbod motivated a defining of the moment. This brought my focus to the deeper context of the binanog practice. In this state of interruption, and later, from the ecstatic continuation of the patawili and the people's daily life, I was led to find síbod as core to the various interlinks within and around the binanog phenomenon.

CHAPTER 2
The Ideologue: Panay Bukidnons

FILIPINO ANTHROPOLOGIST PROSPERO COVAR (1993) SUGGESTS THAT FOR ONE to study and fully understand Philippine culture, one should

> tangkaing isalarawan ayon sa konteksto ng kultura . . .
> ang mapapala ay pag-uugnay ng mga pangyayaring
> nagtatalaban sa isang larangan–ang pagkataong
> Pilipino at ang mga salik nito.

> try to describe the context of a culture . . . so as to
> discover the relationships of contesting events in one
> field–the human qualities or "personhood" of the
> Filipino and their sources.

Síbod is articulated and contextualized through the *binanog,* and with it, the understanding of conflicting or harmonizing elements in a single area that encapsulates the *pagkatawo,* or *pagkatao* (personhood), of the people and their sources. Sources refer to one's history, influences, and ongoing experiences, such as those within one's community and identity. Personhood is related to the concept of communal self, which Covar (1995, 19) explains in this context: "A hundred years later, a new set of values will be necessary in our quest, not for *kalayaan* (freedom) any longer, but *kasarinlan* (communal self)." The self in the communal self is the community deeply valuing itself, having a strong cultural base from which to evaluate any form of action related to communal good and interest. Kondo (1990) digs deeper into the epistemology of the self, connecting it to ethics: the value of action in work and the consequence of such action on the refinement of the self in heart and spirit. A specific example of this value is, "If you polish the floor, your heart too will shine."

The equation between act and effect is further resounded in Kondo's words: "Physical action can in fact be perceived as isomorphic with spiritual change."

The binanog performers' intense verbalization (as noted in the previous chapter) posed questions about the Panay Bukidnons, the ideals that they hold, and the significance of such ideals. Reading through the Panay Bukidnons' reactions, their observation of sound and actions, and why they made verbal interjections in the performance, showed that I was observing a critical and thinking people who evaluated their practices.

In this chapter, I provide background information about the Panay Bukidnons in order to provide various perspectives about them as a people emerging from an interesting past, as they continually carve out a sense of self amid flux and salient influences. In the process, their ingenuity in (re)forming tools for an ideology and expression that will assist them in the practical pursuit of sustaining life in the community will be discussed.

Felipe Landa Jocano's 1968 book, *Sulod Society: A Study of the Kinship System of the Mountain Peoples of Central Panay*, vividly portrays the group. Jocano refers to the people as Sulod (people of the interior parts of the mountain). I finally met them personally in the year 2000 through dance choreographer Nila Gonzalez of Iloilo City. She commissioned me to compose music for the musical-dance production Alayaw, a Panay Bukidnon epic. Anthropologist Alicia Magos, then director of the Center for Western Visayan Studies within the University of the Philippines Visayas (UPV), has documented this epic. My acquaintance with Gonzalez and Magos eventually connected me to my research participants based in the Panay highlands.

The group name, Panay Bukidnon, is widely employed, particularly by Panay-based writers who constantly communicate with their community members. Magos initiated the change of the term, from Sulod to Panay Bukidnon, after a series of field interviews and research efforts with the people. I also attended community gatherings or barangay meetings in my research areas, in Calinog and Tapaz, as well as in their town municipalities. In one of these meetings, the people voiced out that they preferred to be called Panay Bukidnon.

GENE MIX AND TRAITS

Before the coming of the Malays, the early Panay settlers were the Aetas, an ethnic group short in height, darker skinned, and kinky haired compared to the present Malay-looking Panay Bukidnons (Lago 1968, Unpublished Manuscript).

FIGURE 5. Panay Bukidnons during a parade in the Panay Bukidnon Arts Festival in May 2012. Tina Jimenez-Castor and Gaudencio Gilbaliga hold the banner.

At present, most of the locals have a brown complexion similar to the Malayo-Polynesians. There are also a few who may have descended from the *Siyaw* (Spanish colonizers); these fair-skinned descendants are *mestiza/mestizo*.[1] Their skin complexion has become a beauty determinant among Panay Bukidnons.

A family's chosen daughter would be *bukot* (kept in a room) for years, shielded from sunlight in order to have fairer skin. Thus, she would be called a *binukot* (hidden maiden). To keep her skin soft, she would refrain from hard labor such as farm work. Her feet would barely touch ground, and she would be carried on someone's back when moving out of doors. Her tasks included learning cultural knowledge such as epic-chanting, dancing, playing of musical instruments, making musical instruments, and mastering embroidery, among other such activities. Today, it is rare to have a binukot in the family. Nowadays, female children assert their will to go to school instead of staying home and waiting to be married off for a good bride-gift.[2]

FIGURE 6. Modina Diaz-Damas, or *Balanak* (white fish), was a *binukot* during her early years.

There are traces of Bornean influences mentioned in the Panay Bukidnons' *sugidanon,* such as addressing men of power as *datu,* which is also typical among Muslim groups in Mindanao, a group of islands found in the southern Philippines. Robert Fox correlates similarities between the people of Borneo and Mindanao: "There is on Mindanao a strong Bornean alignment of specific traits" (Maceda on Fox 1963). The cited example of such similarities between Mindanao and Borneo also appears in Panay Bukidnon practices to this day: ". . . drinking wine from jars with reed straws, the concept of multiple soul . . . blood placed in a post-hole during the building of a dwelling" (ibid., 29). *Sibulan* (jar), *agung,* and other items of material culture reached the Panay highlands through trade with Borneo.

In earlier times, Panay Bukidnons were referred to as *Mundos* (Burrows 1905, 460), people involved in both insurrection and religious heresy. Such interior people are called *Monteses* (Jocano on Burrows 1968), the same term used by Eugenio Ealdama (1938) in his article, "The Monteses of Panay."

Montes means people of the mountain. Jocano, however, employed the term Sulod to distinguish them from the Ati, or Negritos, also found in the mountains.[3] Lowlanders, especially Christians, have given non-Christian groups specific names depending on where people are based, their behavior as perceived by lowlanders, and their appearance. Some of these names include *Buki* and *Putian* (Jocano 1968). Buki means people of the mountain, but carries with it a negative connotation of people who have backward or outmoded ways. Putian, on the other hand, refers to someone who is fair; this distinguishes such people from the dark-skinned Ati.

My research participants told me that it was mostly the *tagabanwa* (townspeople) or other lowlanders close to the town who referred to them as Sulod. Among themselves, however, they name each other ". . . according to their distance from a body of water or their proximity to land types" (Jocano 1968). These names include the *Panayanon* (people living near the Pan-ay river's headwaters); the *Ilawodnon* (those who dwell near the Pan-ay river's delta); the *Halawodnon* (those who live close to the Halawod river's headwaters); and the *Akeanon* (those who live near the Akean river). The *Iraynon* live near a river's headwaters, specifically in a mountain's interior or upland parts.[4]

During the sixteenth century, they were also referred to as *Vagamundos*, a name associated with the group's habit of changing places to escape Spanish religious conversion. These were the people living in the barangays of Daan Sur and Daan Norte (Tapaz, Capiz). Pfeiffer (1976, 49) writes about the Sulod and the Ati as two ethnolinguistic groups in Panay, noting, "Neither group is remarkable for its use of indigenous musical instruments, but the Sulod maintain an epic tradition, which is unique in the Visayas." However, I challenge his claim because my long immersion in their community proved otherwise; the Panay Bukidnons have many interesting and widely integrated-into-life instrumental traditions aside from their epics.

LINGUISTIC ATTRIBUTES

The majority of Panay Bukidnons speak Kinaray-a,[5] a language similar to Haraya or Hiniraya, particular to Antique and the interior (Hosillos 1992). Mulato (1991b, 37) gives primacy to the term Hiniraya rather than Kiniray-a when referring to the language of the people living in the hinterlands of Tapaz and Jamindan, Capiz. This follows, since Hiniraya comes from the word *iraya*, "an upper area of a place where water passes through as it flows to the lower parts" (ibid., 38).

Hiniraya, now popularly known as Kinaray-a, is the root language of Hiligaynon, which is spoken by most Iloilo dwellers. Both of these languages "belonged to the branch of the Hesperonesian subfamily of the Austronesian language stock to which also belonged the language of North Borneo" (ibid.). Deriada (1991, 11–12) explains:

> Unlike Latin and Sanskrit, Kinaray-a refuses to die. It is the mother of mellifluous West Visayan lingua franca, Hiligaynon, and the less well-known child, Aklanon . . . there are more speakers of Kinaray-a than Hiligaynon speakers: all of Antique, most of Capiz, all the central Iloilo towns, and the coastal towns south of Iloilo City . . . Hiligaynon, having been shaped by the mestizoid ilustrados and the Chinese merchants (and their linguistic deficiencies) of old Parian, now Molo, has been associated with the elite. And so, while the people from the Iraya have retained the brash r's, the peculiar intonation pattern and the middle vowel sounds of, presumably, the ten ancestral datus from Borneo, the affluent people of Iloilo City and Bacolod have changed practically all the r's to l (examples, *wara* to *wala*, *harigi* to *haligi*, *kurong* to *kulong*) and loaded their Hiligaynon with Spanish loan words.

Panay Bukidnons use Kinaray-a in daily conversations. They employ *Binukidnon* (mountain language) when they chant their sugidanon. According to a chanter and Panay Bukidnon tribal chieftain, Mr. Federico "Tuohan" Caballero, Binukidnon is their poetic archaic language. The elders use Binukidnon when chanting epics; however, the majority of their youth do not understand this language.

In one of his earliest writings, Jocano (1968, 33) points out that "most of the mountain people are monolingual." In the present time, the influx of various influences blurs this state of monolinguality as social interactions with the lowland people have become more frequent. In the lowland markets, schools, and other commercial hubs, interactions circulate from different social angles. It would be realistic to say that the highlanders' conversational language is *kasugiranon*-based (reliant on whom they talk to), even if the majority of them speak Kinaray-a. Some of them can shift to Cebuano, Ilonggo, and Tagalog. Very few of them know some English words, which they mix with Kinaray-a. Whatever language they shift to, the way they talk is gene-rally called Binukidnon. The manner of talking involves intonation marked by contour (up-down pitch variations) and common speech patterns such as repeated tones in particular words as well as syllabic stress. Even if they mix the use of terminologies from local languages such as Hiligaynon, Cebuano, or Tagalog, with something international like English or Spanish, they still produce the Kinaray-a intonation. In this regard, the sound of the language can become a basis for determining one's place of origin and a marker for one's identity and association with a place.

SOURCES OF FOOD AND INCOME

Agriculture, hunting, and fishing are the main sources of domestic produc-tion within the Panay Bukidnon community. For those who have contacts with the lowland traders, logging, selling agricultural produce, and offering labor have become common means to make a living as well.

Agricultural production depends on the climate. Weather conditions are observed by their sense of regularity and change. In Panay areas, "There is no specific or pronounced rainy or dry season" (*Tapaz Municipal Brochure* 2000). The schedule for kaingin, planting, and harvesting varies every year.

Fishing is done in many ways: via installed bamboo pens that capture swimming fish; through underwater hunting via a *sarapang* (three-pointed spear); or, in certain times of the year, via *túba*, a natural way of catching river fish. The word túba comes from the name of a tree; its bark is pounded into fine powder and mixed with water to make liquor.[6] Panay Bukidnons pour this mixture into the river, rendering the fish unconscious eventually. This enables villagers to quietly harvest them.

Aside from securing a food supply, Panay Bukidnons exert themselves on other money-making means to acquire certain material needs. Exchanging their rice harvest for money enables them to purchase other household sup-plies such as salt, oil, sugar, and toiletries. More pressing needs, such as their children's education, would require bigger earnings. Some of them resort to logging.

Problems regarding the Panay Bukidnons' living conditions include malnutrition, insurgency, unscrupulous cutting of trees, and illiteracy. Few can afford to send their children to school in the town or city. To solve this economic problem, the natives put their children in work-study situations.

The children, working for people who can finance their studies, are commonly called schoolgirls or schoolboys in the town area. They attend school for part of the day, then work for the rest of the day. Primary grade instruction is available in local areas, but the lack of upland-based teachers and the frequent absence of those who do teach in the highlands make for a low-grade educational environment. Lack of books and school supplies, poor quality of physical facilities, and minimal budgets needed to maintain and expand such facilities also negatively impact access to and the quality of education. In spite of these obstacles, some parents succeed in sending their children to school. Most children complete only their primary education, then quit to help out in their parents' farm. There are specific situations where parents decide who among their children should stay with them to farm the land, and who should move to town to study. Keeping the ancestral land is vital to families: there has to be a family member to continue the task of farming and cultivating the land. There are also Panay Bukidnon families that recognize the importance of educating someone within the immediate family. Doing so ensures other sources of livelihood for the family. Transactions with non-natives are much easier when there is someone literate among them to bridge understanding.

THE PRESENT-DAY MATERIAL CULTURE

Among the Panay Bukidnons, the term *tumandok* takes on different meanings and associations related to nativeness. The word can refer to physical appearance in terms of skin color and bodily features. It can also refer to the presentation of that appearance by the manner of putting together accoutrements to adorn the body. Apparel, accessories, weaponry, baskets, and other objects connect the body to particular culturally expressive activities.

A people's material culture consists of objects and expressions that reflect how they perceive and make use of elements inspired by sight, sound, and touch. The process of forming these elements into something tangible is revealing, as it organizes and makes manifest materiality and function. Eventually, the act of forming can take on a ritual role or force through repetition. This is how tradition, and traditional culture, is conceived, constructed, and reified.

In my periods of immersion within the Panay Bukidnon community, I realized this materiality-value process from observing and participating in their creation of tools and wares, using musical instruments for music-making, and bringing the community together through music signaling everyone to dance. I wrote of one experience in a journal entry dated April 2002:

> When one enters a *puruy-an* (house) of a Panay Bukidnon, one sees a mixture of things, old and new. Old would refer to things used by their forefathers and hence, carried over to their generation (including the technology to make these things, like basket-weaving implements, for instance); and new would mean the things they can access from the *banwa* (town), when they would go down from the mountain. But what would be claimed as that of their own are the things they make from their own hands. There is a portion of the house where they store dry goods in a *tabungus* (big baskets for palay, or grain). This container extends from the floor reaching almost to the ceiling (estimated 6-8 feet/1.8-2.6 meters or more). They also have the *sabacan* (small basket for produce). Their house is a lively containment of sorts—chickens coming in and out (nesting baskets are inside the house); dogs and cats interacting in civility (except when food becomes an issue). Behind the back door is an open kitchen where food is cooked with firewood. They have the modern-day plates (made of plastic or metal) but when they have to serve for more people, like in communal gatherings, they use the *simat* (banana leaf plate) to put the rice . . . I also noticed that their walls are adorned with posters showing women in skimpy dresses, modeling liquor brands. According to teenagers living in that house, they got those posters from dry good stores in the town of Calinog. At night, since they don't have electricity, they still use kerosene lamps for lighting. It is during night time when they sing their songs, play musical instruments and tell stories while insects like *sitsiritsit* (crickets) provide the background chorus.

Material culture straddles tradition and change. Objects considered their own are those crafted by their own hands. This points to the traditional use of resources within reach or around the natural environment. What is considered not theirs, but assimilated into household use, are things acquired from the lowland.

For Panay Bukidnons, the tangibility of material things is not always what it seems. In their sugidanon, material things cross worlds between the realm of reality and imagination. A non-native or outsider may question if such objects are real. Magos (1999) documents a sugidanon hero named Humadapnon who has a *sakayan nga bulawan* (golden boat). The sakayan nga bulawan is true and real as their ancestors chanted it in their sugidanon. The sugidanon is the basis of their history, a revered narrative of the community. For non-Panay Bukidnon, the sakayan nga bulawan—a boat made of gold!—may be a product of one's imagination.

Since collective identity includes the things used, or inversely, things that are associated with a particular group of people, one would wonder what happens when the material culture ceases to be functional or relevant for use. The Panay Bukidnons, in their present state, interact with lowlanders and city dwellers, already adopting various aspects of lowlander lifestyle. As noted, it has become common to use advertisements acquired while grocery-shopping in town, as functional and decorative wall coverings in domiciles. The natives acquired the posters while shopping for groceries in town. The tumandoks also reflect the lowland culture in their choices of clothing, kitchen utensils, and even food flavoring. It has become common to use *vetsin* (monosodium glutamate) in various dishes, even traditional Panay Bukidnon preparations.[7] Ongoing flux is inevitable, yet the people choose what to give up and adopt, and at what rate to absorb it into common practice.

Contact with outsiders has other effects as well. The native sense of valuing is changing due to the visits of researchers and social workers. These researchers work with government institutions, such as the National Commission for Culture and the Arts (NCCA), to fund the establishment of Schools of Living Traditions (SLT). Natives also join the officers and staff of the National Commission for Indigenous Peoples (NCIP) to organize projects with the Panay Bukidnons, such as the annual Binanog Festival, in different areas of the highlands. These efforts have helped to revive the Panay Bukidnons' interest in creating more traditional costumes, housewares, and musical instruments, among other things. There has been a growing awareness among the people to take pride in their personal and community handmade works.[8]

I see the reinforcement of what is valued as crucial and relevant. This has motivated me to go beyond conducting objective research, becoming an advocate for such efforts. As it is, the people have cultivated self-perceptions based on multiple threats and changes in lifestyles caused by and leading to migration, communication, transportation, and movement of people and exchange of goods. The devaluation of community-produced materials produces particular consequences. Aside from its impact on human relationships, the community's social order may be affected extensively as the use of things (e.g., Panay Bukidnons' forehead bands with old coins called *pudong*) linked to a particular social order (e.g., wealthier status in the community) may lose its meaning. When the use or creation of the community's objects and practices stops due to adaptation of urban areas' more prevalent utilities, there would be transformations in the way people think, live, and perceive material culture in relation to identity, social order, creativity, and value.

The discussion of material culture in this chapter ushers in the various channeling of Panay Bukidnons in the integration of their thought processes with physical expressions, including the importance of incorporating tools (e.g., weaponry, costumes) for representation. This integration demonstrates their ingenuity in adjusting to changes and appropriating what would be relevant to the people in the event of inevitable transformations.

TIES THAT BIND: FAMILY RELATIONS

Kadugo (blood relations) is a strong word that entails a deep connection among Panay Bukidnons. When two Panay Bukidnons are kadugo, they are committed to help one another financially or materially, or to provide moral support.

In *Sulod Society: A Study in the Kinship System and Social Organization of Mountain People of Central Panay*, Felipe Landa Jocano (1968) explicates the Sulod's bilateral kinship structure and gives thoroughgoing details on how, among others aspects (e.g., culture, economy, politics, etc.), the Sulod gather and socially interact during different agri-seasons and life cycles. The linkage between kin relationships and social activities conducted among members of the community reinforces the sense of connectedness of the family in home as well as in work environments.

Social units in the Panay highlands are organized either by kadugo or affinity through marriage. Families are bilaterally connected. In *Filipino Social Organization*, Jocano (1998, 23) explains:

> Bilateral means two lateral groups of individuals, related or not, are brought together, by virtue of the marriage of their kin. When a child or children are born, the relation is shifted from affinal to consanguineal, with the child or children as the points of reference. This means that a person reckons blood relations equally with his paternal and maternal relatives, with no marked structural distinctions placed on either side.

An example of this bilateral structure is given in Figure 7. Through this illustration, Estella Gelaiz-Gilbaliga explained that her kindred includes the relatives of her mother, Milagros Gilbaliga, and her father, Magdaleno Gelaiz.[9]

The Gelaiz Family of Barangay Nayawan, Tapaz

(source: Estella Gelaiz)

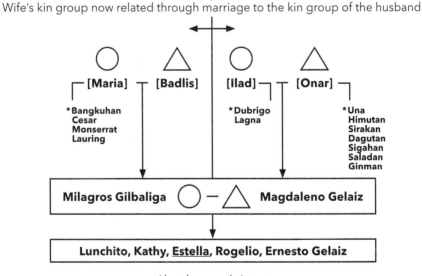

Wife's kin group now related through marriage to the kin group of the husband

[Maria] — [Badlis]   [Ilad] — [Onar]

*Bangkuhan
Cesar
Monserrat
Lauring

*Dubrigo
Lagna

*Una
Himutan
Sirakan
Dagutan
Sigahan
Saladan
Ginman

Milagros Gilbaliga ◯ — △ Magdaleno Gelaiz

Lunchito, Kathy, <u>Estella</u>, Rogelio, Ernesto Gelaiz

*brothers and sisters

FIGURE 7. The bilateral family structure of the Gelaiz family.

Marriage of first-degree cousins to each other as well as to higher degree relations is common among Panay Bukidnons. However, Estella Gilbaliga stated that some church and state authorities discourage the marriage of first-degree cousins as there can be physical defects among their offspring. Despite this, there are cases when parents who are first cousins find ways to conceal their relations so that their children would be admitted to schools. The problem arises if educational institutions require the family's legal documents, such as marriage licenses. A license would ostensibly display or at least imply the legal marriage of first-degree cousins because of their similar surnames.

Polygyny (a custom in which a man has more than one wife) is an old practice in most Panay Bukidnon families. Aurelio Damas, the tribal chieftain of Barangay Taganhin, referred to the customary *waluhan* (giving eight days to each wife). He maintained two wives and made a separate house for each of them. In another instance, a barangay leader from nearby Barangay Taganhin related that he enforced harmony among his wives, which is why his two families live in a single house.

As food is basic and mainly sourced from the land through farming, having several hands to work the land is an advantage. A large family consists of a man, his wives, and their children. The children would assist in farmwork as *timbang* (helpers), those who can help balance the weight of work among his/her fellowmen. Hence, more children means easing labor and time, as well as increasing agricultural production. Having many wives is a sign of wealth, power, or proof of good management skills. Damas referred to this as "Mayad magdumala ka barangay (someone who can manage his community well)." It also validates male prowess. Damas remarked on the practice of polygyny as proving the males' ideal—*Laki siya mo* (Because he is a man). Men in this community are seen as naturally born polygynous creatures, helping create more people to till their land. They believe that having many wives is part of nature's course.

Today there are more families having monogamous relationships, although there are still men who maintain many wives. The influx of various religious groups, particularly Catholic and Protestant sects visiting and operating in different areas of their community, has brought in values that encourage monogyny. There are converted members of their community who embrace such dictums, but others remain rooted in traditional ways.

MEDICO-SPIRITUAL PRACTICES

There is no single way to treat the sick in the Panay highlands. Even as there are commercially available medicines and the municipalities of Tapaz and Calinog provide public health services through local health centers, Panay Bukidnons still actively seek traditional healing. They believe that spiritual and physical health are inextricably linked. When sickness occurs, both the spirit and the body are affected. A person with physical manifestations of poor health may have consciously or unconsciously caused his/her spirit's affliction; in some cases, he or she may indirectly be responsible for illness by unknowingly inflicting harm on another being. Thus, healing involves performing rituals supplicating spirits and their aides: the ancestral spirits. These rituals include chanting, food offering, and dancing that includes food being presented to the spirits.[10]

There are many kinds of healers: the *serruano*, the *dalungdungan*, and the *babaylans*. Unlike doctors, who decide to pursue the medical profession, Panay healers do not consciously become healers; rather, powerful forces select them. If the task is resisted, the person will feel his/her heart constrict, causing an inexplicable pain. According to Menchie Diaz, a healer in Barangay Tacayan, signs of being chosen as a healer came when she felt an intruding force. She would shiver and feel cold. Eventually, she would execute a *kibang* (rhythmic pounding of feet on the ground). Even though she had first been selected many years ago, she still experiences these physical signs of being "re-selected." In 2003, I witnessed her going through these experiences, including constrictions in the chest area, shivering, and the kibang, as she began a ritual.

Each healer must go through ritual phases, initiations, and learning experiences with an older, seasoned guide healer. When the initiation rites are completed, the transference usually occurs when spirits in the older healer move to the body of the protégé.

Most healers have certain preferences in their diet. They largely eat vegetables, fish, or sometimes chicken. They avoid red meat or food from larger beasts, such as pig, cow, carabao, or dog. They also avoid *sapat* (insects) and forest reptiles such as the *halo* and *ibid* of the monitor lizard family.

The spirits in the Panay Bukidnon mystical typology are called the *putian* (white) and the *ituman* (black) spirits. The *sirangans* I met in different barangays identified the putian as good and the ituman as evil. Sirangans are those who can see the other dimensions of beings normally invisible to the human eye. I also learned about these spirits from those who experienced healing brought about by a putian's assistance or, on the contrary, those who got sick because of an ituman's cruelty.

The Panay Bukidnons acknowledge the existence of various beings called *tamawo* (strange beings who look like men but without an upper lip canal), *enkanto* (the enchanted), *dwende* (dwarves), and other unseen life forms. These beings can be putian if they are kind and helpful, or ituman if they are harmful and violent.

There are ways of identifying an ituman from a putian. Violeta Damas, a dalungdungan from Barangay Taganhin, explains:

> When *lati* (moonlight), becomes full or in a capacity to fill the night with some degree of visibility, you can see things around; that's when you can see the ituman. They have black human form but with faces outlined like a wild cat with whiskers. (Directly translated from Kinaray-a to English during an interview in September 2003)

This explains an ituman's visibility though it has no light, hidden from sight. Damas also called the ituman a *malaing ginhawa* (evil spirit) usually seen at night, when most entities' presence is determined. The moonlight provides a pitch-black night with a clearness against which the ituman gains an identifiable form. The contrast of light against dark makes the ituman visible.

A putian is visible, taking the form of a human being without flesh; its body filled with light. Menchie Diaz-Caspillo of Barangay Tacayan said that she implores the putian, which come to her rescue in times of need, for healing.

There are exceptions to the binary concepts of white and black. While general perceptions prevail, exceptions exist, based on specific experiences. A few mountains away, in Cabatangan, Lambunao, Iloilo, serruanos like Noning Lopez attest to seeing the *pulahan* (the red ones). These spirits punish people who disturb their state of peace and order. A person who cuts a tree occupied by the *pulahan* or who desecrates the land that these beings respect would be punished. The *pulahan* may turn the offender's skin red. Noning Lopez says the skin looks like *ga-banog na panit* (swollen skin).

A realization of belief differences and gradations of light and dark hues is a step to widening one's perception from the usual white or black binary construct. This tells us that not all cultural communities limit their beliefs to pure forms, be they opposites, hierarchies, or some other structure. Furthermore, this example demonstrates that expanding research prospects often brings us to the "in-betweenness" of entities, or ideas, and how they may differ.

A serruano heals with guidance from a *saragudun* (spirit-guide), a being that is fed. In a serruano's healing practice, offering food is one way of appeasing angered elemental spirits. Common cases include stepping over a spirit or its territory. It is customary for a Panay Bukidnon to inform a spirit that s/he will trespass their believed occupied space by saying *panabi-tabi* (Please step aside because I'll be passing by). As a precaution, this word is automatically said, since the person cannot see the spirits inhabiting a place. Observing respect prevents danger, as the aggrieved spirits can bring sickness upon those who anger them.

The dalungdungan has a *dalungdung* (spirit-guide), among seven other possessing spirits, to assist him/her in healing the sick. Pagsandan, the mythical hero of Panay cosmology, is the leader of all these spirits. The dalungdungan is tasked to take back the *dungan* (soul) from an evil spirit theft. The dalungdungan is also good at detecting the presence of the *maranhig/aswang* (witch) and the ituman. He or she counters their bad intentions against humans. He or she also uses medicinal herbs and *dalungdong* (a healing oil).

The babaylan (healer) calls on the *diwata*, or spirits associated with fairies, by tinkling a ceramic bowl or plate with a metal beater. The resulting high-pitched sound is believed to reach the diwata's ears in the *kalibutan* (upper level of the cosmos). A *tebongbong* (bamboo tube) can also be used while chanting. The chant is a dialogue between the healer (a mediator of the guide spirits) and the community or relatives of the sick, as represented by another chanter.

The *hilimuon* (task) of the babaylan involves saving the lives of infants. The *kinamnan* (an infant's double) should be retrieved from the spirit world and returned to his/her physical body. A food offering is made to those spirits responsible for the kinamnan. A babaylan can also assist a dead man's soul to move towards the spirit world without being harmed by the evil ones. This process is called *pagbilog* (forming) so the soul will solidify and not liquefy, preventing the aswang from easily devouring it.

In Barangay Nayawan, the drum player Alfred Castor knows of a family whose seven adult siblings are all babaylans.[11] They perform their healing tasks individually, but they agree to work together in cases when they have to help someone with acute or serious illness. Castor said that spectators of the babaylan's ritual are not allowed to leave, even if it takes days until the ritual culminates. He once attended a healing ritual offered for Florinda Castor, who was suffering from a ballooning stomach. A hospital in Iloilo deemed her condition incurable, so her family sought the babaylans' help. Alfred Castor described the event:

> When the seven healers altogether did a kibang, it
> was scary. The whole house shook; their kibang was so
> powerful that they seemed to produce an earthquake
> effect.
> (Direct translation from Kinaray-a to English, Field
> Notes, January 2004)

Castor said spectators had to abide by the rule of staying, even if the healing event was frightening.

Ethics and procedures are relatively constructed, depending on individual healers. They are made part of a healing ritual's overall program that assist in healing efficacy. I once witnessed a ritual in Taganhin. While the spirits were supplicated, people around me warned that no one should laugh at the babaylan's tasks, or else, live coals used in the ritual would attack and burn the person who laughed. The *saragdahon* (spirit-dwellers) that occupy a babaylan's body would feel insulted by skeptics among the spectators.

Some Panay Bukidnons have extraordinary capabilities, other than healing, to help their fellowmen. The *dalagangan* performs unusual feats like jumping from the ground to a rooftop, or running around a rooftop to chase harmful spirits. According to Aurelio Damas, his deceased mother was a dalagangan who rescued people in immediate need. A dalagangan like her can also supplicate certain spirits to make available rain or sunlight.

The *buruhisan* is a medium to nature's spirits. He or she performs rituals by the river to ask the spirits for rain. To request continuous days of sunshine, she performs the ritual on dry land. This happens most often during periods of kaingin.

With the Panay Bukidnons' many healing practices, one learns that an individual is not just a physical being who lives on his/her own plane of existence. The connection of the individual's body to nature, the spiritual realm, and the various strains of relationships among the seen and the unseen keep the equilibrium of his/her beingness constantly attuned and harmonized.

POLITICAL STRUCTURES

Today, the barangay is the Panay Bukidnon's second smallest political unit after the family. Barangay comes from the word *balanghay/balangay*, a boat used by early migrants for island hopping. Onofre D. Corpuz (1989), in his book *Roots of the Filipino Nation,* regards the barangay as a preconquest social grouping.

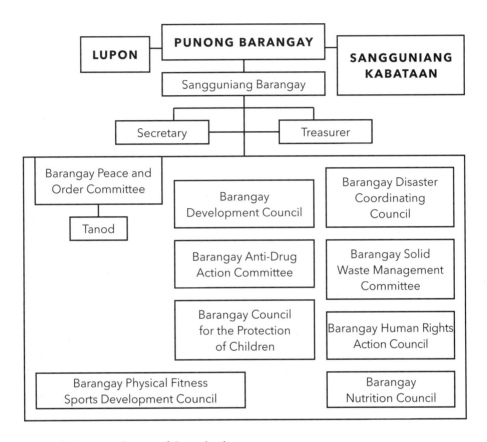

FIGURE 8. Barangay Structural Organization.
Source: *Participant's Handbook: The Role of Barangay Tanod Governance*

A *barangay kapitan* (barangay captain) heads each barangay and is elected by the people to lead for three years. S/he may be referred to as *tinyente* (captain), the present-day title for the one who leads a barangay. A barangay kapitan has a vice chairman and seven *kagawads* (councilors) who are in charge of specific tasks: finance, budget, and appropriation; women and family; peace, order, and public safety; ordinances and legal matters; and human rights.

Meetings between barangay officials and municipal leaders cover local concerns as well as matters that extend outside the community that nevertheless demand barangay officials' collective attention. The issues covered in meetings require follow-up. A few days after a meeting, the barangay officials meet with the people of their respective barangays to echo their municipality's concerns. The people's feedback regarding these concerns, either for or against, is heard and noted. Barangay officers and members also discuss other specific problems, which are brought up in every municipal meeting.

Though this political structure is in place for every town and barangay, some government-related operations are more fluid and flexible. The present-day Panay Bukidnons occupy different barangays, although they consider themselves a single indigenous group. In practice, these barangays merge the traditional ways of governance and the formal, imposed structure. Today, a fusion of customary and government-provided structures works together. Note that this hybrid form comes quite close to fitting the definition of "Alternative Dispute Resolution" (ADR), which includes negotiation, mediation, and arbitration, all of which come into play through the process elaborated below.

Customary practices operate in basic groups such as the *panimalay* (the household). The *ginikanan* (parents) function as leaders of the household and carry authority in extended family networks. In cases when parents working through extended family networks reach an impasse in dealing with an issue, either within the family or in the broader community, they can seek out the *parangkutan* (adviser). Based on the advice of the parangkutan, the ginikanan or any aggrieved individual will consult with a *husay* (arranger) who mediates between contending parties.[12] A husay should be from a *kalawakaw* (a neutral ground or place from which neither of the contending parties belongs) in order to avoid personal prejudices. This condition helps the husay give a fair hearing of the evidence provided by both parties. A case between Minan and Aglupakan (2004) illustrates these points. According to Federico "Tuohan" Caballero, their husay came from a kalawakaw. He entered an area controlled by neither of the two parties in conflict in order to mediate the problem between them. This is one of the traditional ways of settling problems within the community.

In a government-sponsored structure such as that shown in Figure 9, Panay Bukidnons have a *lupon* (group of leaders) headed by a *punong barangay* (barangay leader).[13] S/he forms a *pangkat ng tagapagsunod* (group of followers that has a leader and a secretary) functioning as community peacemakers. This group consists of voluntary members appointed and assessed by the community as fair, nonpartisan, independent-minded, decisive, and

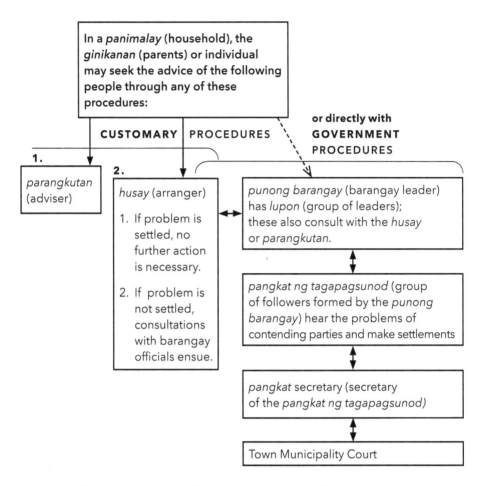

FIGURE 9. A fusion of customary and governmental structural procedures.

investigative of the truth. For every dispute, any member of the community can file a complaint with the pangkat who, consequently, summons the complaint's respondent and witnesses, if any. Both parties are heard by the pangkat ng *tagapagsunod*, and a settlement is arranged. The pangkat secretary submits a report of the minutes of the proceedings, signed or attested to by the punong barangay, to the local court.[14]

Husay is the Panay Bukidnon word used for settling problems through a person (usually an elder) who resolves the dispute. The government uses the legal term *amicable settlement*. The fusion of these systems in the community is significant. The Panay Bukidnons have combined a system introduced from outside of their community (in this case, the national government) with a system found within their culture (the traditional parangkutan/husay). Such a fusion is currently operational in their community and recognized by the Philippines' organization for indigenous peoples, the National Commission on Indigenous Peoples (NCIP).

A barangay kapitan may also consult with a parangkutan and husay, and any of the three can assist each other in resolving problems. A group of respected elders come together to informally discuss a problem over *tubà, likit* (smoking), and *mamà* (betel nut-chewing). If the problem is resolved via the husay, then the barangay officials need not forward the problem to the town area. If not, the barangay kapitan discusses this with the kagawads, especially if the problem needs representation on the municipal level in legal and criminal matters. Court trials are deliberated in the municipality where the relevant local court is based. In case a higher level of the justice system is needed, a trial will be held at a city's Justice Office. If a problem arises in Calinog, the case will be brought to Iloilo City; if in Tapaz, Capiz City will take the case. There are also instances when cases filed in municipal courts are deliberated on and arranged with the barangay for an amicable settlement before the onset of the trial.

Conflicts arise among elders as well. A particular case arose in one of Calinog's barangays, in which the contending parties did not agree with the husay's arrangement. They consulted a second husay from another place, insulting the former husay. To placate the first husay, the contending parties agreed to pay him a penalty fee. The payment, they felt, symbolized the redemption of the husay's lost honor.

Barangays are under a municipality's jurisdiction and management. As is standard operating procedure across the Philippines, a mayor and vice mayor govern Calinog and Tapaz. A group called the *sangguniang bayan* performs specific functions implementing the mayor's ordinances. The group consists of committees such as Finance, Budget and Appropriation; Women and Family; Human Rights; Youth and Sports Development; Environmental Protection; Cooperatives; Rules and Privileges; Senior Citizens; Ordinances and Legal Matters; Peace and Order and Public Safety; Health and Social Welfare; Agriculture; Education and Culture; Public Utilities and Facilities; Market, Slaughterhouse and Plaza; Public Works and Highways; Housing and Land Utilization; and Barangay Affairs.

The community's youth (18 years old and below) also choose their leaders. Their organization is called the Sangguniang Kabataan (SK) and their leader (whom the natives also call SK) is tasked with addressing the youth's social needs. On their behalf, the sᴋ leader represents their complaints and proposals to the municipal government. Most of the time the youth have access to sports and other social activities aimed at reinforcing communal bonding as well as at diverting them from various forms of delinquency, such as drug or liquor use and theft.

This system of combining the traditional system and that of the government's is one of many instances when human agency is at play, sensibly deconstructing and consequently reconstructing a system that is effective for all; that is, a well-negotiated merging of customary and national government practice according to communal norms. Panay Bukidnons have a local ideology, sibod, which involves this negotiation and fusion.

CHAPTER 3

Understanding *Síbod* and Its Expressions

MUSIC-MAKING, DANCING, COSTUMING, AND OTHER CULTURAL EXPRESSIONS of the Panay Bukidnon depend on an important source of thought and action, an ideology that they call síbod. In this book, the use of the term ideology deeply involves a communal belief, a belief of achieving an ultimate state of workability by involving the self and the community, just as the *banog* in the story presented in Chapter 1 achieves a unified state of wholeness in its embodiment of numerous birds and animals.

Síbod constitutes both: a process and a point of destination. To achieve síbod, one must think and act on it at the same time and by extension, to do both things with others as well. But why should one aim for actions to be in síbod? That's because Panay Bukidnons believe it is the life and energy of music and dance, or any activity for that matter. Without it, a dance step is lost, a rhythm is missed, or the relationship of a man and a woman involved in *binanog* gets entangled in conflict.

Many music researchers focus on a local culture's music theory. Choreographers center their attention on dance structures. In this book, I write about an ideology that weaves together these pursuits, but it also does something larger and deeper: it motivates the Panay Bukidnon who see their expressive practices as channels for continuing cultural transmission through various successive generations. Within this narrative I intersperse in the explanation of this ideology my subjectivity as to how I see language, gender, and spacio-temporalities involved in the mix of these elements or as substrates of these practices. Starting from a general definition of ideology, I gradually bring this word's applications to local and actual examples. I do so in order to set the context of síbod in clarifying its manifold definitions, constituent elements, and functions.

Ideology is usually a term employed in politics, economics, philosophy, and sociology. It is defined as "any coordinated body of ideas that reflects the aspirations of an individual, group, class, or culture" (Gove and Merriam 1968). Somehow the theoretical position of ideology in the cultural domain is not so widely discussed nor established as a focused subject of a study. Descriptions, symbolic meaning, and power constructs have become predominant modes of structural and data analyses that highlight an analyst's voice more than the insights offered by/through the researched source.

Ideologies mostly occupy a limited space in certain fields of disciplines. Railton (2005) argues that even if it is generally a "science of ideas" of examining its elements and relations (Destutt de Tracy 1754–1836), its "important usage in contemporary philosophy and politics is narrower and more normative, standing for a collection of beliefs and values held by an individual or group for other than purely epistemic reasons, e.g., bourgeois ideology, nationalist ideology, or gender ideology" (Railton 2005). Noticeably, ideology has become popularly associated with mass movements: something that invokes radicalism, resistance to power/class positions, and the advocacy of social change.

Bourdieu (1985; also Dorn 1991) points out that an ideology may not be explicitly demonstrated in language, but may be implicit in nonverbal articulations such as the arts. In this study, I look at both articulations of the síbod ideology—the verbal and the nonverbal and how the Panay Bukidnon explain meanings by acting on meanings. Panay Bukidnons aim for síbod when they use the term *pasibudon* (to make things work). They remind performers verbally of the task of pasibudon to encourage performers in a nonverbal way (or through music and dance) to bring about síbod.

An ideology is a dynamic, living force and it "not only interprets reality but actually organizes every kind of social practice" (Dorn on Godalier 1991). This brings up the nature of ideology as not static (Gove and Merriam 1968, 1123), which offers a plausible reply to Railton's question: "What is the critical force of calling a belief ideological?" The people's maintenance of their beliefs via traditional rules and practices, the shared values of music/dance structuration and play, and the continuous evaluation of performances constitute the people's ideology and its expressions.[1]

Síbod is deeply embedded in the expression of cultural mediums. I define expressivity in this book as any form of externalization—a gesture, dance movement, story, chant, or playing a musical instrument or musical performance—that is potentially able to demonstrate and relay meaning. Externalization involves the manifestation of an affect that to Armstrong (1971, 43–44) is "the interior condition of feeling relating to the presence or absence of socially articulated values or the presence of felt, "visceral" values." Such values, like síbod, are intrinsic to Panay Bukidnon musicians and dancers as they involve their affect to substantiate or bring expression to an ideology.

Síbod as an ideology consists of a coordinated body of concepts actualized by performers in an activity. Such concepts form the taxonomy of expressive forms (Feld 1984, 391), or specific words that define síbod in particular situated contexts. If music theory presents structures and their use in musical practice, síbod, through its related concepts, largely explicates the mechanism or a structure's working principle in the context of people, place, their relationships with other expressions, and its effects on a community's construct. It clearly affects the living community in its present state, but more so, síbod catalyzes the re-formation of the community as a group; thus, the rationale of why I use a community's construct rather than directly alluding to the community as a nonchanging unit.

Panay Bukidnons work on macro- to micro-materials. They refer to síbod as a general term for an overarching ideology that encapsulates specific concepts. The details of these concepts involve language-based mnemonics as their way of representing sound/movement. Linguistic patterns and other applied language components guide music-making and actuating dance movements.

In the next Figure, the concepts of síbod are illustrated based on the Panay Bukidnons' motif of *buhok ka adlaw* (hair of the sun), which is customarily used as an embroidery design in their traditional clothes, accessories (including their coined necklace), and even as an ideational base for music and choreographic directions.

These concepts are explained in this book according to how Panay Bukidnons employ them from mind to body, and to their *kalibutan* (surroundings). These embodied concepts are *sunú* (bases, conventions); *hampang* (play); *salú* (catch, remedy); *santú* (synchronization among performers, music, dance, space, affect, gender); and *tayuyon* (flow, physical and spiritual linkage). In the next section, I explain how cultural expressions manifest these concepts in laying the groundwork for realizing síbod.

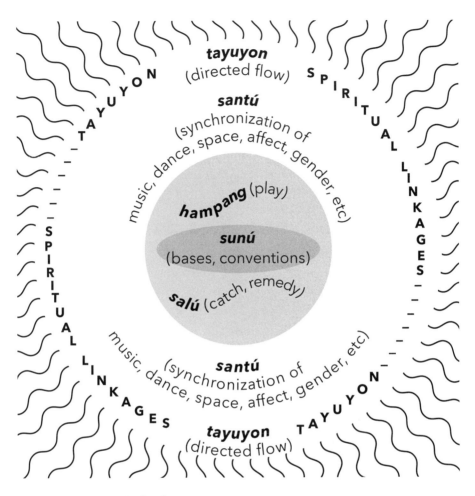

FIGURE 10. Síbod as a body of concepts.

MODES OF EXPRESSIVITY

Around the periphery of tradition and performance lies a symbiotic relationship between modes of expressions, or between music and dance, traditional
clothing, accessories, or even the constitution of these aspects in epic-chants
and other expressions. These modalities channel síbod through the bodies of
the dancers working the details of music's sound and silences; and inversely,
the musicians playing the instruments with the dancers' movements and
footwork in mind. These interphases of sound and movement work together
with the donning of embroidered clothes and related accoutrements; all are
elemental to the performance of the binanog with síbod.

The various expressions of Panay Bukidnon cultural life are projected on the banog story (see Chapter 1) during a *patawili*. For instance, the banog captures the attention of the crowd when it dances or flies with grace. The specific actions that the banog makes are described in the myth:

Ti, nag-umpisa ya kunu	And so the occasion started,
ukasyun, dasun nagsa-ut ya	then the hawk-eagle danced.
kunu banog. Nagtiririk gid ya	It circled around, its wings
kunu banog nagpalakpak ya	clapped; it chirped around as it
kunu pakpak kag naghuni na	was happy to dance.
nalipay gid nga nag-saut. Ti,	
sa subra ya kuno tara-taririk,	As it whirled around in an
nagasarurut ya kunu banog nga	extreme way, it hastily flew
paibabaw.	upwards.

Part of what constitutes the bird's sense of authority in the animal kingdom is portrayed in its dancing abilities, musicality, and showmanship. It circles around, claps, chirps, and flies upward. The dance also manifests the presence of affect as the banog is said to be happy while dancing. The banog can lose itself in the dance as it *subra . . . tara-taririk* (whirls round and round in an extreme way). Freeing one's physicality from certain conventional boundaries raises the question of whether there is a level of transcendental expression in the banog's dance, a kind of a letting go from any form of restraint. In healing rituals, it is commonly perceived as a way to enter an altered state. At the extreme, the healer enters a trance. In this state, one can cross the bridge toward the spirit world in order to mediate a person's healing.

The *huni* (bird's chirping) sounds out a call to get someone's attention. The bird's sounding depicts the most vital element in human existence: survival. The call finds a corollary in the Panay Bukidnons' dance as a vehicle or expression of courtship; various elements in the dance, especially the climactic *pinanyo* in binanog that features a play of handcloths, involve getting, and holding, attention. Courtship is an important process leading to marriage, childbearing and rearing, propagation of family life, and through this, maintenance of the Panay Bukidnon community. Jourdain (2002, 307) similarly notes that humans expend so much energy on making sound for survival drives. The same holds for dancing and other creative expressions. These expressions also provide human beings with opportunities for opposite-sex attraction. Thus, the dance supports the continuity of life.

FIGURE 11. Lucia "Mehoran" Caballero demonstrates the use of her body in dancing.

Another source for expressivity is the body. In Binukidnon, the archaic language of the Panay Bukidnon, the body is called *tubu-an*. *Tubu* is growth and *an* refers to a place from which growth comes. Thus, the body is a springboard for growth. Romulo "Amang Baoy" Caballero enumerated the traditional names of body parts: "In the upper part of the tubu-an, there are the *sigbong* (shoulders); then the *butkon* (hands) with the adjoining *ingay ingay* (fingers) and *buladon* (palm); the *siki* (feet) come out from the lower part of the tubu-an, joined by the *tuway-tuway* (knees) and the *kitenkiten* (soles of the feet)."

The body has *boses* (specific movements). This is in contrast to the Hiligaynon-speakers of Iloilo (the southeastern part of Panay island in Western Visayas, Philippines) who employ boses to mean voice, which may be in reference to the word *voces*, a Spanish and Italian term that refers to voice. Among the Panay Bukidnon, boses relates to a function of the body, not of the vocal system, although a movement implicitly communicates, just as the voice does.

The qualities of a person's tubu-an have significant connections with manners of dancing and symbolic meanings attached to these qualities. An aging tubu-an is associated with those who are *antigo* (experts), signifying a mature banog. A heavier set tubu-an usually has prominent hips—the emphasized body part during the dance gives the dance more of the appearance of a duck's walk. Young dancers of the Panay Bukidnon community adopted the duck-walk as a new trend in binanog called *pinato*. The young dancers claimed they learned this by imitating some dance styles they saw on television in the town of Tapaz. More about this new trend in later chapters.

Differences in age reflect variations of preferences regarding rhythmic modes. For instance, dancers 50 years old and above would prefer the *purungut* rhythmic mode as this has a slower rhythm; the young ones below 50 generally want the faster *guribal* and sometimes the *turuba*. Ostensibly, one's dancing speed is dependent on one's tubu-an, if not one's physical capacity. There are those who choose certain rhythmic modes to demonstrate skill or simply the subtle but clear and transparent moves of the hands, feet, and body, carefully insinuating the graceful movements of the banog (particularly common among the old members of the community). Older dancers who want to show that they still have physical prowess and speed request the *Dalunga* mode.

My research participants pointed out certain differences in dancing explicitly manifested by the symbiotic relationship of the tubu-an and bird images:

1   An old tubu-an is like a very mature banog. This body type is associated with a dance category called *dinuma-an* (an old way of dancing

the binanog). Movements are *hinay-hinay* (moderately slow) where the simulation of wing flaps is deliberate and bodies are swung forward and backward before advancing to the middle of the dance space. Heads are usually tilted upward, seemingly reaching for the sky.

2   *Bag-uhan* or new/young tubu-an:

- Pinato (like a duck). This is associated with young dancers who intentionally move their hips like ducks while dancing. Usually, an unmarried female dancer who is flirtatious in luring a mate would exhibit this style.

- *Mabaskug,* the energetic dancing from the very beginning of *bayhunan* onward to the pinanyo where everyone is fired up in the spectacle of the event. This is where the male employs the tactics of *pabuyung-buyung* and where the woman elaborates in her strategies to *si-ud* (trap) the male by entangling the neck with the *panyo* (handkerchief/shawl), and where through a series of teases for example, *bingkit* (closing in the distance of the partner) among other challenges are shown.

- *Latun-latun*—The tubu-an in this case is projected as lightweight and flying with ease. A male dancer shows an almost effortless grace particularly at the binanog's beginning. The male dancer sometimes does this in the dance's last part to project a suave and manly image. This is a term also used in playing the agung to mean "beat it lightly"; it also suggests not using accents.

These modes of expressivity are significant to mention as we proceed to the next discussion about the binanog. The word tubu-an, or body, becomes animated in the ritualized as well as in the performative aspects of the dance, in motion.

THE BINANOG DANCE

Hampuro is believed to be the predecessor of the modern-day binanog. According to Amang Baoy (a *parungkutan* of the Panay Bukidnon community), hampuro means dance. It is as old as the sugidanon, which predates the Spanish conquest of the Philippines (circa 1521).

FIGURE 12. Dancing the Binanog in a communal gathering.
(Photo courtesy of Museo Iloilo)[2]

Amo gani nga sang waay pa ma-praktis ka mga tawo ang binanog, sa history nga daan hay katong una . . . ang sugidanon duna gid na; sa kabuhay buhay na gid nga mga istorya nga kada-a, antes nga wala pa mapraktis ka kamal-aman namon. Daya na ang ginatawag nga hampuro. Ugaling ang gin-ngalan katong hampuro, may isa pa nga daya nga tinaga, bale ang hinampang. Hampuro ukon sa du karon, kasadyahan ukon sinaot. Nga amo nga binanog dun; naghalin daya sa sugidanon, kung paano gin-praktis. Kay kung mag-history ka, imaginun mo lang bale ano ang ginatawag nga hampuro, bahin sa hungaw; kung sa aton pa, ginapasaot ang nobyo kag nobya antes . . . matapos ang tanan nga istorya nga ayos dun, hampang lang sila ukon i-hampuro lang sila, ukon sa dukaron pasa-uton.

In our history, long before man practiced the binanog . . . the sugidanon was already around; a story of generations past, our elders chanted. In it was already what we called, the hampuro. However, there is another term, the hinampang (to play a game). It was hampuro, or nowadays a form of celebration or dancing. Such is known today as binanog; how it was practiced came from the sugidanon. Because when you make a story, you imagine the hampuro based on the hungaw (traditional wedding); in our terms, we make the betrothed couple dance prior to the wedding . . . after the formal discussion of the elders, we let the betrothed play, or let them render a hampuro, or as it's said today, "let them dance."

In another sugidanon, the hero Humadapnon and his wife Mali danced the hampuro during their wedding day. As mentioned in the epic, it is danced with the music, particularly the playing of the agung, tambur, and other instruments. As Amang Baoy expounded on the fact that the binanog was originally called hampuro, he recounted an epic story that noted the names of specific dance steps during that wedding ritual. Below is a transcription of the chant, as rendered by Amang Baoy.

Hmmmm...........di...........
...n...
di.......di...i...nan...na.....di...i

(Intoning)

And so we continue where we once had stopped

Gani idulug tuga-in madungan
Mabalikid maubling
Si Uwang Matan-Ayun
Kay Uwang Ginbitinan na di kunu
Ay uwahin dun tadang sabayan

Uwang Matan-ayon turns around to face Uwang Ginbitinan,
Telling her,
   "Let the betrothed dance together":

Si Buyung Humadapnun
Si Nagmalitong Yawa
Tuhawa hay pahungaw

Datu Humadapnon,
Nagmalitung-Yawa
Of course,
   because they will be married
Let them dance with each other

Tuu hay talighuman

Stand up, gentleman

Matindug matinbayu
Ginuu Harangdun
Ni Datung Parangkutun
Sa Puhawa Kapangbay
Sa punu ka pangasi
Pasahi man tuladan
Bagayan parihu-an, tuladan
Si Nagmalitung-Yawa
Si Nagmaling Diwata
Danuk danuka'y agung,
Dupi Kadula karatung
Gatamburan, agungan Datu

The respectable Datu
Advisor Datu
In difficulties our guide
Head of the rice-wine drink
One-of-a-kind,
Role-model we can follow
Beautiful Mali
Enchanted Mali
Play the agung
Beat the musical instrument
Datu, strike the tambur and the agung,

Gakaratungan, ihampurong	Beat the instruments, dance the hampuro
Ma daw gani saut	Get to dancing
Madaligan tindug	Stand up immediately
Magbayhun bayhun, Datu	Do the *bayhunan*
Palisyun lisyun,	Dance gentleman, Bachelor
Ginuung Harangdun	with *lisyon* movements,
Ni Datung Parangkutun	Datu, Advisor
Si Nagmalitung Yawa,	Beautiful Mali
Si Nagmaling Diwata	Enchanted Mali
Purmelisyun, gapunta ga-lisyun	Do the lisyon from one end to another
Gakalibutan bulos makilikili	With style, execute the dance steps,
Iwanon tarun lamang	Move it (the panyo)
Madaligun daligan	
Daw gapagsimbaludan	While swaying
	Like the simbalud movements
Ihampuro ka Datu	
Isaut, Kamalangga	Dance, Datu
	Dance, Bachelor

(English translation by Maria Christine Muyco from the Binukidnon to Kinaray-a based on oral translations of Masaroy Councilor Amang Baoy, who is also the chanter of this excerpt.)

The dance steps mentioned in the sugidanon include the bayhunan, which typically marks the beginning of the binanog; the *lisyon-lisyon,* which is considered synonymous to the bayhunan; and the *simbalud.* Lisyon-lisyon is identified in the epic as an arm movement simulating the opened wings of a bird while leisurely walking; not flapping but steadily suspending them, the arms positioned at the shoulder level in a soaring pose. There is a portion of the dance where the panyo is used; the epic states that it should be swayed with the body while executing the simbalud. These various movements are drawn from the observed behaviors of birds, primarily the banog, but as noted in Chapter 1 includes steps taken to represent other animals' movements as well. To recall, Miningkol describes the banog's flight as flying to greater heights at a gradual speed; as it spots a target landing, it tirik-tiriks (hovers around as it flaps its wings faster), so it can get closer to the place of destination; similarly, the binanog music and dance have the same progression as the banog's as it flies gradually from a relaxed to a heightened pace. (Directly translated from Kinaray-a to English in field notes, August 2003)

Amang Baoy described the other dance phases in addition to the information he provided through the sugidanon.[3]

pinanyo (handcloth game)
simbalud (like the flight of the rail)
sadsad (heavily accented steps)
repaso (dancer warms up steps; no stamping or heavy accent)
bayhunan/lisyon-lisyon (leisurely walk)

The binanog starts with bayhunan or lisyon-lisyon. It is a relaxed walk-like movement where dancers go to and fro across the dance floor. The man holds a panyo, while the woman has a shawl on her back held by both hands. The man and woman usually face each other on opposite ends of the dance space. They walk while passing each other, eventually arriving at opposite corners of the dance floor.

1. After the bayhunan/lisyon-lisyon, dancers start to make dance steps in time with the rhythm of the music. This is called repaso (dancing without stamping). The woman dancer's hands are free of the panyo (women usually put it on their shoulders or tie its ends; men just hold it). At this point, arm movements start to extend sideways. This simulates the banog's outstretched wings while in flight. Other pre-sadsad dance steps are *kaykay* and *isduyung*. Kaykay makes use of brush-like footwork simulating birds that are scratching the ground. Isduyung manifests a semicircular, or arc-like motion of the body, when dancing.

2. Sadsad is a general term for footwork. It also means heavily accenting once or twice one's foot on the floor, or ground in a stamp. Other types of footwork are *turuba*, which is marked by accenting one's foot

thrice; *burtu, isul,* and *pahangin* are backward or reverse steps with pedal accentuation.

3　In simbalud, dancers execute more arm movements as compared to sadsad, where footwork is more active. These include wing flaps. Sometimes the wings are held upward and immobile as if in preparation for a sudden flap. Footwork is continuous, regularly paced, and looks like a quick walk. This sort of quick walk is halted with a knee bent, like a temporary pause. Then, the dancers proceed again with the quick walk. There is a shift of dynamics in this phase. Dance partners hastily circumvent each other, mimicking the banog's tirik-tirik (whirling in an extreme way). This is a prelude to the heightened portion of the dance. Here, dancers are finally close to each other and ready to compete with wit and strategy in a game of panyo.

4　The pinanyo is alternately called hinampang. Here, the woman attempts to pursue the panyo of the man. The art of acquiring the man's panyo entails a strategy. The woman spreads and tightens her panyo with both hands. With good timing, she inserts the mid-portion of her panyo at the center of the man's panyo, forming an X (see Appendix 3). Instead of focusing only on the panyos' intersection, they can slide toward each other's edge to form an L (see Appendix 3). By moving to the edge of the panyo, the woman can loosen a man's grip on his handkerchief. This improves her chances of grasping his panyo. If the woman succeeds in getting the panyo, the dance ends. Otherwise, she can try again using the *wayway* and si-ud:

a　The woman can initiate the wayway (holding a pointed corner of the panyo as it hangs down); when she does so, the man follows suit. A widow particularly employs the wayway. While dancing, the woman continues attempting to capture the man's panyo (see Appendix 3).

b　Another attempt can be the si-ud (see Appendix 3). In this case, the panyo is hurled around the neck of the man. The male dancer is considered smart if he can be good with pabuyung-buyung (fast twirling of the panyo in different directions), so the woman will have a hard time grasping the material.

The dance phases define the climactic shape of the binanog, starting with the relaxed walk-like manner of the bayhunan, to the more rhythmic repaso, followed by sadsad, which builds more tension with the sectional change of simbalud, and finally towards the exciting game of shawl or handkerchief play called pinanyo.

Diosdado Jimeno of Barangay Bato-Bato explained the challenge of wits between a person and his/her dance partner in pinanyo. The woman artfully devises ways to get the man's panyo while the man positions his panyo so that the woman cannot get it. There are different strategies employed by a man to retain his panyo. For instance, he can raise his panyo higher than his head with arms stretched upwards. This technique is an advantage if he is much taller than the woman. He may also swing it around his legs or back. Even with all this trickery, the woman usually captures the panyo. However, there are some cases when the binanog ends without the capture of this handcloth.

Miningkol sheds light on using the panyo as a form of communication to convey intimate messages between lovers. Culturally, this is an accepted practice for men and women in courtship, and sometimes is used by couples having extramarital affairs. A man hangs his panyo loosely in one hand in front of a woman to relay the information that he is interested in her. When a woman swings her panyo around her neck, this would mean that she returns his interest and wants to pursue a relationship. However, if she shakes a panyo in front of the man, this means that she is not interested in him. Miningkol noted that dancers should be warned of how to relay intimate messages particularly when there are people in the crowd who are relatives of the dancers. If the man, for instance, is married and he uses a panyo to send love messages to another woman during the dancing, he and the other woman are in trouble. Relatives and friends of dancers are usually watchful of incidents like this to protect the people they care for.

One particular message that a woman could relay to a married man via a panyo is to demand that the man leave his wife. She does this by holding her panyo as it lingers around one of her shoulders; she looks directly at the man with an expression of interest. In these ways, the pinanyo has become an interesting avenue to express affection, but also for the audience to read "private" matters between the dancers. This has become a source of conflict for families in the Panay Bukidnon community. The use of secret codes can be creative and playful, but it ceases to become a form of play when relationships are destroyed and result in the loss of a sense of communal order.

FIGURE 13. Melvin Castor and Concepcion "Miningkol" Diaz in a Pinanyo.

Panay Bukidnons dance the binanog in both ordinary settings and on special occasions. By ordinary, I do not mean insignificant. Rather, the activity is a typical part of the people's way of life. People coming from the farm or from a day's work, mothers carrying their young, children playing outside the house, and teenagers chatting with each other by the doorstep may at any time gather inside a house and casually lift the gong and drum to initiate the binanog. About this, Filipino scholar Felipe de Leon, Jr. (1990, 318) has written:

> In people's culture, art is not a highly specialized activity that calls for highly exclusive places . . . since artistic activity occurs right in the places where people live and work, in the context of everyday human activities.

Inside the Panay Bukidnon household, the binanog is a pastime for everyone. It is an activity for family entertainment, like playing musical instruments, telling tales and sharing experiences of a day's toil; singing about the heart's concerns can be undertaken at any time of day. Sometimes after supper, they have the binanog while drinking tubá. Moreover, family members cajole one another to take the next turn to dance. Adults challenge those who are alert or skillful to use the panyo, and teenagers tease each other about partnerships. In this type of gathering, the binanog exists side-by-side with various activities that consume the whole evening until the time to retire for sleep.

Aside from its "ordinary" practice, the binanog is also present in formal functions like courtship rituals where community members come together and enjoy *punsyon* (feasting), music-making, and dancing. Feasting is synonymous with abundance of the harvest. Because the banog is mostly seen flying during the season of planting or during harvesting when the sun is out, these times are usually the ideal time for punsyon. There is much to celebrate and food is plentiful. Performances of the binanog are common in this period. A hungaw is typically held in a punsyon, but harvest season is not the only time when weddings take place. If a man can afford to provide for the wedding feast and bride-gift, then the punsyon can occur anytime of the year.

In discussing the function of the binanog, I include the discussion of pre- and post hungaw as these events constitute part of life cycles—birth, puberty, adulthood, courtship, marriage, and death. Such events form the figurative procession of rites for the institutionalization of the family and the process of taking on responsibilities in the community.

The binanog is an opportune event where young men and women meet and get acquainted with each other, whether their marriages have or have not been arranged. An *alyandador* (expert dancer) serves as the mediator between individuals to help them choose their dance partners. Some relationships develop from these chosen partnerships although sometimes a problem can occur when these partnerships run contrary to the parents' wishes or plans. Parents traditionally choose the partners for their children, but during the binanog there is less control over circumstances that lead to partnering, and this can influence how relationships form, and with whom. There are those who follow/act on their parents' arrangements but there are those who defy tradition, exercising their will to select the person they would like to court and eventually marry.

When the binanog has successfully brought a young couple closer to each other, marriage plans are made. There is *pabagti*, an act undertaken by the man to inform the parents of the woman about his serious plans to marry her. The man meets with the woman's parents and they discuss the bride-gift, consisting usually of heirlooms, livestock, and/or poultry. After the pabagti, there is a *pahimpit* (the agreement of the parties involved). The agreement

may revolve around roles and responsibilities of the couple as well as ownership of certain material culture. After this, another meeting will be set with
parents and elders to discuss final plans. This will include the discussion on
the revised or finalized bride-gift and the date of the punsyon.

A punsyon starts with *pangasi* (drinking of the rice wine) from a sibulan using a *tayok* (ladle). The betrothed and their parents face each other
or sit close to each other as they alternately drink the rice wine; facing or
sitting close to each other on this occasion is called *gina-itib*. The parents of
the bride leave the groom with *pamilinbinlin* (reminders) as their daughter
would have to live with her husband soon and will not be with them any
longer.

In Taganhin, tribal chieftain Aurelio "Kune" Damas recalled the old style
of the *patalanha*, or *sikreto* (a secret meeting), between a man and the parents of a woman.[4] According to him, this secret meeting usually takes place
without the woman's knowledge. It serves the purpose of giving the man
the chance to discuss with the parents his serious intention to marry their
daughter. Traditionally, this meeting takes place after about a year of *pan-
gagad* (rendering service to the woman's parents). Service would include such
acts as chopping firewood; pounding *palay* (rice grains); and helping out
on the woman's parents' farm. The patalanha is followed by the pabagti, or
announcement of the man's intent to marry. If the man, however, decides to
sleep with the woman before the punsyon, he needs to *pabayaw* (announce
publicly) to the community. He would then offer the woman's family a pig.
Other forms of compensation are typically offered. Traditionally, the man
prepares a number of *bi-it* (tokens): a *sanduko* (knife weapon) is given to the
sister/brother of the bride; a *biningkit/kulintas* (necklace) and *terno* consisting
of *saipang* (outer blouse) and *patadyong* (barrel skirt) are handed over to the
mother of the bride, among other gifts. These are given after the *bayaw-biit*,
an introduction of the groom to the community; a *dapay*, a bedsheet with
a bird design, is usually prepared for a woman's *amang* (grandfather) who
should be kept warm during the punsyon.[5] He is usually tasked to sing the
ambahan, a vocal chant praising the betrothed.

Below is an example of an ambahan from Taganhin, as sung by Kune on
February 2004:

Hmmm . . .	Hmmm . . .
Kaayad ka tigamhun	You are good, ideal
Kahimput, kahuron-huron	Sincere, dedicated
Ulalis ka sa puno	You came from your ancestors
Ilis ka sa pinudlan	You take on their tasks
Tal-os sa ginpukanan ka guknan	From where your parents
Ginpudlan ka ginikanan	originated
Ginpangrugalan nga Taganhin	Taganhin is the place
Lugar nga makalilingin	A place of dizzying wonders.

After the ambahan, the participants prepare for the binanog. Punsyon attendees put money inside a container made of bamboo, which is a custom called *ala-salud.* This is optional, though, and is dependent on the parents' approval of the match. The binanog is then initiated by the antigo, with musicians playing the instruments to call on the dancers—first, the parents of the couple in the following order: mother of the bride partnered with the father of the groom; father of the bride with the mother of the groom, followed by the couple, and lastly by the community and *pangayaw* (guests). The dancing of the binanog goes on overnight and sometimes for a couple of days.

The married couple resides in the house of the bride's parents for three days. The night when they sleep together and consummate the marriage is called *duot-panit* (touching the skin). Sometimes a ritual called *pag-sagda* (supplication to the spirits of dead relatives) where a white chicken is offered as a sacrifice, precedes this. After three days, the celebrated couple begins life together in a separate *puruy-an* (dwelling), which has been prepared or built by the groom and his family months before the punsyon.

The wedding and punsyon of Miningkol (incumbent tribal chieftain of Tacayan) and Rodolfo Diaz (former barangay captain of Tacayan) in 1973 involved a ritual by a babaylan who did a pagsagda using the *kamangyan* (incense) from an *almasiga* tree. The babaylan asked the dead relatives and spirits not to *hikaw* (envy) the couple, but instead to give them good health, fortune, and the blessings of children. After the ritual, the participants consumed pangasi and *daha* (prepared meals). These meals consisted of rice, *tinola* (boiled vegetables), cooked pork and chicken. These were served in *simat.* The entire set of preparations was made to please the spirits. If the served food failed to satisfy the spirits, ill fate would come to the couple.

To this day, family and relatives as well as acquaintances and members of the community attend the punsyon. They first enjoy eating the punsyon meals and then relax with pangasi and socialization. The music of the agung and tambur together with the *kahuy* (wooden percussion) is soon heard, and the music ushers in the binanog. The couple may initiate the binanog; then their families, other kin, and guests follow. People join the binanog until the wee small hours of the next day; sometimes this lasts for several days.

Besides being a tradition in a wedding feast, the binanog is also danced at funeral wakes. On occasions like weddings, funerals, and other rites of passage, it is important for people to gather, to express communality and concern. In Barangay Tacayan, Romulo Diaz died of a heart attack while dancing the binanog. To commemorate his love for this dance, his family and friends danced the binanog during his funeral wake.

A babaylan, in a healing ritual, also dances the binanog while offering food to the spirits. This act of dancing and simultaneously making an offering is called *ginalaglag*.[6] What makes it a binanog even as the arms are not executing bird-flying gestures is the involvement of the feet moving in time with the music of the binanog. In some instances, this dance is also called *binabaylan* since it features the healer as the dancer and not just any ordinary member of the community.

If more hands are needed on a farm, whether for kaingin, planting, or weeding, the landowner will call for patawili. Sometimes my research participants call it *patabang*. To distinguish patawili from patabang, I further researched it and learned that patawili is a community gathering to help in planting while patabang involves clearing weeds, burning plants, including shrubs, and other ways to prepare the land for planting.[7] The landowner or the family who called for either of these gatherings should serve food. After lunch, or in the afternoon after farmwork, the attendees relax and usually play music and dance the binanog.

Carlos Parle, 77, of Bato-Bato (Tapaz, Capiz), recalled his younger days when he witnessed a warlike performance of the binanog. Based on his recollection, he demonstrated to me how the dancers used weapons while dancing the binanog. He also acted out his description of the movements and the overall action:

Mag binanog, ga-taming laki ug bayi; may bangkaw halin sa bugsuk ka kawayan . . . tusok sa ibabaw . . . daw gin-sinda ikaw. Una ang labu sing laki, singku sa idalum ka pamunu sing bayi. . . .

When the *binanog* was danced, men and women used the *taming* (shield); there was the *bangkaw* (spear) taken from the uppermost part of the bamboo tree . . . I pierced it upward (Carlos demonstrated with an imaginary spear) . . . as if cursed. The man did the striking first, then the woman followed the same thing five times using the bottom of the spearhead. . . .

Functions vary as to the performance of the binanog. As part of fish harvest, the binanog is held at the side of the river as a form of celebration for abundant fishing. Túba is a day marked specifically in the month of May when fish are abundant. Panay Bukidnons pour túba into the river. Several hours afterward, the fish get drunk and "fall asleep" as expected. The binanog is an offering of thanks to the spirits of the river who provide people with fish.

Amang Baoy added that the binanog is part of the ritual activities employed to conjure spirits. He said: "*Ang buhis ka to naga-ihaw ka baboy sa suba kag gagamit binanog; dyan mo makita ang sari-sari nga mga klase ang mga tawo naga-dugo kag naga-praktis ka binanog.*" (The offering those days was to slaughter/prepare a pig for cooking by the river and the binanog would be held; there you could see different kinds of people doing various offerings and actuating the binanog.) In this regard, the binanog has a crucial role aside from courtship and the ritual of binding (as mentioned in the beginning of this chapter). These are to mediate between man and spirits for the provision of good weather and good harvest; to intercede with the spirits for man's physical/material needs; to bring about the balance of nature; and to express gratitude for wishes fulfilled.

Binanog for Panay Bukidnons is also called *sinulóg*. This is spoken with accent on the last syllable: sinulóg. This is unlike the *sinúlog* of Cebu, a dance form practiced in the Eastern Visayas that is pronounced with the accent on the second syllable: sinúlog. Binanog, though a customary name among the elders, is met with a less accepting reaction from some young members of the community. I bring this up since I encountered a situation when the Panay

Bukidnon used the term sinulóg while the topic we were talking about concerned the binanog.

According to Nida Gilbaliga of Barangay Daan Sur, Crossing, they have always used the term binanog; this has been what their parents and the older generation used to mean the dance of the banog. There was a time, however, when they were invited to perform in the town plaza of the municipality of Tapaz. The tagabanwa who comprised the audience called their dance sinulóg. Youths adopted this term after hearing it repeatedly from townsfolk, especially in school and during cultural presentations. Some community members adopted the term sinulóg since they regarded it as a generic term for any native dance in Tapaz.

Various factors motivated the adoption of the term sinulóg. A key factor involves derogatory name-calling by tagabanwa against the Panay Bukidnon. Townsfolk call the highlanders *bukî* (backward or out of fashion) since they live in the *bukid* (mountainous areas). Affected by this, some Panay Bukidnons, especially youths who had more contact with townsfolk, changed some of their ways and manners of doing things in order to gain social acceptance in the town area. This included imitating the townspeople's language, such as using the term sinulóg, which seems to be the townspeople's general term for a native dance. Another factor is the Panay Bukidnon's reference to a *sulóg* (rooster), thus the term sinulóg that refers to dancing like a rooster. Considered a bird as it has wings, the rooster is part of the kingdom ruled by the banog in a story previously narrated in Chapter 1. Therefore, in the Panay Bukidnon conception, specific bird and dance steps associated with that bird can be alluded to as the binanog since species in the bird kingdom exist within the larger form.

Evidence of Panay Bukidnons' use of musical instruments, such as the bossed gong and drum, has been extensively documented in the early twentieth-century Accession Records of The Philippine National Museum. This collection includes Emerson B. Christie's purchase of an agung from a Panay chief.[8] This chief (name unrecorded) is said to have obtained the agung from Borneo through trade in 1930. As documented in the Records, it was then in use by people of the upper Panai River. During his visit to the Kapis[9] province in 1912, this collector also bought a tambur for the price of one peso and fifty centavos.[10] The Record referred to the people as *Montescos*, a Spanish term meaning people of the mountains.

BARASALUN AND OTHER MUSICAL INSTRUMENTS

ENSEMBLE FOR BINANOG (HAWK EAGLE DANCE)

tambur (drum)   kahuy et sarug (wood   agung (gong)   tata (vocalizations)
                       percussion and bamboo floor)

SOLO INSTRUMENTS

a   tikumbo (idiochord)

b   tulali (flute)

c   subing (Jew's harp)

d   suganggang (buzzer)

e   litgit (zither)

FIGURE 14. Panay Bukidnon Musical Instruments.

Tribal chieftain Tuohan mentioned that his elders had exchanged goods with the *Sangleys* (Chinese merchants). They traded because the Panay Bukidnons do not personally produce or manufacture gongs. I do not assume, though, that all Sangleys were just traders moving gongs from one place to another. Some gongs had direct connections to makers, as evident in historical accounts. Pigafetta, a chronicler who travelled in the Philippines with Magellan in the early 1500s, provides some of these accounts. He reports that "gongs were made of brass and are manufactured in the regions about the *Signio Magno*, which is called China" (Blair and Robertson 1909, 33: 149–51; also Maceda on Blair and Robertson 1963, 32). The gongs that Pigafetta referred to were "suspended gongs . . . and two small gongs held in her hand" (one of the girl musicians of the prince of Cebu met by Pigafetta) (ibid). Although Panay Bukidnons currently do not use small gongs in the binanog, Amang Baoy recalled his younger days when he held one of those small gongs in his hand to provide music for the dancers. In his other hand he held a wooden beater used to strike the gong's bossed area. The small gong was about the size of his outstretched palm, approximately 8 inches (20 centimeters) in diameter. He specified that two small gongs joined the rest of the binanog ensemble composed of an agung suspended on a tree or on a ceiling post of a house, a tambur, kahuy, and other bamboo instruments.

An excerpt from the sugidanon provides the names of musical instruments. Panay Bukidnons believe that the people who play the instruments are their heroes and ancestors from the olden days:

Si Nagmalitung-Yawa	Beautiful Mali
Si Nagmaling Diwata	Enchanted Mali
Danuk danuka'y agung,	Continuously play the agung
Dupi Kadula karatung	Fast, beat the *karatung* (instrument)
Gatamburan, agungan	Datu, strike the tambur and the
Datu	agung

This excerpt mentions the agung and the tambur that comprise the music ensemble of the binanog dance. The agung is a bossed gong suspended/hung from a stand. It is played by *danuk*, where the player lightly bounces a rubber-padded beater on the gong's bossed area. Another way is through *kadul*, or striking the bossed area of the gong with a rubber-padded beater; this was referred to in the epic text as *kadula*, telling the person to strike the gong.

Other types of beating the gong is *basal*, or striking an instrument using a rubber-padded beater on a gong's boss; and *patik*, which involves beating the rim/side of the gong using a pair of thin bamboo sticks.

On the other hand, the tambur is a two-headed drum beaten by a pair of thin bamboo sticks. This drum has heads made of deerskin. In the absence of deerskin, goatskin may be used. Only the upper part is beaten. This part is called *bayi* (woman) because it produces a higher pitch compared to the lower part called *laki* (man). The Panay Bukidnons assign gender types to the drum's parts because of the materials used to make it. The drum's bayi is taken from a *lipay* (female deer). The laki side is taken from a *sungayan* (male deer).

Amang Baoy noted that more instruments/sound sources have joined the ensemble. These are the following: the *kahuy nga ginabasal/ginabatil* and *sarug* (bamboo floor). Kahuy is a wooden percussion struck on a sarug. The sarug is considered part of sound-making as it resonates when beaten. Most Panay highland houses have bamboo floors with wooden supports. The kahuy is used to repeatedly stress rhythmic accents as well as mark the two heavy steps called sadsad in the binanog section of the same name (details below).

In the sugidanon, gongs have names. Note that although the Panay Bukidnon gong has the generic, or common name—agung—particular examples of the agung with proper names exist in the epic. Each possesses various sound qualities, or timbres that are implied in the specific name. Amang Baoy enumerates:

Kay man sang una, may agong man nga daan, amo tu nga ginhambal ko kanimo nga may mga ngalan ang agung: agung ni Burulakaw, agung si Buysawang; si Makaylong-hunusan, si Magkahunodhunod – hanggud-hanggud nga agong; agung ni Abaw, agung si Tawag-Linaw; si Makahibong Banwa. Ti dya ang agung namon dun karon si Danao ang ngalan na.	In the olden times, the gong already existed, and as I told you before, the gong has many names: the gong of Burulakaw (an epic character) is gong *Buysawang*; of Makaylong Hunusan's (another epic character) is *Magkahunodhunod*—a very big, big gong; the gong of Abaw is *Tawag-Linaw*; also *Makahibong Banwa*. But our gong, the one we use now, is called *Danao*.

Amang Baoy continues by providing more detailed descriptions of gongs included in the epic, adding more names to the list in the process. He enumerates their roles in evoking magic, light, and sound qualities. He also notes various characteristics associated with these gongs:

1   *Tawag-Linaw* means, "clear sound; clear call." The gong of Abaw (short name for Labaw Donggon), it represents magic, charm, and power.

2   *Magkahunod-Hunod* means, "many resonances." Makaylong Hunusan, a strong man mentioned in Panay tales, owns this gong. This gong represents power and strength.

3   *Libusawang* means, "much potency; can win favors." Being the gong of Datu Humadapnon, a brave man with a golden body, this gong represents power, value, and strength.[11]

4   *Maka-hibong Banwa* means, "one that can bring the whole community together." A female symbol of motherhood, it represents an embracing arm and congregational prowess.

5   *Buysawang* means, "fire and light." This is the gong of Burulakaw, another epic character who hails from the upper cosmic world. This gong represents magic and spells.

6   *Magkahuwang-Huwang* means, "echoing sound." In the *sugidanon*, it is the gong of Datu Humadapnon, the hero of the Earth and Cosmos/Afterlife. It represents power and wealth. It is usually played in *hungaw*,[12] healing, festivities, etc. It represents power and wealth.

Amang Baoy's brother, Tuohan of Barangay Garangan, further embellishes these points,[13] providing information on who keeps or owns the gongs held by Panay Bukidnons, where the gongs are found, details regarding their physical and sound properties, and the associations that come with the names:[14]

1   *Lamba* means, "huge sound like the cow's moo." It is associated with someone in authority. It is played in the *binanog* courtship and wedding rituals as well as for healing, festivities, etc. It is currently with the Takuron family of Barangay Siya (Tapaz, Capiz).

2   *Sungayan* means, "piercing sound and has the capability to outdo others by volume and quality of sound." It is associated with fauna, or animal imagery (*sungay* means horns of an animal). It is used in binanog courtship and wedding rituals as well as for healing, festivities, etc. It is owned by Amang Badlis, a tribal elder of Barangay Nayawan (Tapaz, Capiz). It is also shared with the family of tribal *parangkutan* (advisor) Federico "Tuohan" Caballero. Even if Caballero resides in Barangay Garangan (Calinog, Iloilo), he traces his roots to Nayawan.

3   *Kamangyan* is likened to the tiny particles of burned leaves of the Kamangyan tree. This is the smallest Panay Bukidnon hanging gong, but it has a so-called "wide resonance, like smoke." It is currently with the family of Aurelio Damas, the tribal leader of Barangay Taganhin (Tapaz, Capiz).

4   *Lumakday* is from the root word *lakday,* traveling. Thus, the sound of this gong seems to travel far and wide. It is now with Lakuan (whose whereabouts are unknown).

5   *Danao* means, "shape able to hold anything, including water." This word is actually taken from a household story about a woman who improvises using a gong as a basin. It is used in *binanog* courtship and wedding rituals as well as for healing, festivities, etc. The former barangay captain of Barangay Daan Sur (Tapaz, Capiz), Jaime Olido keeps this gong.

6   *Magkahurao* means, "calming like rain that eases out." The sound of this gong creates a peaceful feeling. It is now with Roberto Diaz of Barangay Tacayan (Tapaz, Capiz).

7   *Pabu-ay* refers to "a big turkey sound." It is presently with Tar-og of Barangay Buri (Tapaz, Capiz).

Gongs named *Maginsung, Butawan,* and *Agindan* have unknown keepers. Their whereabouts are unknown as well.

The reader will note that these agungs are kept in the houses of well-positioned individuals such as barangay leaders and tribal chieftains. Alcina's history of the Visayan islands in the 1660s (translated by Kobak and

Guttierrez 2002; also in Yepes 1996; 1998) showed that the *principales* (people of high position and wealth in their community) have agungs.

> In their antiquity, the principales had in their houses these agung, which were many and very large. It was by means of these that they summoned the people to their tasks and festivities. They also used these as accompaniment to their dances. . . . When their drinking sprees and their drunkenness were at their height, they rang these bells faster and louder. (Kobak and Guttierez 2002, 200, 91)

Clearly these ownership traditions continue to the present day based on the earlier accounts of Caballero about those people who have the gongs.

Solo instruments typically produce less volume than instruments used in the binanog ensemble. However, playing and listening to these instruments provides a different form of entertainment. More importantly, playing these instruments helps young community members to learn basic rhythms. After mastering these rhythms, young players can prepare for more challenging tasks such as playing the agung and the tambur. Typically, master players mentor these developing musicians. With the approval of the elders, players trained on these solo instruments can eventually join the binanog music ensemble.[15]

The *subing* is a jaw's harp. Although it is played solo, it is also employed once in a while to accompany someone to rehearse and become a skillful dancer. With its soft sound projection, it is suitable for an intimate space, say a small room, where the sound can be confined to the player and the dancer so that the concentration of synchronization can be well rehearsed.

Panay Bukidnons believe that the subing serves as a link not only between animals and men, but also among the animals themselves who strategize and possess varying levels of cleverness in carrying out tasks. One repeated phrase in the folktale with the subing as its focus is *Kurubingbing Kurubawbaw*, an onomatopoeic sound heard from the jaw's harp. According to Tuohan, these are nonsensical but teasing words. This phrase is also utilized as a rhythmic pattern for subing playing. This pattern, orally conveyed as a sung narrative, helps in memory retention. It is recalled by performers to practice on this rhythm and experiment on its variations. A master player also employs this as a pedagogical tool when teaching a learner.

Alcina (translated by Kobak and Guttierez 2002, 89) gives remarkable details of how a subing is constructed:

> The manner of fashioning them is to cut a splinter the width of a finger or even less and as long as the palm of the hand and thinning it out and smoothing it with care and retaining the solid portion of the bamboo which appears behind the bark. When cleaned, it will be about the diameter of a *real de cuatro*, three parts, about one finger-length apart and leaving the lower extremity always entire. They cut two from both sides and leave the one in the middle which projects itself into two fingers, more or less, beyond the other two; on this they put something like a small dent, which juts out in the middle and falls in line with the other two short ends that are fitted into the mouth, while the other end remains outside of the mouth.

Various factors affect the sound of Panay Bukidnon instruments. The way the instrument is played, particularly how a percussion instrument is struck, affects both volume and timbre. For instance, I mentioned earlier that danuk means to lightly bounce on a gong's boss. However, kadul means to hit this instrument forcefully. Note that in the sugidanon, the gong is associated with Humadapnon and Mali, two forceful, powerful characters. The type of beater also impacts the sound. The pair of sticks, patik, not only makes for a lighter sound, but also allows for faster striking. In patik, the player or players strike the agung's rim. The part of the instrument played or struck matters as well. Playing the rim produces a high sound and emphasizes higher overtones. On the other hand, kadul is associated with beating the agung's bossed area by a padded beater. The sound produced in this part of the gong is usually lower as a boss is thicker than most of the gong's other parts. Furthermore, a padded beater tends to absorb high-frequency sounds, which emphasizes the lower, fundamental tones. In the same light, the pronunciation of the word kadul gives a lower sound (specifically because of the syllable "dul" in kadul) compared to the word patik, which sounds more brilliant and emphasizes higher overtones. All these associations are onomatopoeic and important to consider when categorizing instrument types and groupings.

VOCAL EXCITATIONS

I consider *tàtà* and *hiyaw* as part of the Panay Bukidnons' music-making sources. As vocalizations of the audience, these contribute to the overall spectrum of Panay Bukidnon ensemble music. Both types of vocalizations use repeated vocables used to intensify the music-making and dancing of performers. What differentiates them? Tàtà are verbalized with much gusto in time with the ensemble's musical instruments. Hiyaw, on the other hand, can be in a form of calls and hoots expressing excitement over a music and dance performance. This type of verbalization can be fluid, spontaneous, and does not have to adhere to the rhythmic pattern of the mnemonics used.

Members of the audience do not merely watch the binanog as a spectacle; they are not passive onlookers. They play an important role in sound-making, forming dynamics, and in enlivening the total mood of the acoustic environment. As the event progresses, they actively participate as they loudly tàtà, such as whooping, "Hirli, hirli, hirlikita!" The tàtà, sounded in time with the music, is based on a mnemonic sequence, which further reinforces the sense of structure and connectedness between all who attend the binanog.

The syllables employed by the audience when they tàtà often do not mean anything. However, the manner of sounding them, especially in terms of volume and pitch, suggests that dancers should move with more gusto and zest. Most often, while doing the tàtà, the audience claps in time to the music (particularly with the rhythm of the mnemonic).

In tàtà, it may seem like the audience puts together the sounds in some random sequence, but in fact this action is the audience's conscious effort to synchronize with the total spectacle involving music, movement, embroidered apparel, and social interaction. A tàtà adheres to the beat, particularly when the sadsad is well pronounced. An example below shows how a tàtà is spoken in time with a mnemonic rhythmic pattern:

Example of tàtà: **hir-li_ , hir-li_ , hir- li-ki- ta_**

(Mnemonic):   **tak-da_ , tak-da_ , tak-da-lu-nga_**

(_ indicates a slightly prolonged vowel tone)

As noted, the hiyaw is more spontaneous, fluid, and loose than tàtà. In some sense it is a direct expression of excitement or serves as an effort to inject more excitement into a binanog event.

In the western European tradition, performers and viewers (via the setup of a platform or stage) remain separate, but this dichotomy does not exist in the binanog tradition. Everyone is on the same ground level; binanog is traditionally held without an elevated floor for the performers except in organized cultural shows outside of the community. This emphasizes togetherness, a key value in Philippine traditional societies.

Together with the instruments and dance, the audience contributes to the cluster of sounds and sights, affect and interconnectedness by commenting on a good—or improper—music-dance rendition. The cluster is a combination of various sensory experiences. The tàtà and hiyaw fuel and focus these elements, bringing power and drive to musicians, dancers, and other community-participants.

Both tàtà and hiyaw provide a way for anyone to join in the task of building fun and liveliness within a binanog event.

SANGKAP

Community members extend participation by donning the proper apparel in connection with their music and dance tradition. I first noticed the attention paid to wearing traditional embroidered clothes when I invited a group of dancers to demonstrate the dance to visitors. They hesitated to dance on the spot, excused themselves and moved to a room containing embroidered tops paired with barrel skirts and accessories. Wearing proper attire while dancing fits with the concept of santú. Combining music and dance with embroidered apparel completes the preparations for a performance; leaving out any element breaks connectedness.

FIGURE 15. *Sangkap* **for binanog.**

Clothing materials and accessories are referred to as *sangkap* (implements) of an activity, whether used for the binanog or something else (see Appendix 4). Sangkap hold special relevance to the dance tradition's (1) visual or aesthetic impact; (2) memory; (3) acoustic, or sound enhancement, as most accessories are made of coins that rattle and tinkle when dancers move their bodies while they dance; and (4) linkage to the different spiritual domains of their kalibutan.

The sangkap visually differentiate the binanog clothes for women and for men. Male dancers usually wear either of the following: (1) *barong* (shirt); (2) an embroidered black long sleeved-shirt called *sinumbrahang itum,* or *supa;* or (3) any ordinary long sleeved-shirt that is available. Men pair any of these shirts with *delargo* (pants). On their forehead they wear a *sampulong* (an embroidered forehead band) that typically covers the entire forehead and stands up above the front of the head. The male holds a panyo in either of his hands.

The female dancer also has a panyo (also called *subrigo*) but usually drapes it over her shoulders. She also wears a headband, but the ornate and weighty pudong includes numerous coins and covers the forehead extending over the front of the hair, clinging close to the head. The pudong rests on a *takurong* (veil). The saipang is worn over a *kimono* (inside blouse) or any blouse available. A patadyong (barrel skirt) wraps the hips and legs. A good patadyong is one that is "durable, well made because the weaving is close and tight, not loose . . . and whose colors do not fade" (Doromal 1993, 5). Traditionally, a patadyong would be layered by wraparounds like the *pulus* and *tapis*. This layering is called *hinimbis* (like fish scales). Pulus is usually a *sinorkan* (deep purple) cotton cloth. However, with limited access to the materials needed to make the dyes, Panay Bukidnons now use other colors. Tapis can be any *ginaplang* (flower-printed cotton fabric), although sometimes Panay Bukidnon women substitute a plaid wraparound. Typically, the ginaplang is the upper layer with the pulus immediately underneath. Sometimes a *lagwas* (a sheer material with lace edges sometimes known to Filipino urbanites as a half-slip) is worn under these layers. I have seen the lagwas worn below the pulus with its lace edges shown. So typically, there would be three cloths shown before the patadyong.

Clothing accessories function as visual and acoustic enhancements. A woman's biningkit is mostly composed of coins but also has the *girong-girong* (a small round bell) and a *bao-bao* (turtle-like) silver pendant. The most prized coin is the late 1800s Mexican currency that has on one side the sun (which the natives call as *buhok ka adlaw*) and *agila* (eagle) on the reverse. Panay Bukidnons regard this coin as an heirloom; as such, it can figure into a bride gift. According to Panay Bukidnons who possess such coins, a single such coin can fetch thousands of pesos from coin collectors in Tapaz or Calinog. Families pass on such heirlooms to their children. Such heirlooms occupy a special place alongside other assets such as land and other precious commodities. Women's accessories with coins signify wealth: the more coins, the wealthier the woman.

Coin accessories are usually made of *dumaan nga pilak* (age-old silvers) that adorn the Panay Bukidnons' forehead band, necklace, waistband, and anklet. These coins are important in Panay Bukidnon costuming of Panay Bukidnons as these contribute to the texture and timbre of the music as dancers move to the beat of the gong and drum.

PANUBOK (EMBROIDERY)

Panubok, or embroidery, is an age-old textile art practiced in the Panay highlands. It is more than just the final product; the term panubok also refers to the process. As a needle passes in and out of the *katsa* (cotton cloth), a landscape comes to life, the colors and forms reverberating with patterns drawn from nature. Such creative self-expression is an encapsulation of forces within and without the self's inhabited environment.

Panubok is done on both men and women's upper wear used for dancing: headdresses, wristbands, neckbands, and even men's *oyampi* (loincloths) include needlework. When women dance the binanog, they wear the *sinumbrahang puti* (embroidery on a white blouse) or the *sinumbrahang pula* (embroidery on a red blouse). Men, on the other hand, wear the sinumbrahang itum, sometimes called supa.

Panay Bukidnons translate various organic forms from nature into pieces of cloth. Aside from the cloth used by the Panay Bukidnon, some evidence points to an earlier tradition of using the body as a canvas for such creative expression.

FIGURE 16. Sinumbrahang pula worn by Jally Nae Gilbaliga (left) and supa worn by Alben Gilbaliga.

Cultural historian Zeus Salazar (personal conversation, August 2006) points out the striking resemblance between painted skin patterns of the *pintados* (Visayan painted/tattooed people) and clothing embroidery of the Panay Bukidnon. Figure 17 illustrates the skin painting of the pintados.

FIGURE 17. Similarity of Pintados' skin painting to Panay Bukidnons' clothing.
Source: Boxer Codex.

In particular, there is a stark parallelism between the female pintado and the male clothes. The use of the *girgiti* (zigzag pattern) in a vertical manner instead of the usual horizontal placement as shown on the pintado women is, inversely, a pattern used in the male binanog apparel. On the other hand, the girgiti on the neckline portion of the pintado man with flower designs beneath it, along with the high waist, midriff oblique "stripes" appear in the female clothes of the Panay Bukidnon. This appropriation of tattoo designs from skin to canvas brings to mind a transmission of visual culture that cuts through time and space.

The similarity between skin paintings of pintados and the natives' embroidered clothes has more specific linkages—both allude to the hierarchical positions of the kalibutan. The different dimensions of the kalibutan have a role in the balance and function of the Panay Bukidnon universe. Likened to the sun or the upper cosmos and below it, a series of flora and fauna (with the reptilian or snake skin base design), the preference for positions is interesting to notice. These dimensions are believed to be directly or indirectly influential to their people's activities, including the panubok. The Figure below describes the partitions of the Panay Bukidnon kalibutan and with each dimension, the corresponding embroidery designs:

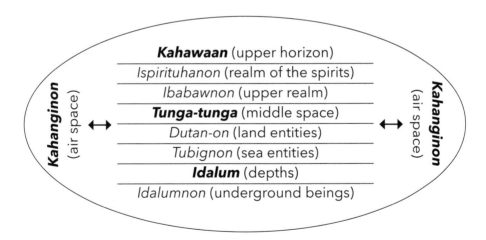

FIGURE 18. Panubok and the Kalibutan.

Everything has its place in the different dimensions of the kalibutan; the same is true of each stitch's arrangement and placement on a given cloth. In a woman's sinumbrahang pula, the neckline has an appliqué using the girgiti design that resembles zigzag forms associated with mountains or the sun's rays. Directly below this would be creatures with wings, such as *pakpak ka aguring* (bee wings) and the banog; below this level are flowers and plants, such as the *bulak ka labog* (flower of the *labog* plant) and the *pako-pako* (fern). Aside from *dutan-on* (living things that occupy the land), the middle portion of the cloth sometimes includes *tubignon* (creatures that live in the water). Conchita Gilbaliga from Tapaz, Capiz, usually embroiders a *kataw* (mermaid) in her work; it is a signature of her style. She does this to commemorate her grandfather's sighting of such a creature. Gilbaliga explains that the thread colors she chooses match the mermaid's coloring as described by her grandfather. The cloth becomes a canvas for recording the visual details from her grandfather's memory keeping his story, his sugid, alive.

Reptiles and sometimes snakes, as well as other water animals, appear in this level of a given panubok piece. A pattern called *inagsam* portrays the crocodile's pointed teeth; the snake's skin can be seen in *Matang Punay* (eye of the *punay* bird). Some snakes live underground, explaining why the lowest part of the woman's blouse has the *sobrekama,* or *panit ka magkal,* which portrays the image of a snake's skin. The snake positioned in the lower domain of the Panay Bukidnon's kalibutan is associated with idalmunon (underground spirits).

The *Buhok ka Adlaw* (Hair of the Sun) motif often appears in whole and is sometimes suggested in part throughout Panay Bukidnons' material culture. This motif can be analyzed in many ways. The most apparent is to look at the outward direction of the rays that come from the center. However, I illustrate and explain the opposite, the ray's inward direction. For example, in this traditionally embroidered panyo by Gleceria "Igli" Gilbaliga of Barangay Garangan (Calinog, Iloilo), we see a series of lines leading toward the center of the cloth: a large embroidered flower[16] (Figure 19). This flower contains sets of petals, each set with a different color that seems to reveal more insides—a flower within a flower. This embroidery design directs the eye to its center and draws deep attention, as if entering an unfathomable abyss.

In the analysis of dance space and this panyo design, I would like to allude to the word "intension" (Armstrong 1971; Keil 1979) that figuratively means "folded in upon itself" (Keil, 196). Unlike its complement, extension, which

FIGURE 19. Embroidered panyo by Gleceria "Igli" Gilbaliga.

conjures structure or motion expanding into space, intension encloses or reaches inward, exploring and inhabiting the interiors of a space. The prefix *in* with the root word tension substantiates the sort of implosive characteristic of its meaning. Material builds, sometimes powerfully, but is still contained. The word *intense* in intension is quite appropriate with the binanog dance use of space (see Figure 45, Chapter 6). The more inward the direction of the dancers, the more intense the relational effect of the affect. Covar (1993) adds another dimension to this analogy—*lalim* (depth) aside from *loob* (inside) and *labas* (outside)—in his structural examination of the body and jar metaphor of *pagkataong Pilipino* (Filipino personhood). He places the categories of *budhi* (conscience) and *kaluluwa* (soul) in the lalim, signifying the deepest and most profound settlement of one's self. Covar's lalim and Armstrong's actualization[17] of affect in time and space are important factors to see beyond the physical appearance of cultural objects; note that these factors exist in a continuum where everything is connected.

When a Panay Bukidnon wears an embroidered cloth, there is self and communal pride. In it lie the linkages of dance, of chants, and of playing musical instruments. It reinforces a person's pride, emboldening him/her to express or perform a traditional art. As mentioned earlier, dressing in traditional apparel lays the foundation of performing, or even demonstrating, the binanog dance. One should wear clothes made by one's own hands or by the hands of kith and kin. Only then can one dance truly, completely, and be in connection with the tradition.

CHAPTER 4

The Foundational *Sunú*

IN HIS ARTICLE "THE RANGE OF DIVERSITY OF VOCALIC SYSTEMS IN ASIAN Languages," Lawrence Reid (2003) asks the question: "To what extent has this set of features, particularly the phonological and rhythmic ones that characterize the linguistic area, affected the musical traditions of the area?" He raises this query through deliberating that

> just as the characteristics of the languages are the unique expression of the natural, underlying phonological processes that bring about the richness of vocalic expression, the characteristics of Asian music are just as much the unique expressions of the underlying musical processes that permeate the inner being, and that ultimately have their same source as those that motivate language development. (267)

How this language and music relation, as well as physical expressions such as dance, makes sense is a function of how people in a culture embody tradition via structural and creative use of their natural/physiological resources. In this section, I will point out the structural relations of language and music in Panay Bukidnon dance and music tradition. I will focus on how underlying creative elements play out through the process of a courtship ritual.

THOUGHT-OF-SOUND

As a tradition that transmits knowledge orally and aurally, the Panay Bukidnon depend on language/speech for patterning music and dance structures. Panay Bukidnons encapsulate these references in the term sunú, a subsidiary concept of *síbod*. This concept is relational—it involves and manifests itself through a particular understanding of physical movements embedded in a wider semantics of bodily motions and sound vocabularies, both used in performing the ritual as well as those accompanying performers. Síbod, according to Lucia "Mehoran" Caballero of Barangay Garangan (Calinog, Iloilo), is sunú: "*Ga-sunú ang basal sa tikang amo man kadya ang tikang sa basal*" (A musical instrument is played based on the timing of one's dance steps, and similarly, dance steps should cohere with the music). Referring to timing, she pointed out that síbod relates to time structures and relationships between music and dance. These time structures depend on language-based mnemonics. I explain these later in the chapter.

Sunú can also be perceived as a distinct resource in the realization of ideas, that is, an index to producing music or enacting sound structures through the body. This base, given that local language is part of its constitution, is emic to the musician or dancer. Given, however, the public exposure of *binanog* through town festivals and mass media, including the Internet, people from outside of the community who want to learn its music and dance merely listen to the structure and watch the steps and movements and bring imitation into action. Without the tradition's context, the performance's presentational aspects cannot move to the fore. This leaves aside the deeper cultural essence of ritual, representation, and meaning. Nevertheless, sunú for the Panay Bukidnon comes into being where fundamental performative conventions link to an organization of sound and into language-based rhythmic patterns. In turn, evaluating the propriety of actions between the male and female dancers as they occupy and move through the dance space, and between dancers and musicians in the keen observance of a rhythmic mode, plays a role in evoking and understanding sunú.

Mehoran demonstrated how playing an instrument should adhere to the basics of mnemonics to align with the dance movements. On one occasion, she did not approve of a binanog performance in her home barangay because the music-making and dancing did not connect on the strong beats. The various performers did not synchronize their movements and playing, either. She underscored the importance of marking the music's accented beats by demonstrating a kind of heavy footwork—graceful and rhythmic stamping—and then contrasting these accented beats with unaccented beats. In this way, sunú provides guidelines for a musician to adjust his/her playing to the dancer's movements.

FIGURE 20. Lucia "Mehoran" Caballero.

To understand the intricacies behind the dancers' and musicians' markings of accented beats and the use of mnemonics, the next section will discuss the articulation of the Panay Bukidnon language and its use via various morphological processes.

MNEMONICS FROM LANGUAGE

Pronunciation is the utterance of certain sounds used in words. It involves the articulation and production of sound. Sound is elemental to various aspects of communication such as speech (both oral production and aural perception), music, and dance. In relation to a mnemonic, spoken sounds provide the structure of speech rhythm determined by the presence and absence of stress and the glottal/stopped or otherwise extended vowel sounds. In turn, these rhythms and accents play a structuring role in music-making and dancing. These speech determinants are part of a larger body of phonetic analysis and examination of sound from spoken language. Before looking at binanog mnemonics' phonetic details, I provide rudimentary information about *Kinaray-a*:[1]

1   Vowel sounds are not equated with the English vowels; only three vowels
     are used—a̱, i̱, and u̱.

2   Every word has monosyllabic stress (only one syllable is stressed, e.g.,
     giri.lìng). There is no secondary stress except in cases of repeated syllable
     words, e.g., the word tàtà (vocal excitations). Monosyllabic stress usually
     falls on the penult or last syllable of the word.

3   Degrees of stress may vary. /ˊ/ is a heavier stress as compared to /ˋ/. Thus,
     in this mnemonic: patakdanga Dalunga, a heavy stress occurs in da̱ of
     patakda̱nga and another in Dalu̱nga: [patak.dáŋaʰ dalu. háʰ]. Patakdanga
     is sometimes shortened to takdanga and in this case, the stress based on
     the people's manner of articulating it (in voice or instrument-playing) is
     applied on the last syllable, the nga of takda̱nga: [takda.háʰ dalu. háʰ]

Reid (2003) quotes Donegan (1993), who wrote the article "Rhythm and Vocalic Drift in Munda and Mon-Khmer:"

> . . . rhythm in music clearly echoes rhythm in language.
> Both are brought about by an internal rhythmic clock,
> or "neural metronome" which emits a flexible but
> regular beat upon which we attempt to map the words
> that we speak. . . . (258)

This relationship between rhythm in language and rhythm in music helps in
understanding the pronunciation of mnemonic words and the particular phonetic structures inherent in Panay Bukidnon language.[2] Reid explicates the
aspects of time in language as well as time in music by discussing rhythm and
syllabic stresses (12). For instance, Austronesian languages in the Philippines
have a phrase accent at the penultimate syllable or at the end of the phrase.
Kinaray-a, being of this language group, manifests this characteristic. This
differentiates Kinaray-a, a syllabic-timed language that has features related to
stress-timed language in other parts of Asia such as Thailand and China.

mnemonic: patakdanga Dalunga
(sometimes as takdanga Dalunga)
phonetic transcription: [patak. dáŋah dalu. ŋah][3]

Reid posits that the "phonetic realization of accent in such languages (stress-timed/syllabic-timed) is usually *pitch* [emphasis mine] since accented syllables can only be lengthened if any other syllables in the same beat are shortened" (5). I explain this in describing the mnemonic system in greater detail after Figure 21. Furthermore, Hyman (1978, 2) says that "pitch is the most reliable perceptual cue for stress (the most common kind of accent)." This aspect about pitch is relevant to understanding the relative differences of tonal production from accents used in the mnemonic phrases of the binanog drum patterns, like so:

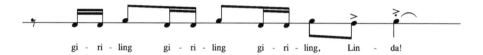

gi - ri - ling   gi - ri - ling   gi - ri - ling,   Lin - da!

FIGURE 21. Intonations on a Female Rhythmic Mode.

So "ling" and "da" are accented, or lengthened. They are realized through a high pitch as compared to shortening gi and ri of "giri" to occupy one beat. This results in a low pitch for these latter syllables. However, the *lin* in "*Linda*" falls in-between the relatively high and low pitches, placing it in a middle range. This outcome arises as a result of two factors: 1) being the only syllable occupying a beat so it does not come out as low as the *gi* and *ri* of "*giri*," which are shortened to fit in one beat, and thus sounded at a lower pitch; and at the same time 2) this syllable is not accented so it is not sounded at a high pitch.

This brings us to a discussion of phonemics. This is the examination of distinct sound units in language and how these allow words to be distinguished from one another. Those fluent in a language can distinguish sounds, organize them into identifiable words, and assign meaning to the resulting words and phrases. This much is obvious. However, fluency in language extends beyond these basics. Mastery of phonemic elements gives rise to individual differences in expression and the meanings drawn from such utterances. This brings us into the realm of culture, which makes use of conventions regarding expressions and meanings, and individual style. Studying the phonemic characteristics of Kinaray-a helps us understand how sound structures comprised by words contribute to local meanings and how the people use words to construct meaning.

Such meanings depend on literal definitions and at the same time reach deep into the realm of connotative meanings. Connotation here is multi-dimensional and open-ended. Many words used by the Panay Bukidnon, such as síbod, have richly layered definitions. Precision is not the point in the sense of a singular, one-to-one mapping of a word's meaning to a particular thing, feeling, or idea. Rather, words suggest, imply, and subsume all kinds of related meanings and feelings into a network of meanings. For instance, síbod connects to sunú, *tayuyon*, and half-a-dozen other named concepts. Taking away any of them reduces the whole constellation of relations and meanings connected to each and all such components and the words associated with them.

In the binanog, a connotation can be suggested, or made explicit through a particular word, phrase or story. It can also be physically manifested. In expounding on patakdanga, a dancer showed me the gestural interpretation of the word. At the same time, I had to read and interpret the suggestions regarding what the word and the gestures meant and how they related to other ideas and movements based on my interviewer's demonstrations.

I asked a number of Panay Bukidnons what patakdanga in *Dalunga* meant. Most of their answers broke down into two types: 1) That the word has no concrete or direct meaning; the syllables contained in that word just serve to guide musicians and dancers in realizing the rhythms in the binanog; 2) That its meanings are indirect and implied. I clarified these two types of perception and built supporting evidence for my interpretation by talking with other binanog performers. One of my most trusted and informed interviewees, Amang Baoy, directed my attention to his dance steps while saying "patakdanga." He pointed to my feet and said "patakdanga" at the same time, commanding me to make the step. From his voice's intonation and by pointing to my feet, he suggested these meanings: to act on the word by dancing; to imitate movement based on a given model (specifically from the word's syllabic structure or from the steps he exemplified); and to communicate with another person or to channel sound and physical rendition as suggested by the prefix pa- in "patakdanga." "Pa" means "to" or "to do something." Although takdanga does not have any denotative meaning according to Amang Baoy, it can suggest any form of action that corresponds with making a sound or physical movement.

So in binanog, a mnemonic becomes a substantial dynamic entity when it is transformed from abstraction to sound, and simultaneously, to other symbolic and discursive forms of communication. Patterns of speech-rhythm, intonation, stress or syllabic accents, among other elements, are reflected in, and made manifest through, mnemonics. Since Panay Bukidnon music and dance rhythm arise from speech rhythm, performing music and dance accords with the pronunciation of local terms in the mnemonics. Knowledge and use of local language (including syllabic constructs, accentuations and intonations) are relevant, even crucial, to actuate sound-to-body transference, and vice-versa. Familiarity with local speech articulation allows speech rhythm to be channeled from the mind to other expressive systems: to hand movements used to beat the drum or gong; to head, trunk, hands and feet, as in the case of dancing; and most significantly, to the affect or emotion, which gives life, force, and vitality to the whole music-dance performance.

Panay Bukidnons translate the *tiniglalaki* (male) or *tinigbabayi* (female) sound patterns into music or movements by the segmentation of 1) affixations and root words; 2) resultant tones from speech inflections; 3) perceived important word-sound segments marked by syllabic stress; and 4) all syllables regardless of function. These processes are explained immediately below.

Affixations refer to prefixes, infixes, and suffixes attached to a root word. Below is an example that demonstrates how parts of mnemonics can be segmented. In this case, the mnemonics are patakdanga Dalunga and *giriling giriling giriling Linda*:

1   Dalunga mode: *pa-tak-da-nga Da-lu-nga:* 'Pa' is a prefix to the root word 'takdang' and 'a' is a suffix. The 'Pa' is a causative prefix attached to a verb. This signals a command or request to an addressee to *takdang* (implying to make a step of). What specific dance step? The 'a' suffix (in *pa-takdang-a)* points to an object topic and in this case, it is *Dalunga.*

2   *Giriling Linda* mode: *gi-ri-ling gi-ri-ling gi-ri-ling Lin-da:* The root word is *giling* and *ri* in the *giriling* is an infix. *Giriling,* to gyrate, is addressed to the object topic, which is Linda (representing the female, in general).

Components of a mnemonic, e.g., affixations, root words, and names, are segmented into their tiniest forms—the syllables. Syllables function like atoms. They can be fashioned into larger and more complex sound/movement/meaning systems. These, in turn, form even more elaborate patterns and systems. Each pattern comprises one cycle repeated throughout the event. Each cycle is a set of mnemonics and this set comprises the structural foundation of binanog music; thus, this set is a sunú. Below is an example of one cycle using mnemonics:

Dalunga	pa	tak	*da*	nga	Da	lu	*nga*
mnemonics or the *sunú* of music	♪	♪	♪	♪	♪	♪	♪

FIGURE 22. Structural bases as sunú.

Each syllable (that is, each mnemonic of the mode Dalunga) represents a single pulse. The agung player works on each pulse and creates a rhythmic pattern thereby varying the given mnemonics. Musicians base their playing on the indicated pulses. In turn, the pulses provide the basis for making rhythmic variations. As shown above, the agung player works on the sunú, or mnemonics, to vary certain pulses. Further details about variations will be discussed in the following chapters.

Syllabication and speech inflections from mnemonics result in varying tones. Musicians produce the varying tones on their instruments by using different playing techniques. Heavy beats contrasted with unaccented or neutral beats translate mnemonics into performance on musical instruments. Another technique, the *pangmidya* (damping of sound), produces pitch change on both gongs and drums. Dampening an instrument is used to produce a relatively low pitch. Doing an unaccented stroke could create a mid-range pitch. A high pitch can come from a strong stroke on an instrument, which results in an accent. Each pitch corresponds to a phoneme in the mnemonic. These relative pitches can be identified below in Giriling Linda, a tinigbabayi rhythmic mode—using this mnemonic: giriling giriling giriling Linda. These varying tones are sometimes heard in the playing of the *agung*:

Mnemonic: giriling giriling giriling Linda

(_ *low pitch*   + *midrange pitch*   ^ *high pitch*)

FIGURE 23. Pitch differences in Giriling Linda.
Note: A higher pitch difference can sometimes be noticed in the mnemonic's last syllable. A high pitch is produced by an accented stroke on an instrument; midrange with an unaccented stroke; and a low pitch by dampening the instrument's sound with a free hand.

Tambur player Mansueto Parle explained that the hand executing the pang-midya makes síbod happen. This hand should be positioned on the upper rim part of the drum. To dampen the sound, one must hold down the stick on the drum skin after the other hand strikes the drum skin. By executing the pangmidya correctly—that is, in rendering the mnemonic accurately and with the proper feel—síbod happens. The production of sound from damping and striking is the key. Synchronization between two hands is another source of síbod.

Damping, in effect, eliminates the decay of a particular sound. This causes the succeeding pulses to be clearly heard. In other instruments such as the agung, the process of damping a sound involves *patik*, or use of sticks played on the gong's rim side. Here the player holds the stick down on the gong's rim after the other hand strikes first. Another form of pangmidya is tightening one's grip on the string that holds the gong to stop the sound reverberation. This is applied to damped syllable sounds as shown in Figure 24.

Pangmidya assists the dancers in easily perceiving tones and synchroniz-ing their steps to the gong. It helps them hear, feel, and move with the musical contour of a phrase. Articulation, whether in playing instruments or dancing, is a form of language that works with pitch differences and tone utterances.

Affect is expressed in damping tones. The kadul player tightly holds the rope or string connected to the agung to deaden the gong's resonance. While doing this, the player would usually *kidò-kidò* (move their shoulders in time with the music). I also noticed the kidò-kidò with tambur players while damping. The shoulder lift is not just for aesthetic effect; rather, it expresses the performers' affect. I mark the areas of pangmidya with a cross (+) and a bracket below where the off-hand damps the instrument.

FIGURE 24. Specific locations where damping is usually applied.
X means beating the instrument according to the guide mnemonic.
+ means pangmidya, usually after another hand or beater has struck the instrument.

Sunú is illustrated in dance through footwork or steps. It does not include the specifics of arm or body movements as these complement the footwork;

however, wrist flexion most often occurs on accented steps. Details of body movements, including footwork and arm motions, will be described using Benesh notation (see Appendix, A5). The reader can see that the notation does not indicate the kinds of steps being made—light, heavy, brush style— that are conventionally required because, as sunú, the syllables only serve as a guide for placing each foot in each event cycle. Of primary importance here is that the movements alternate between the two feet and this pattern of alternation continues for two or three cycles.

mnemonics or the sunú of music	gi	ri	ling	gi	ri	ling	gi	ri	li-	(ng)	Lin	da
DANCE PHASES	♪	♪	♪	♪	♪	♪	♪	♪	♪	♪	♪	♪
bayhunan			step							step		step
repasu		step	step		step	step		step	step			step	step
sadsad			step			step				step	accented step	accented step

FIGURE 25. Sunú of music and dance.

The three dance phases indicated above are customary in the female rhythmic mode. From bayhunan, where the solo female dancer moves sparingly with few steps, she proceeds to repasu where more syllables of the mnemonics are delivered through the footwork. Then she renders the accents of the mnemonics by stamping her foot on their last two syllables: this initiates the sadsad. The dancer eventually exits from this phase. Notice that the Giriling Linda mode as shown in the Figure does not have the pinanyo phase, which is typical in Dalunga. This is because the dance is not a partner dance and does not call for the cloth game. Instead, the female dancer can just stop the dance anytime during the sadsad. Choosing when and how to stop is solely up to the dancer since she does not have a partner who would complement or respond to her movements as she moves toward closure. When she does stop the musicians also cease playing. However, they can base their "feel" for this closure from the dancer's display of dance styles in sadsad. As this female rhythmic mode calls for the woman's display of her physicality and grace, she demonstrates this and exits when she knows she has fulfilled the purpose.

As a sunú to playing instruments and dancing, these mnemonic segmentations shown in Figure 25 are merely guides or bases for creative variations in playing rhythmic patterns. In actual practice, musicians apply hàmpang to the mnemonic segments. This gives rise to many patterns and variations.

According to Mehoran, síbod means "*ga-sunú ang basal sa tikang amo man kadya ang tikang sa basal*" (a musical instrument should be played based on a dance's timing, and dance steps cohere with the music). She said this while watching a binanog performance she did not approve of because the music-making and dancing did not attain a balanced effort. Worse, the musicians and dancers did not synchronize to the rhythm. After explaining this, she demonstrated how an instrument should adhere to the basics of mnemonics to align with the dance movements. She underscored the importance of marking the music's accented beats by heavy footwork, and then contrasting these with unaccented beats according to the underlying linguistic structure.

There are designated references and relationships in sunú. To initiate sound, a binanog musician has a *gina-isip nga limog* (thought-of sound/mnemonics). According to Mansueto Parle of Barangay Bato-Bato (Tapaz, Capiz), a thought-of-sound precedes the initiation of action. It is a mnemonic that serves as a memory guide to mentally organizing and then performing rhythmic patterns in playing instruments.

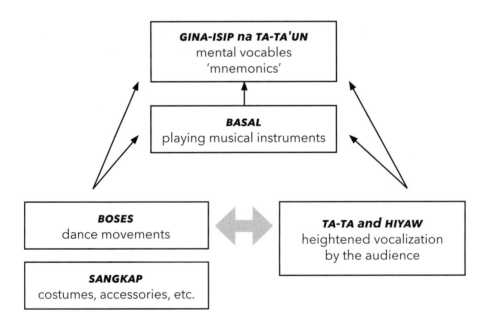

FIGURE 26. Dependence on mnemonics.

The mental vocables are translated into sound via the *basal* (instrument playing). Dancers first listen to the music performed on instruments. Then, they determine whether the music calls for a dance by a lone woman or a male-female couple. Aside from basal, some dancers also base their boses on mnemonics. They bring life and additional energy to the basal through their boses via sangkap. These accessories act as rattles, adding rhythmic emphasis and shimmer to the music. As the dance proceeds, the audience becomes more active with *tàtà* (vocables). The tàtà should be performed in time with the basal and the *ginapaino-ino nga limog* (thought-of sound). Taken together, this collective sound motivates dancers and musicians. It heightens the spirited atmosphere of the binanog-in-action.

Some factors are considered before using a specific mnemonic. Typically, a dancer would ask himself/herself what music would best correspond to the celebration. The lead dancer would also observe the other dancers, noting their body types and ages. A heavy body would require a slower rhythmic pattern; the same logic would hold for older dancers. The dancer's preferred rhythmic mode would also be considered. S/he may be familiar with certain dance steps that go with particular musical patterns. Musicians and dancers need not discuss this if they are familiar with each other's favored rhythmic mode *ex ante*.

Upon deciding the type of mnemonic, instruments would begin to play. The music would start on the agung playing patik. The tambur follows, also played using a pair of sticks, although not on the rim of the drum. The kadul on the agung complements this. Both the beating on the tambur and on the rim of the agung would maintain repeated rhythmic patterns. The tambur and agung using kadul may vary mnemonics used by segmenting the related syllables and forming patterns from rhythmic combinations of these syllables. More explanation about the details of patterning is given within the discussion about hampang.

CONSTRUCTS OF GENDER

Sunú also involves Panay Bukidnon gender constructs. This connection comes through two main binanog categories: the tinigbabayi and the tiniglalaki. These binary categories are assigned to specific music and dance types within the binanog. *Tiniglalaki* literally means "for men" and *tinigbabayi* "for women." The use of "for" in the phrase "for men/women" directly presupposes a purpose or function. "What does the binanog do for a man or for a woman?" This question is addressed in the paragraphs below.

Gender consideration arises from appreciating natural physical and sexual distinctions between males and females. This naturalness is evident in replies to my question, "Why is there gender differentiation?" My informants typically replied, *Kay amo dai-a* (Because that's the way it is; or: it has always been that way).

This difference translates to various aspects of music-making, dancing, and the mnemonics underlying both. Tuohan once observed a peculiar dance in Barangay Garangan (Calinog, Iloilo). A woman danced alone to the music of a male rhythmic mode. He corrected the performers: *Dalunga dai-a! Unsa man di sya mag tinigbabayi?* (That's a Dalunga! Why doesn't she dance the tinigbabayi instead?).

In terms of music and dance, the primary sunú, or bases for gendering, is the mnemonic. The resulting sound from combining syllables and structures in mnemonics implies specific meanings. One of these meanings suggests stylized movements. Sound structures suggest certain sensations, which Bolinger (1989) refers to as phonestheme. Articulations in these word families mimic sensory-based semantics of word groups that provide associations to particular tactile, visual, and other sensory experiences (Shore on Bolinger 1991, 19). Among the Panay Bukidnon, the mnemonic *giriling giriling giriling Linda* used for a female rhythmic mode suggests grace and a certain finesse. Women move their feet over the ground in an especially fluid, elegant fashion when dancing with this mnemonic in mind. Perhaps the recurrent use of the vowel "i" in the repeated mnemonic *giriling* suggests these physical acts and intimate gestures. On the other hand, the mnemonic *patakdanga Dalunga* for a man's rhythmic mode suggests to the Panay Bukidnon certain aggressiveness and freedom of movement associated with male action. One way that gendered dances differ is that men raise their feet high while women barely lift their feet off the ground. Perhaps the use of the vowel "a"—which requires a more open posture of the mouth and of breathing—in the mnemonic *patakdanga Dalunga* contributes to the openness in how the feet move and the way the whole body refers to the space around the dancer.

Just as a mnemonic is associated with a particular rhythmic mode, gender also acquires identity through the reiteration of certain behavioral patterns and acts by men and women. The dichotomy between the sexes is reinforced, differentiated, and made to appear natural in this way. "Performativity is thus not a single 'act,' for it is always a *reiteration* (emphasis, mine) of a norm or set of norms . . . to the extent that it acquires an act-like status in the present . . ." (Foster on Butler 1998, 3).

The tinigbabayi's Giriling Linda rhythmic mode displays a single female dancer's grace and skill. A group of women sometimes join the dance for fun. In a formal setting, dancing the Giriling Linda introduces a young unmarried woman to society. The binanog is executed in a public sphere that displays her womanhood in stylized movements. This is when men can assess and select whom they will partner with in the tiniglalaki. Traditionally, this becomes an especially exciting moment for a binukot who is first seen publicly in the binanog. She dances wearing a *takurong*, which almost covers her whole face. She raises curiosity among the men in attendance and this encourages bidding on her bride-gift.

Traditionally, the tiniglalaki is performed after the tinigbabayi. However, Panay Bukidnons no longer strictly follow this rule. Dancers and musicians can deviate from the traditional sequence, especially on occasions where gatherings emphasize fun over formality.

It is interesting to note that the tiniglalaki is not danced by a solo male but by a duet—a man and a woman. This dance serves as a venue for a man's quest for a wife. It is for a man because it directly benefits him. A gathering is important because some of the community's barangays are quite remote from each other. It is his rare opportunity to meet, learn about, and screen different women as a prospective marriage partner. Through the gathering, everyone becomes visible and publicly known.

The man or his parents in the Panay Bukidnon community can choose his wife and not the other way around. The tiniglalaki is the man's domain of power, and of course, where he can practice power. In it, he draws the woman toward his aim. This is not to say that the woman is powerless. A woman expresses her power and prowess when she attempts to outsmart a man in the pinanyo. The pinanyo is the final phase of the binanog where the woman takes the lead role in moving the dance forward by pursuing the man's panyo. Here she brings the man into her turf. Her approach and aim is distinct from the actions taken by the man in the tiniglalaki construct I mentioned earlier.

Between male and female binanog dancers, there is a sunú as to how each one moves in conjunction with one's partner. For instance, the man should observe and match the steps of the woman. Amang Baoy says it is important for the man to sense when the woman will shift her steps from repasu to sadsad. As soon as he sees this shift, he must adjust his steps and dance the sadsad. He must also pay attention to where his partner is headed. If the woman is heading towards the center of the dance floor, the man must follow her. These conventions are traditional parts of the binanog's function, particularly in its courtship setting.[4]

Figure 27 shows the dance phases in a tiniglalaki. These phases correspond to the stages of courtship in the Panay Bukidnon tradition. Although presented in a structured and chronological way, in practice they may follow other sequences of order, overlap or change position depending on individual situations. Research participants have provided the phases below. They are in the order most faithful to the binanog tradition's conventions:

DANCE PHASES	bayhunan	repasu	sadsad	simbalud	pinanyo
	(leisure walk)	(dancer shifts from walking to dancing using un-accented footwork)	(use of accented footwork)	(flying like a pigeon, encircling partner)	(game of handcloths)
COURT-SHIP PHASES	meeting	orientation/ observation	Show of character/ abilities	Familiar-ity/moving to a closer relation-ship	Challenge of wits and strategy; closer space/ intimacy

FIGURE 27. Phase correspondences.

The binanog dance phases reflect the gradual but developing process of courtship—from meeting, to orienting/observing each other, showing each other's characters and capabilities, until familiarity with one another brings the couple into a closer relationship. Unlike the tinigbabayi where a woman dances alone (traditionally to show her talent and to publicly display her availability for marriage), the tiniglalaki establishes that the dance partners have met and have interacted to know each other more deeply. It is important to note the gaze and expression of the dancers. In the first three phases, dancers hardly look at each other. As strangers, there is a certain level of ambivalence, mixed with shyness, between them. This perception of each other as strangers changes as partners perform the pinanyo. This is because it necessitates eye contact and focus on the panyo. Increased eye contact also suggests an intensified level of involvement with the other person.

The sunú also varies as the dance moves from one phase to the next. Women enact certain traits in the tiniglalaki. These are particular to the Giriling Linda of tinigbabayi, such as their earthbound footwork. As they move from the bayhunan and repasu to the sadsad phase, there is an observable shift of sunú. A portrayal of a contrasting aggressive role for the woman prepares and anticipates the coming of the pinanyo. In this latter phase of the binanog, the woman pursues the man to obtain his panyo. As they move from the bayhunan to the sadsad, men have already established a spirited and free dancing form. Then, in the pinanyo, a man shows his resistance to the woman's pursuit by positioning his panyo away from the woman.

Shifting between dance phases requires crossing thresholds that are subtle, but not quite invisible. Traditionally the woman guides the dance through these phases. The male dancer follows her lead by keenly observing the shift in body movements, especially her feet and facial expressions. The direction of her gaze is one way to indicate such a change. Because these changes may evade simple observation, the process takes on a liminal quality, a sense of standing on a threshold. Sometimes it is subtly sensed even in the slightest gestures of her body. It could be how her fingers untie the ends of her panyo, which at first is tied around her shoulders, to spread it widely on her back, before moving it to the front of her body. These gestures—first nearly undetectable then, finally, open—signal her preparation for pursuing the man's panyo. I once witnessed an audience member loudly comment that the male dancer did not see the very beginnings of a dance phase's changes. Instead of shifting from simbalud to pinanyo, he kept his panyo folded in his hands. The audience brought him back to his senses by shouting *Pinanyo na!* (It is time for pinanyo!). With this, he began spreading out his panyo and initiating his strategies of dancing with the panyo, as expected.

The woman brings the intensity level of the dance from a relaxed pace in bayhunan to a quickening of movement in sadsad and simbalud. The audience encourages the transition of dance phases as they initiate the vocal excitations. These participatory sounds are tàtà and *hiyaw*. They drive the dancers to come closer and connect with each other via the pinanyo. Instrumentalists may also raise the music's dynamic level. The dancers and the audience drive the shifts from one section to another. They also drive the resulting changes in energy and intensity.

Traditionally in the binanog, men become the challenged gender. They become prey in the so-called *si-ud* (entrapment of women). Si-ud is an alternative approach to seizing the man's panyo when the subtler and stylisti-

cally appealing techniques fail after repeated attempts. In si-ud, the woman
hurls her panyo around a man's neck, trapping him and preventing him from
moving. All of these approaches serve to more deeply involve the dancers,
both as binanog performers and as men and women. Because connection is a
central aim, multiple means exist that encourage a man and a woman to relate
to each other. In these ways the binanog partly mirrors life cycle processes
recalled within the period of 'doing' the dance, playing the music, and performing related practices. The conventional—or model—man and woman in
the binanog are tasked with enacting their traditional roles. However, they are
actually exemplars of flexible or versatile sexual agents who adjust their roles
in particular situations or circumstances.

In executing kadul on the agung, Panay Bukidnons vary the beating intensity on the gong's bossed area. Tuohan says the beating should be *ginadu-on
du-on* (intensified) in the tiniglalaki gender modes by pressing the beater on
the agung's bossed portion. In tinigbabayi, the beating should be *latun-latun*
(lightly pressing on the gong's boss). This contrast of playing the gong relies
on an explication concerning an act rather than the effect of sound from the
degree of beating the instrument.

As with many Southeast Asian music-dance forms, Panay Bukidnon music
and dance rely on one another. The relationship of these two forms is crucial,
even to the point of the two being essentially unified. For instance, musicians
depend on the dancer's boses for cues about when to shift to a given rhythmic
variation or tempo. This happens particularly in identifying when the sadsad
dance step starts. Mehoran said dancers often sense when a patik or kadul is
not properly executed, which affects their dancing. When this happens she
stops dancing and reprimands the player. When dancers or musicians first
sense poorly played music, they initiate a salú, or catch to correct the timing.
If the catch or correction does not work or sustain itself, the whole music and
dance activity ends.

THE BODY TRANSLATING SOUND

Sunú are guidelines to actions and have implications for action beyond the
music-dance tradition. Here, we focus on the binanog in understanding
these guidelines/actions. The rendition of these guidelines generates various musical and movement forms where the *tubu-an* becomes the actor. The
epistemology of the local term tubu-an is interesting, as it is rooted in the

word *tubu* (growth). The suffix "an" connotes the base or main source of out-growths. Tubu-an translates into one's trunk. From there, the arms, legs, and head extend out as appendages of the trunk. When applied to musicians and dancers, the tubu-an's generative capability points to the practice of human creativity. This creativity primarily works through a given base that provides ideas or structures for action. Cultural structures (e.g., life cycle and aging) and activity (e.g., rituals, courtship dances, and daily activities, like hiking and farming) stimulate creativity through the body. This is why we must "not think of the dance simply as a *play activity*, (italics mine) but as forming part of an . . . undertaking" (Williams 1999, 124). The binanog is the pursuit of a prospective mate by reading their gestures, body movements, and use of the panyo. The tubu-an is a channel by which the different parts of one's body become active, involved, and responsive to sound. This brings up the notion of embodiment in realizing a goal of action.

Miningkol shared her experience as a child:

Sang ga-edad pa lang ko sang una mga lima ka tuig, naga-adtu kami sa punsyon. Kung magsaut gani, ang magurang ko lang pirmi ga-saot; ako iya waay. Tapos natanom sa isip ko, para magabantog man ako nga manog-binanog, magatu-un ako kada magparigus ako sa suba' . . . kis-a ginapadala ko lang paagi sa hampang (play) . . . kung paano mag-arte, kag paano ko maintindihan ang saot nga binanog . . . magasaut ako sa baras, sa tubungan, sa idalum ka among balay . . . para ya Makita ko ya agi ko sa baras, kun pila ka purgada . . .

When I was five years old, we went to a *punsyon* (feast). When dancing sessions would come, my older sister always danced; not me. Then I thought if I would be a famous binanog dancer, I should practice whenever I would go to the river to bathe . . . sometimes I did it through playing . . . how to creatively act, how I would understand the binanog . . . when I dance on the sand, in the *tubungan*, the lower part of the house . . . so I could see my footprints on the sand, how long is the distance . . .

Miningkol was exposed to various binanog activities in punsyon. Her sister often showed her dancing prowess while Miningkol just watched. This challenged Miningkol, who wished to be like her sister, a well known expert dancer. Inspired, Miningkol spent her childhood days practicing the dance by the river. Instead of playing sand and water games, she played with dance. According to her, it was like a child's play.

In another conversation, Miningkol observed dancers while she was an audience member. She noticed that some of them were muttering words while dancing. This muttering, called tàtà, seemed to be done in conjunction with their arm and footwork. She recalled using tàtà so that even without accompanying music, her dancing became better when she muttered. Her feet executed the rhythm in the sand while she focused on vocalizing the mnemonics. She did not ask to be taught. She equipped herself by means of observation, resourcefulness, and confidence to learn. This theory, shared by most Panay Bukidnon dancers, differed from the commonly held principle "the visual/kinesthetic senses are primary in dance, whereas the auditory/kinesthetic senses predominate in music-making" (Hanna 1992, 319). In binanog, there is no notion of the primacy of the visual sense vis-a-vis dancing, nor is the auditory sense of singular import in playing music. Miningkol posits that the visual and auditory senses are both actively involved in dance.

There are other physical and affective motions of dancers that may be considered sunú. When Miningkol taught me to dance, I remember her telling me to li-ad. This is where the dancer bends backward, pushing the chest forward while flapping the arms. I found this to be a test of balance. In the first few training sessions, I nearly fell backwards several times because of the stance's difficulty. I came to understand their sense of balance after hiking with them. I have joined them through rugged hills, farm paddies and narrow, steep trails. They could keep their bodies pliant and their strides fast and unbothered. Meanwhile, I could hardly cope with their speed. I gradually improved after numerous hikes, coupled with continuous training. I eventually developed the balance needed to dance without falling backwards.

Everyday routine and activities form and dynamically reconstruct the body's kinesthetic memory. Pierre Bourdieu (1980) explicates that practice, and its related workings, is structured and predisposed to (re)structuring through the body. In *Body, Movement and Culture: Kinesthetic and Visual Symbolism in a Philippine Community*, Sally Ann Ness (1992) connects the movements of everyday practice (what she calls routine or raw behavior) to the patterns of dance as learned collective experiences or explicitly as "symbolic public action." In other words, experiences pattern movement, balance, and physical awareness. In the words of Wacquant (2011), experience is pedagogical. As a boxing apprentice, Wacquant organized his ongoing observation of pugilistic pedagogy, and participation in practice of the sport, while consistently drawing from Bourdieu's anthropological works to personally test and validate the many concepts about actions. He notes that in the *Outline of a Theory of Practice*, Bourdieu retrieves habitus "from a long line of philosophers, stretching from Aristotle to Aquinas to Husserl, to develop a dispositional theory of action recognizing that social agents are not passive beings pulled and pushed about by external forces, but skillful creatures who actively construct social reality through "categories of perception, appreciation and action." In the process of learning the li-ad with Miningkol, I saw myself as an active learner in that I circumvented the pedagogy of mere imitation (the apprentice imitating the teacher's movements) to make a connection with work-related techniques such as walking the narrow borders of paddies, navigating the sudden drops on hillside trails, and moving over other challenging contours of curving highlands. I observed the balancing act of farmers walking through narrow paddies and how this act conjoins with their li-ad when they danced the binanog at nighttime. In the same light, mastering the balancing of my strides while moving through upland farms developed my li-ad stances. I therefore add to Bourdieu's and Wacquant's perception that a non-dance experience, which I was previously a passive learner of, has become a relevant dance-learning skill that can be constituted and embodied in the formation of practice.

Another body movement that Miningkol taught me was kidò-kidò. This consists of shoulder lifts done in time with the music. It is a felt motion. Once a dancer gets the groove of the music, his/her natural tendency is to lift his/her shoulders continuously in time with the music. Kidò-kidò is a skill at a higher level of mastery in dance and music-making. At this level, emotions can be externalized and skills are well-developed. This type of expressivity in the binanog ascertains a performer's comprehension of the music and dance. This is determined by tactile or physical stimuli and responses. Panay Bukidnons find kidò-kidò a visually pleasing and beautiful element in the binanog.

Who can gauge and evaluate if the sunú have been well incorporated in performance? Amang Baoy remarked that a systematically effective binanog performance could best be seen from the eyes of a true dancer. This is assuming that the dancer he was referring to is not at this time performing but rather is part of the crowd viewing a performance:

Makita mo ang tunay nga   You can see a true dancer: the
manog-saot: malantaw,   dancer watches, can determine that
mahambal tana nga santú gid, everything is working well, there is
uniform gid, santú-anay gid ya   uniformity of movements and the
ang ika-sarang sa sa-ut.   capabilities of dancers matched.

Amang Baoy's point is that a dancer would qualify as true if he/she could judge an effective dance. An effective dance goes well with the music and with the performers' capabilities. Thus, alignment and compatibility fall into place naturally. An experienced dancer is often a good evaluator. The communities' elders usually watch and determine a performance's quality. They have rich music-making and dancing experiences, allowing them to understand and feel what works, expresses, or embodies síbod. They know the whole network of operations in a performance. They are versatile enough to switch roles. They can be musicians and dancers, audience participants, critics, and teachers.

CHAPTER 5

Hàmpang as Play on Structures

PANAY BUKIDNONS CONNECT HÀMPANG TO THE *BANOG*'S NATURAL HUNTING tendencies. When it flies, it takes off from a tree branch; it wanders the sky, scanning for prey, before returning to the trees. Patrolling the skies—wandering, as the Panay Bukidnon put it—is a serious prelude to capturing prey. It exemplifies the banog's freedom of movement in space. In the same manner, hàmpang is purposeful even as it is open and playful. A serious regard for *sunú* exists even in the process of playing. So the banog's homing back to the tree is like a dancer's recalling of patterns from sunú.

The ability of a musician or dancer to play around the sunú, or to manipulate rhythmic structures and work around conventions of movements/sound, is reflective of a good player. Panay Bukidnons would call a said player an *antigo*. Thus, hàmpang is another concept within *síbod* that refers to the act of playing through personal and creative interpretation of structures found in language, as well as other nuances that articulate these structures.

Hampang's process and conceptualization are mirrored in *larò*, its Tagalog equivalent. Larò plays a significant role in the practice of *subli*, a traditional music-dance form found in Bauan, Batangas (southwestern Luzon, Philippines). Mirano (1989) sees the interplay between song, music, and dance as a result of a larò around the formula and procedures of these expressive forms. Above all these performative elements lie the seriousness and meaning of subli in its main intent: to please the *Poon* (God). Play in subli is essentially an act of performers praying deeply as a form of personal devotion.

The notion of play and manipulation also appears in the article "Sacred Camp" by Alcedo (2007). He utilizes the word "navigate" to work around participative processes in the *Ati-Atihan* Festival of Kalibo, Aklan (Western Visayas, Philippines). It is a street dance embodying Panay Island's *Ati* (dark-skinned natives). They embrace the Catholic faith and venerate the

Santo Niño (the child Jesus). Alcedo gives particular attention to one's gender identity and general playfulness even to the point of eccentricity. In Alcedo's words, it is Carnivalesque, or costuming as forms of self-representation. At the same time, a deeper feeling flows through the festivities. One's participation is a religious devotion incorporated in the very spirit of the festival. This echoes my earlier discussion about larò in a dance called subli (Mirano 1989). In it, play and pray are intertwined in the devotion to Poon.

I see Alcedo's definition of the word navigate as being close to the meaning of hàmpang as defined by Panay Bukidnons. Alcedo's treatment of gender and blurring of gender definitions links to hàmpang in the way gender roles can be reversed and negotiated in the binanog. Although the Panay Bukidnons' binary gender categories do not entirely align with Alcedo's discussion of multiple identities, I see the point of gender transformation as a reality within the very frame of a music-dance performance such as in the Ati-Atihan and binanog.

This notion of play and reworking structures is not limited to the Philippine context. In *The Pin Peat Ensemble: Its History, Music and Context* (1988), Cambodian ethnomusicologist Sam-Ang Sam writes about the notion of *bamphley* (to cheat; to alter; to change). Applied to various professions, from magicians to meat sellers and businessmen, bamphley is also associated with musical processes. It enters with the intent of making various elements different from their original forms via embellishment, or making a simple melody or rhythm more complex. Variation is done to avoid monotony as well as to express freedom and creativity in music-playing and dancing.

Connecting hàmpang to larò, bamphley, and other concepts of play provide a wider ground for discourse on restructuring conventions and renewing expressions.

In binanog, hàmpang is playing around normative structures found in language. This includes the order, arrangement, and sequence of mnemonic syllables. At the same time, it makes considerations regarding accentuations. The term hàmpang is also used in place of *pinanyo*. I heard it used once in a binanog event; the people exclaimed: "*Hinampang na!*" (It is time for play!) This means it is time for the pinanyo to start. In this game, female dancers try to outsmart their male counterparts to gain possession of his *panyo*.

There are also visual representations of hampang. Feliza Castor, an elder from Barangay Nayawan (Tapaz, Capiz) showed me the *batong-batong* (tattoo) on her chest. It was a figure of a man dancing the binanog. His arms flapped like the wings of a banog in flight, and his legs showed the curve of a binanog dance step. I asked her what it meant and her answer was "*ga-ham-pang.*" She did not tell me that the man was dancing, but rather, that he was playing.

In different forms, play as an act or a symbol (e.g. tattoo) is embodied in the individual. It also comes about through social interaction between people. In binanog, it is between different musicians, musicians and dancers, and especially paired dancers. This active and overlapping web of participation manifests and animates the complex relationships of people involved in the music and dance activity. Hampang is a vital part of living, particularly in building the communal spirit among members of the community.

RHYTHMICIZING MNEMONICS

Panay Bukidnons play the agung and tambur in the same way that they play with language. They treat musical rhythms like natural speech. Panay Bukidnons interchange vowels in words just as they sometimes abbreviate words. For instance, the words tiniglalaki or tinigbabayi have puzzled me. Sometimes locals would say them as *tinaglaki* or *tinagbayi.* Sometimes the term is *tiniglaki* or tiniglalaki, tinigbabayi or *tinigbayi.* As I learned conversational Kinaray-a's nuances, I realized that pinning down exact definitions missed the point. The terms tiniglaki or tiniglalaki and tinigbayi or tinigbabayi have the same meanings, provided one refers to the root words *laki* (man) and *bayi* (woman). Thus, *tinig[laki], tinag[laki], tinigla[laki], tinagla[laki], tig[laki]* all mean 'for a man' or 'representing a man.' Panay Bukidnons interchange affixes to the root word laki such that *tinig, tinag,* or the even shorter *tig* may all be employed and yet mean the same thing. The root word may also be augmented or repeated; for instance, laki is sometimes spoken as *lalaki.*[1]

Regarding the spontaneous use of language, Robert Jourdain (2002, 174) writes in his book, *Music, the Brain, and Ecstasy.*

> There is nothing extraordinary with improvisation. We all improvise constantly in words. . . . We begin a conversation with a topic, draw in related observations, digress to subtopics, and add moments of emphasis or wit.

In Panay Bukidnon practice, whether in music or dance, variances are made possible by creatively using affixes to root words of the mnemonics. The creativity and variation Jourdain observes flows directly into musical and kin-esthetic expression, since linguistic mnemonics underlie both structures. In particular, Panay Bukidnons improvise on syllabic segmentation by choosing segments of syllables from words to form specific patterns, for example:

1. *Giriling Linda* mnemonics: *giriling giriling giriling Linda*
    In Syllabic Segmentation:
    gi/ri/ling, gi/ri/ling, gi/ri/ling, Lin/da
    Play of Syllabic Segmentation:
    gi/ri/ling, gi/ling, gi/ling, Lin/da

2. *Dalunga* mnemonics: *patakdanga Dalunga*
    In Syllabic Segmentation: *pa/tak/da/nga, Da/lu/nga*
    Play of Syllabic Segmentation:
    tak/dang, tak/dang, tak/dang/a, lu/nga

    This play with segmentation results in a rhythm that is similar to a mnemonic used in playing the *litgit* (bowed two-stringed zither) and *subing* (jaw's harp): *"kadul, Tisan; sadsad, Ingkitan"* (play the *agung* Tisan, dance Ingkitan) or as segmented: *ka/dul, Ti/san; sad/sa/(a)d, Ing/ki/tan*

As shown in the above examples of play via syllabic segmentation, syllables can be diminished, sped-up, or short-cut, such as in the cases of *lu-nga, lu-nga, nga, nga* in *Dalunga*. Certain syllables can be augmented through doubling, tripling or embellishing: *pa-tak-da-nga pa-tak-da-nga, pa-tak-da-nga Dalunga*. Performers insert the variations after the basic patterns have been played through. Sometimes, changes directly follow the introductory beats. Other times, due to these combinations' complexity, the basic pattern becomes almost unrecognizable.

Some instruments in an ensemble can hàmpang. This is because instrument techniques like the *patik* maintain the basic musical materials, allowing other instruments to vary. The repetitive material is often called an *ostinato* in Western musicology. According to Bonnie Wade (2004), an ostinato is an-other form of drone. Here, I use the term drone to refer to repeated, founda-tional sound patterns:

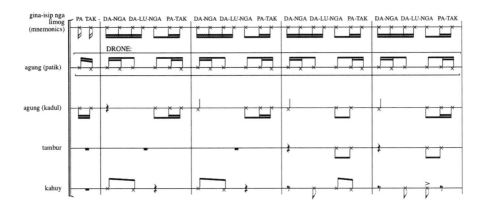

FIGURE 28. Drone or repeated patterns.

In this example, the patik on the agung and the *kahuy* provide constant drones. Sometimes, the kadul on agung as well as the tambur reiterate each other's patterns briefly. However, they can improvise their parts at any point.

The musical drones can drive the dance activity by stabilizing the relationships of dance phases, say, from sadsad to simbalud, then to pinanyo. The development of dance phases may be seen as dynamic forms moving in time with the repetition of musical patterns or drones. This kind of dynamic relationship continuously brings music/dance into a sense of balance. This is due to shared roles, connected materials, and support in building the excitement of the communal event.

Panay Bukidnon musicians use repetition strategically. Repetition is the bedrock of their creativity as expressed in elaborated rhythms. As they repeat patterns, they reach an almost thoughtless state. Their hands play the rhythm over and over until their natural reflexes take over. Thoughtlessness should not be equated with being unthinking. Thinking is taken over by the body in habitual motion. This state of automatic movement provides players a chance to work out and render the variations they plan to execute.

Repeated sections are like moments of stasis, during which nothing seems to be happening. This was my experience when my mentors Mehoran and Alfred Castor coached me. They taught me to dwell on the stasis. When I asked why, they said my hands or sticks had to stay in motion and sound for a long time. I did not need to think about them moment-by-moment and should concentrate on creating patterns later. In this realm of stasis, I realized that there was potential or stored energy. The stasis is a thought reservoir for the formation of other rhythmic combinations. It could embellish or vary the constant, repeated pattern. I saw—and felt—the purpose of repetition. A repetition prepares one to alter or embellish. As one dwells on the patterns' habitual repetition, one looks for change. As I played, I thought about introducing dynamic elements to the music while repeating the cycle. There was something about repetition as a form of stasis that made the need for dynamic articulations more evident and convincing.

Panay Bukidnons call the changes introduced after a continuous stream of repetitions *palabor-labor*. This means going around—not going straight to the point. Palabor-labor can also imply embellishment of a repeated pattern or a short improvisation based on a rhythmic pattern. Typically, these improvisations are short. In Panay Bukidnon's culinary language, palabor-labor can mean giving *sabor* (extra flavor) to bland food.

Players may respond to each other by playing repetitive patterns, with variations, as in hocketing. In the example below, a kahuy responds to the kadul. The kahuy hockets as it occupies the kadul's empty space and helps complete a united string of rhythms as seen below:

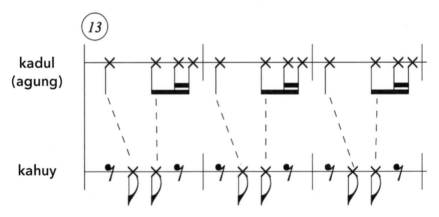

FIGURE 29. Hocketing between the *kadul* (beating the gong's boss) and the *kahuy* (wooden percussion).

Some instruments provide a contrast to the repeated rhythmic patterns by embellishing them. The contrast does not eradicate the sense of balance and stability that the repeated patterns provide. It is the embellished patterns that provide contrasts and reinforce the strong beats. These beats serve as key signposts where dancers and musicians can synchronize movements, intensity, and emphasis.

The next example illustrates how gong and drum musicians interpret the Giriling Linda mnemonic with hàmpang.

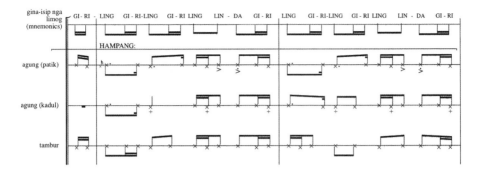

FIGURE 30. Instruments at Hàmpang.

People who are not part of the Panay Bukidnon community may look down on a simple repetition of rhythmic patterns. One time, as a public school teacher assigned to Barangay Taganhin (Tapaz, Capiz) watched the binanog, he exclaimed: "*Amo man dai-a gihapon!*" (It's just all the same!) His words state that he heard only repetition and he said this with a tone of frustration and boredom. This reaction can be linked to an etic, or outsider's perception, of a tradition. His etic perspective emerges from a particular context. His expertise at work is teaching Math and Science lessons, not dance studies or anthropology or Philippine cultural studies. A few times a month he would make brief visits to the community and leave for town after teaching lessons. Thus, he did not have enough exposure to understand the details embedded in this cultural expression. Given his lack of exposure, and a concomitant lack of guidance in how to perceive the music, he could only hear the music and see the dance on "his" terms.

Many persons who first encounter the binanog do not detect the fine details at work in the music, and therefore, fail to make a meaningful connection to the work. Without meaning, the work seems uninteresting. Typically, we regard meaningless, uninteresting work with indifference. This, in turn, produces distance. This distance weighs heavily on the work of the Panay highlanders. Few outsiders take an interest in their dance and music.[2] The aforementioned teacher falls directly into this trap. In the midst of his observations, he stood apart, missing the point that this is a ritual that requires participation. For instance, he did not chant the vocables that connect the dancers to the non-dancers in the ritual. By leaving before the full "narrative" of the dance had played out, he did not see that the dance moved toward the game of handcloths, wherein the female dancer works to catch her male dance partner's handcloth. This being a courtship dance, such interaction operates at the center of the dance's meaning. He was neither attentive to nor completely aware of the subtle changes in rhythms due to the players' palabor-labor. Such ignorance, which can happen to us as a consequence of our inattentiveness as well as our holding onto ideas that hinder meaningful observation, can lead to making judgments that lack sound bases.

The people's rendition of the binanog is an all-encompassing and integrative form of sugid that is achieved in certain forms of performativity, or states of projection. During an active state where performers and audience-participants are involved, display has a central role. In this formal setting, the binanog is executed at its best with the least error possible. This allows the audience-participant to watch, listen, and interpret, with sharpened focus, what is being expressed in the performance.

Another way the binanog projects sugid is through the preparation state. Here, people gather and casually rehearse their music-playing skills, or learn new steps from their elders. This state has an informal atmosphere compared to the active state. Performers can be interrupted and interviewed while they act. During this state, I took the opportunity to learn the details of mnemonic segmentation. The dancers and musicians explained these points to me verbally, with physical demonstrations. The sugid becomes two-dimensional or more as the binanog performers respond to questions while playing instruments or dancing. Multi-dimensional interactions could happen when non-performers share their views, or demonstrate dances on the sidelines (due to shyness, among other inhibitions). On some occasions, others pulled me to the dance floor, encouraging me to dance. Often, they would let me experience the dance or the music rather than explain them.

ORGANIZATION OF TIME

I learned various lessons about the binanog while the Panay Bukidnon were in their preparation or active state. One lesson is about organizing time. The binanog has recurrent patterns in its mnemonics. Hence, musicians and dancers partition and create a sequence from its syllables. They render this into music and dance expressions. Aside from this process, I have found another way of understanding time organization. In order to convey certain rhythmic ideas to particular readers and academe-based musicians and dancers (particularly to non-Panay Bukidnons), I thought of organizing the said patterns into meters, marked with time signatures. I have used the idea of the time

signature to deal with the sense of precision and to understand the function
and effects of accentuations on the perception of time.

In reality, Panay Bukidnon musicians do not articulate the idea of time
signatures. They have a feel for certain time regularities—a basis for organization. I employ time signatures to deepen the discussion of convention and
play in music-making across cultural boundaries. This is to understand síbod.
I note that the representation of time signature is not without basis. It is taken
from the structures of mnemonics:

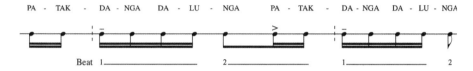

FIGURE 31. Mnemonic: *patakdanga Dalunga*.

The "pa-tak" here is a form of an upbeat. The main measure comes in on "da"
of "da-nga Da-lu" as the first beat followed by "nga patak" as the second beat.
As such, the time signature is 'two-four' (2/4), or two main beats where each
beat is represented by a quarter note.

FIGURE 32. Mnemonic: *giriling giriling giriling Linda*.

The first two syllables "giri" usher in the upbeat. The main measure contains
the rest of the mnemonic, which can be organized into four main beats. These
beats are represented as "four-four" (4/4) or four quarter notes in a measure.

The indicated time signatures are generally true to the structure of the
mnemonics and the feel of two (in the case of Dalunga) and four (in Giriling
Linda). However, these time signatures can be perceived in other ways. This
is where hàmpang comes in to interpret time signature. In certain situations,
there are individual performances, varying articulations, and placements/
displacements of accents that affect how time signature is perceived. For
instance, 3/8 +1/8 is possible in place of 2/4 (Dalunga mode) and 3/4 +1/4 in
place of 4/4 (Giriling Linda mode).

Previously, I discussed the most obvious presence of the 2/4 'time sig-nature' in the Dalunga mode and 4/4 in Giriling Linda. I assigned these signatures based on the structures of tàtà mnemonics—the aspect of syl-labic division, location of stress, and other ways of articulating structures. In performance, there are spontaneous renditions of mnemonics that may change the organization of or the perception of time. This can be viewed in the creative implementation of structure, specifically in hàmpang, that may be used to form other time signatures.

One recorded performance revealed that two time signatures can occur simultaneously and overlap. The performers played independently on differ-ent beats and accents. They collectively affected the resultant time. I observed that the patik on agung was playing a 3 + 1 beat group pattern. This was because the upbeat (which I marked as *) of the patik was played with the same level of intensity as the first beat of every measure. The upbeat, which was the 4th beat, changed the feel of a 4/8 and thus became almost a separate unit. I marked this as "1" in the 3/8+1/8 meter. On the other hand, the kadul on the agung was stressing a 2+2 time division as seen below:

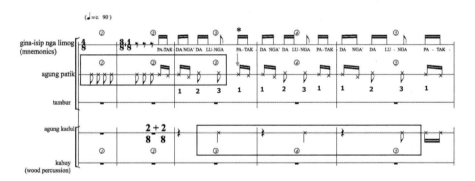

FIGURE 33. Division of time.

As I noted earlier, individual play can yield different perceptions of time. When I heard the rest of the music (illustrated in Figure 34), I made several more observations, which I recorded in written form.

At first I regarded the time signature for the kahuy as ambiguous. By measure nine, the kahuy structure became clearer. As rendered in the score, the kahuy shifts its emphasis from the first beat of measure 6 to the third beat in measure 8. In the next measure, there are already two strong beats

FIGURE 34. Another perception of time.

indicated by the first and the 3rd pulse. This signals a strong division of two strong beats (2+2) in a four-beat measure. The articulation also contributes to the change of perception in the time signature. Because the kahuy accentuates here on both the first and third beats, the division of two in a four-beat measure becomes more prominent.

Hàmpang on the Giriling Linda mode also produces a perception of time different from the 2/4 meter I had identified earlier in the sunú:

FIGURE 35. Division of time in Giriling Linda.

In the example above, the patik gives the fourth beat of every measure a double articulation—an accent played staccato. This fourth beat then becomes a distinct unit of time and fits the meter: 3/4+1/4. The prominence of which beat is also complemented by the kadul and tambur. This beat is produced on a comparably higher pitch compared to the other beats. As discussed in previous chapters, pitch change can be an indication of accentuation related to the mnemonic/linguistic understructure.

The overall feel of the piece still retains the 2/4 structure, but listening to every instrument in a more detailed manner gives various perceptions of time. This realization dawned on me during the process of transferring sound from the recording into transcribed notes. The sense of multiple, distinct meters operating simultaneously strengthens the idea that ordinary meter and the concept of time signature does not work here except as a guide to help outsiders understand some aspects of rhythmic structure. However, this tool serves as a starting point, not as an endpoint. Repeated listening and the experience of playing the instruments also gave me insights on how to differentiate each instrument's contribution to the totality of sound. Moreover, the manner of playing and the musician's play on the mnemonics can further vary the production of sound and its constitution.

There is the in-between aspect of time that cannot be measured. This element is ginhawa, or breathing. When I gave a talk in a graduate seminar in the University of California, Los Angeles' (UCLA) Ethnomusicology Department in 2006, I showed a video of the Panay Bukidnon's drum playing while seminar participants looked at the transcription I made of this music. One of the graduate students in attendance raised the point that the transcription seemed to miss a bit of time, or a "nick" of time, so to speak. This triggered a discussion on the presence of a sound, or a short gap in time, that seemingly delays the next beat throughout the music. I watched the video on my own, repeatedly, and found that the drummer's beating depended on the timing of his breath. However, since I noticed this after I did my immersive research period in the highlands, and have not had the opportunity to delve into conversations on this point with musicians in the highlands during more recent visits, I cannot deal with this observation thoroughly in this book. I do, however, expect to examine this point in upcoming research.

LEARNING MUSIC THROUGH DANCE AND VICE-VERSA

Having more than a single skill related to the cultural expression helps in understanding performances. Even if learning how to play one instrument engages all the motor skills, as well as the visual and auditory senses of a performer/researcher, the inclusion of dance while playing an instrument helps further illuminate instrumental learning. It also directly engages the different parts of the body in a communication field of act and response. Dancing is a reference to instrument playing as well as an influential factor in maintaining stable physical patterns. This maintenance of patterns is significant in keeping time. Dance has a more direct and completely kinesthetic aspect than playing a single instrument. Thus, tactile stimulus plays a crucial role in correctly executing and connecting moves. This puts feeling into a central place in expressing oneself through dance. So feeling the dance—dancing in one's head, which may well translate into subtle physical movements—aids in expressing oneself while playing an instrument.

While studying the skills and performance techniques of Bawa, an Indonesian drummer, Tenzer (2000, 281) observes, "Eyes closed and torso subtly evoking the choreography, Bawa's body language insisted that it was the connection between music and movement that mattered: the need for the drummer to understand both and act as a conduit for translating between them." The translation happens from "movement into musical quality" (ibid).

Something similar happened to me through studying both dance and music with the Panay Bukidnon. By involving my understanding and feel of music in honing my dance movements, I could more deeply connect tactile and acoustic references to my bodily movements. Learning to play the tambur, agung, and kahuy brought me to understand their rudiments and techniques.

I started visiting Mehoran in her house in Barangay Garangan (Calinog, Iloilo) in 2001. Her house is the stopover of researchers who hike into the mountains. For many days, I lived in her house to learn panubok, as well as tambur and other musical instruments. My sporadic sessions with her were, at first, a disadvantage. I learned unassimilated chunks of lessons, making the continuity difficult to follow. I later realized that the segregated lessons let me absorb her teachings for long periods of time before I took in other lessons. There is no hurrying with the Panay Bukidnon. Adjusting to their sense of time is part of gaining their knowledge. Thus, I waited until Mehoran was ready to teach before taking on a new lesson.

Mehoran first taught me how to hold a pair of sticks before allowing me to beat the tambur. She stressed that incorrectly holding the sticks could cause improper sound damping. As with writing, one must first learn to hold a pen.

Mehoran stands out as one of the most prolific and versatile persons in the Panay Bukidnon community. She is skillful in constructing musical instruments, including chordophones, idiophones and bamboo flutes. She knows how to play these instruments well. Known for her creative clothes-making and panubok, her textile works are most highly sought after. Most dancers in the community wear what she embroiders. She also chants traditional texts. Her multifarious skills partly explain her teaching method—these were wide-ranging, multidimensional, integrated across perspectives and disciplines. Once, while I practiced the rhythm she introduced on the tambur, she not only listened and observed my drum beating but also danced with the music. She showed me the relationship between her drumming and her movements. A series of lessons with her demonstrated and expanded on this kind of linkage.

Between April and May 2003, I lived in Barangay Daan Sur (Tapaz, Capiz). There, I met Alfred Castor, a tambur player. He had a high level of musicality and was more innovative compared to older players. He displayed an unusual mastery of playing with mnemonics. His youth was an advantage, giving him the vitality to drive the music into a more excitable zone and enliven the level of each of his performances. These elements attracted many young performers to his playing. It motivated them to join in the activity of learning.

So that I could further understand the idea of hàmpang in playing instruments, I asked Alfred to teach me. He first taught me how to hold the sticks, then taught me how to beat the drumhead. In the left hand, the stick should pass through the space between the index and middle finger. The thumb supports the back end of that stick so that it cannot be dropped. The thumb and index finger hold the stick in the right hand. He made me repeat the act of striking without musical patterns for many days. It was important, he said, for the hands to get accustomed to the act of striking. I found that striking was not as simple as pounding the stick on the drumhead. One could apply contrasting degrees of force when beating with accented and unaccented rhythms. When he felt that I made drum strokes in a regular and steady manner, he moved on to the next lesson: learning the pangmidya technique.

Alfred was good at improvising from repeated patterns. According to him, these were a matter of personal feel and timing. These involved complex rhythms that were difficult to catch up with and transcribe. I requested him to slow down so that I could discern the rhythms. He first played a certain number of repeated patterns, introducing changes to them. After that, I was able to transcribe the slow version of his adlibs. I then understood part of his technique. I asked him to play these again, this time incorporating damping techniques. If the player is right-handed, damping is executed by the left-hand stick, and vice versa.

Sometimes, Alfred's playing would have more palabor-labor. He would insert unpredictable grace notes and other dampened strokes. His advice was to practice repeating the regular patterns for a long time. He told me that when my hands had gotten used to the regular pattern, I would have internalized and finally acquired the habit of playing the instrument naturally. With practice, I was able to play with spontaneity and less rigidity. Eventually, I could also play more openly, to go with the rhythm that flowed between my body and instrument. This gave way to other impulses, such as embellishing the sound, varying individual pulses, and letting go. Letting go did not mean sounding frenetic or out of hand. I was still aware of the definable parameters of a utilized mnemonic.

Magdalena Jimenez, a respected elder of Barangay Siya in her late sixties, also served as a mentor. She taught me the mnemonic phrase: *lanalana Talda*. She showed me that the pangmidya on the tambur should be synchronized with the syllable "Tal" and the release from damping on the beginning of "da" of "Talda." For many nights, under a kerosene lamp, she coached me on how to render the sound of the mnemonic phrase lanalana Talda on her tambur.

Of all the experiences I had in learning about musical instruments of the Panay Bukidnon, my drumming lesson with Mehoran in July 2006 was the most fruitful. I was learning how to improvise, and she showed me her playing techniques. In her demonstration, she moved her shoulders up and down in time with the rhythm. When I asked her about the shoulder lift, she called it *kidò-kidò*. This manifestation of affect or expression can be seen among instrumentalists and binanog dancers, particularly when they danced the pinanyo. This image of dancing and playing the instrument stuck with me. At that moment, I realized that I should try dancing while playing. This simultaneity in the activities made my drumming acceptable to her ears. This was the only time I heard her say "*marapit na*" (you're close). This memorable moment provided fruitful insights about my body being the closest connection to developing hand/motor skills aside from sound. This mirrors the experience of Chernoff (1979, 66), who was told by Ghanaian Dagomba drummers that he had to mind the dancers, and that his drumbeats should correspond to their movements. My experience went the next step; it taught me not only to look or mind the dancers, but also to be a dancer myself. I intimately evoked and lived the dance while playing the music. This was so I could incorporate my affect. I also channeled the emotional energy of the dancers and the entire group.

MOVEMENTS AT PLAY

There is a difference between the *dinumaan* (old way) and the *bag-uhan* (new way) in binanog. Rolando "Ulan" Caballero of Barangay Garangan (Calinog, Iloilo) said that the dinumaan has more *púntu* than the bag-uhan. Púntu is an accent's bodily manifestation based on the mnemonic's rhythmically punctuated syllable.

In Philippine language, particularly Tagalog, púntu refers to intonation or the general sound of a person's speech. Among the Panay Bukidnon, intonation corresponds to different levels of motions similar to speech tone patterns marked by varying degrees of pitch and intensity. Intonation is part of the sound qualities that make a person's speech pattern. In general, intonation is derived from one's enunciation of accented and unaccented syllables creating various levels of pitch.

One can identify a person and the Philippine region s/he comes from through púntu. A friend of mine once overheard a conversation in a shopping mall in Manila, the Philippines' capital city, where Tagalog dominates. She noted: "*May púntung Bisaya sila*" (S/he has Visayan intonation), referring to people born and raised anywhere in the Visayan group of islands. If familiar with their speech sounds, one could identify numerous varieties of Bisayan languages.[3] Nida Perillo, a *kagawad* (councilor) of Barangay Nayawan, can easily distinguish a visitor from a local resident. This is because of the person's púntu: *Pangayaw dai-a; naga sinà sya* (She is a visitor; she speaks the language of the city people). Púntu can be used to determine a person's birthplace and familial or ancestral origin.

A Panay Bukidnon's tubu-an expresses púntu through boses. If likened to a voice, it can project certain ranges of vertical motions just like the intonations produced in uttering their linguistically-based mnemonics. The use or non-use of púntu in these ranges of movements identifies the bag-uhan or dinumaan way of dancing. According to Ulan, a bag-uhan has no clear púntu; it must be developed through more training. The community elders resent how the bag-uhan disregards the binanog púntu. For them, this reflects the

community's perceived sense of authenticity in binanog dancing. Authenticity
is projected in the traditional ways of doing things fulfilled by the dinumaan.
These ways are: the dancer's tubu-an following the mnemonic structure faithfully; footwork sounding the mnemonic accents and rendering kidò-kidò and
li-ad.

Thus, púntu is part of the details involved in rendering hàmpang in
movements. Figure 36 shows some steps with or without púntu in using the
Dalunga rhythmic mode. I have transcribed the playing as I learned it from
my dance mentors particularly in playing on a mnemonic. I use footwork to
represent some creative versions or interpretations of musical patterns. My
intention is to illustrate how play can be a guide for those who wish to improvise on their own.

MNEMONIC OR SUNU: PATAKDANGA DALUNGA

syllable(s) per beat	(pa)tak	da-nga	dalu	nga	(pa)tak	da-nga	da-lu	nga
hampang example **1**	RF*	RF	RF, LF	RF >	RF	RF	RF, LF	RF >
2	RF, LF	RF	LF	LF >	RF, LF	RF	LF	LF >
3	LF backward step	LF	RF forward step	RF	LF backward step	LF	RF forward step	RF

RF is right foot, LF is left foot

FIGURE 36. Hàmpang on Dalunga.

This Figure shows different footwork patterns using units of sound, or syllabic
segmentations of the sunú's syllabic segmentations: the mnemonic of patakdanga Dalunga. These different patterns are versions of hàmpang. Aside from
footwork and accents, hàmpang also involves directions. Example 1 starts on
the right foot. This opening includes two steps in any direction, e.g., forward,
backward, or in place. This footwork then alternates on three steps (right, left,
and back to the right foot). The right foot makes the first accent in the pattern
after this. All examples shown in the next page (Figure 37), have two types of
combinations: 1) alternating unaccented steps followed by an accented step;
or 2) repeated steps of the same foot (e.g., LF, LF) followed by the repetition
of another foot (e.g., RF, RF). This same foot repetition is done with the body
arched backward, accompanied by arms swung in bird-like motion forward
and backward.

In Giriling Linda, as indicated in the next figure, dancers can choose to make two or three steps on the same foot. One foot can make accented steps successively to stress the last two syllables of the mnemonic *Giriling Giriling Giriling Lin-da*.

MNEMONIC OR SUNU: GIRILING GIRILING GIRILING LINDA

syllable(s) per beat	giri	ling	giri	ling	giri	ling	Lin	da
hampang example 1		RF						LF >
2		RF			LF			LF >
3		RF			LF		RF >	RF >

FIGURE 37. Hàmpang on Giriling Linda.

A dancer's hàmpang can be expressed on what foot to repeat or alternate. Some dancers alternate their right, left, and right foot (or the reverse sequence of left, right, and left if they prefer). However, an accent is made by the next footfall that aligns with any of these syllables in the mnemonic: the [da] or [Lin] and [da] in "Linda."

Both of the previous Figures showed hàmpang on which syllable to align one's step with, and the use of púntu. In the actual binanog, one's púntu provides contrast between movements. One effect of this contrast is evident in dynamics that noticeably build up in each successive phase: from bayhu-nan, repasu, to sadsad. Because of using púntu in sadsad, there is an apparent intensity experienced in the whole music and dance event. Blum (1987, 52) defines dynamics as "qualities in movement that arise from feelings such as delight, anger, fear, sense of power, affection, etc." Blum notes his conversation with Kwabena Nketia in 1981 about dynamics. Nketia told him that in Ghana, onlookers would urge the dancer to show-off, to say something sincerely via dance. Ghanaians regard the public demonstration of one's dancing capabil-ity as a show of dynamics or the dancer's statement about his feelings and beliefs. This belief can be a deeply held principle or strong conviction. Simi-larly, Panay Bukidnons actively motivate performers and their expression of dynamics. Audiences play an important role by using loud vocalizations to increase the emotional intensity of binanog dancing. By hollering suggestions or comments about the performance, they encourage more action and energy.

HÀMPANG ON GENDER

So how does sunú become hàmpang in performing masculinity or femininity in the binanog? At first, gender is projected as a sunú, or the conventional role required of a man or a woman. In the context of hàmpang, there is a sense of fluidity in re-enacting the sunú. At the same time, this enactment becomes an experience of fun. Both sexes, male and female, become open to manifesting the qualities of the other. Either partner in the dance can portray particular qualities traditionally ascribed to a man or a woman. In this sense, the meaning of tradition is reconfigured in the process of change.

Gender play in the binanog demonstrates that certain masculine and feminine projections defy stereotypes. In sunú, women's steps are expected to be more earthbound. Meanwhile, male dancers move more freely in space. They display footwork that lifts up farther from the ground, and leaps that span a larger area. Being earthbound is not a sign of timidity, nor is the male footwork interpreted as signs of aggressiveness. As the dance proceeds, any such impression would not remain fixed. The male dancer follows the female in whatever direction she takes as they work their way from bayhunan to sadsad. He does so whether across the dance space or to the opposite side of the partner's space. He may not turn his back on her. While this may seem subservient, it is really about attentiveness. During pinanyo, the female follows the male's direction in the pursuit of his panyo. The dancers readily switch between the aggressive/active and subservient/passive roles. Hàmpang becomes a play of shifting roles and characteristics as the steps change with each dance section. The bodies' orientation in space underscores and works with certain gender roles. This happens as the dancers move about each other, gradually coming closer. The transposition of roles and the intimacy between dancers eradicates stereotypical gender roles. As men and women go on the offensive and defensive, finally coming to a compromise, such roles cease to matter. A man can either give up his panyo intentionally, or evade the woman's chase by making it harder for her to get the panyo. A woman can take the offensive and, if she does not succeed, resort to si-ud. A female dancer can also give up and accept the man's strength and willfulness.

The actuations in the pinanyo may not necessarily reflect realities outside of the binanog setting. As mentioned, the woman strategizes in obtaining the man's panyo. Logically, we may see the woman as an aggressor. The man who successfully evades her gains an image of intelligence, alertness, and resistance to the woman's dominance. However, if he loses his panyo to the woman, he may be seen as a weakling who has given up, even if only in a symbolic sense. Over the course of the dance, a woman's or man's abilities may not become the only gauge of strength or weakness. Sometimes, decision-making comes to the fore in how dancers plan and execute schemes. The process of rendering such a scheme is, of course, still a form of hàmpang. During one of the binanog activities, I observed some men said that they intentionally allowed women to obtain the panyo. This could be a ruse to get the woman's sympathy or to show compliance to gain her trust. These men would get the women to pay attention to their kindness by losing. This, presumably, encourages women to be more compassionate. Some men believe that women can pity them as they lose face. Ulan (Rolando Caballero), in particular, feigned weakness by letting the woman win his panyo. This was so he could win her affection. One cannot predict women's reactions to such deceptions. Whether women succumbed to pity depended on individual choices or instinctive responses. Based on my interviews, some men did achieve their aim: attention and response. For these men, such steps initiate the process of finding a wife via the binanog.

Hàmpang can help one figure out a potential mate's abilities, regardless of gender. Skillfully playing in and between dance roles may well indicate flexibility and empathy for the other in life. Tuohan was attracted most deeply by his wife's all-around abilities. By this he meant her prodigious artistic skills as well as her abilities in working in the home and at the farm. He did not expect the traditional feminine qualities—beauty, delicacy, and submissiveness—as absolute and unchanging. While these qualities might well be desirable, they could not sustain a lifetime partnership on their own. He was proud that his wife could be assertive, resourceful, dominant, and independent. Yet, she could be submissive if the situation demanded it.

There are men who are unthreatened by and respectful of women's strength and decisions. Hence, some women gravitate toward these men. Miningkol was her barangay's tribal chieftain while her stay-at-home husband tended to domestic needs and their poultry business. He had been sick for some time; Miningkol had to find means to support the whole family. She wanted to pursue some form of leadership even when her husband was the barangay captain. Currently, her position entails looking into her people's cultural affairs. She has gained followers in propagating cultural transmission between the elderly and the young. At the same time, she maintains authority over her sons, does farm work, and makes decisions for the family at home.

Male and female dancers rendering multiple and shifting roles actually perform a hàmpang, or play of sunú. Play becomes habitual when it gains a regular pattern within already structured dance sequences. It becomes a naturalized part of tradition: another sunú. A good example would be the Panay Budkinon youth's experimentation with popular dance. They imitated TV dancers' African-American inspired mediagenic dancing, utilizing more hip gyration and swaying. They would bring dance steps they learned from lowland peers back to their highland barangays. Some integrated these innovations into the traditional dance, giving rise to the pinato. Trimillos (1999, 152) describes this process and its implications: ". . . characteristics embedded in performance feed back into society through repeated presentation. They become both icons and processes for identity formation, enculturation, and gender conditioning."

While new ideas and techniques enter, others wane. Some established traditional forms fall into disuse, an example being the taboo of bingkit, or skin-to-skin contact, with one's partner. Doing a bingkit is like teasing one's partner. In the past, male violators were penalized, which made men avoid getting too close to their partners. Now, penalties for such actions are no longer strictly enforced, leading sexually interested unmarried men to commit this act. Aside from being part of music/dance practice, this form of play is involved in behavioral and social relationships. Once worthy of censure, it passed through a period of inspiring lighter sanctions; in the course of time, no restriction is applied to it. This previously unconventional behavior will likely become more common and achieve social acceptance once it is normalized as and framed within the context of play.

Hàmpang is a creative action, one that is suffused with a sense of purpose. It is an act that entertains while simultaneously pursuing a deeper goal. It aims to render self and collaborative excellence, as well as achieve sociocultural and spiritual linkages. In essence, its goal is to forge relationships.

CHAPTER 6

Catch and Sync

THE CONCEPT OF *SALÚ* IS A FORM OF RECOVERY WHEREIN ONE'S FOOT FINDS A spot in the music to bring the whole body back to the rhythmic pattern's foundation. This Panay Bukidnon concept and corresponding action finds a near-parallel in the work of Desiree DePriest (2003) who has put forward the Human Synchronicity Theory. This theory supports the principle of human capacities to construct, alter or synchronize individual perceptions with that of the shared environment whether by intention or not. Close proximity between human beings establishes a connection. In such a connection, messages are shared, agreed to/disagreed upon and become a basis for response. This brings about an alignment or unity between music and dance participants. Panay Bukidnons achieve this alignment through various rhythmic connections expressed through dance, music, and mnemonics.

Such alignments and connections occasionally break down. DePriest explains that there are allowances for breakdowns in symmetry or connection between an individual's actions and the actions of the others in that group. She attributes such breaks to the inconsistency of human nature with conscious or expected tasks. For instance, in playing gong and drum instruments in a group, sometimes a player will lose his/her sense of rhythm. This causes a discontinuity of the overall music, even if there was a conscious effort not to do so. In an asynchronous moment like this, the remedy she espouses is called multi-homing. This concept is a way to immediately cover up the failed correspondence in the group. It is back-up for the failure until the asynchronous person recovers from the error. The rationale for this is the recognition of diversity and thus, reasoned DePriest, is not a 1:1 (one-to-one) but a 1:M (one-to-many) process.

A group of perceptive teammates can help make the person who made a mistake redeem his/her place among the group. Each member knows, and commits to, making rather than breaking someone's performance. Concomitantly, a performer intending to make his/her co-players fail for personal reasons would break apart the whole music-dance event. In any case, even if salú can largely be an individual task, the network of related people—musicians, dancers, and audience—should readily express an *espirit de corps* to manifest salú. When one catches his/her sense of rhythm with the rest of the group, there is santú, or synchronization. This is another concept embodied in the ideology of *síbod*.

RECOVERING FROM ERROR

When one becomes asynchronous with the music, Panay Bukidnons immediately suggest salú. Noning Lopez, a binanog dancer in Cabatangan, explained this in relation to how Panay Bukidnons remedy a dancing error. She stated how she had once failed to coherently dance with the music because she did not attune her body to the musicians' rhythm. This sense of non-coherence between her dance steps and the music is a situation that calls for an immediate remedy. In the binanog, when one makes an error, the solution is to salú or to catch the beat using one's *kahig* (feet). The act of catching is not merely figurative to one's embodiment of the musical rhythm. Binanog dancers, when musically lost, stamp their feet in time to the music accents. Stamping helps them find their way back to the course of dancing.

According to Lopez, when the kahig would execute a salú properly, there would be síbod. When I asked her, "What is síbod?" Her reply was, *Ang ga-síbod, ga-salú* (something that has síbod, catches on).

Musicians as well as dancers employ salú. If the musicians do not clearly give their accentuations, the dancers will not recover from their error. The audience, by rendering *tàtà*, can help the dancers hear the rhythms via their loudly chanted vocables. Salú depends on and simultaneously evokes a one-to-one-to-one connectivity: between the dancers and musicians; between the dancers and the audience; and between the musicians and the audience. This is the foundation. Note that in the course of the performance, one-to-many correspondences happen as everyone who is receptive and attentive to others vastly expands the range and manifestation of salú.

Salú goes beyond performers. In the Panay Bukidnons' world, even the dancing floor has a part in salú. Manuel "Imas" Gilbaliga, who lives in the crossing between Barangay Daan Sur and Nayawan, demonstrated the male *binanog* dance steps to me. In the course of dancing, he stopped to briefly note that his feet would not síbod if the flooring's material would not respond well to his *sadsad*. "*Indi man mag-síbod.*" (It won't síbod.) He demonstrated the floor's failure to sound, since it did not salú on his stamping. Observing other dancers and their relationship with the floor, I realized that this went beyond resonance. Gauging the response of a floor to one's dance is, in a relative sense, a matter of personal acoustic perception and, possibly, feeling and sensation as well, since the floor bends and moves in response to a dancer's steps. The Panay Bukidnon can determine both resonance and movement: the salú achieved by the quality of floor material that can bring out an effective resonance, *and* the personal feel of síbod brought about by salú.

BEING IN-SYNC

According to Nida Perillo, síbod is synonymous with santú. It has to do with the relationship between dance and music, including the relationship of emotions—what one feels about the santù between dance and music. She explains:

Ang buot siringon ka síbod:	What síbod means:
Naga-santú ang sadsad kag agung, amo dai-a nga kanami magsaut kun nagasantù-anay.	The sadsad and the agung synchronize, that is why it's pleasing to dance if there is santú.

Santú connotes a parallel joining between dance and music. Nida mentioned that a sadsad is danced in time to the agung's rhythm. The connection she notes between movement and dance links up a larger set of factors, such as the ways in which aural and visual perceptions align within musical time.

Nida states her pleasure in the effect of a well-synchronized binanog, and how this synchrony urges her to dance. Synchronization also motivates audience members to stand up and dance.

Santú can be explained in many ways, one of which is the way Panay Bukidnons put together different materials into a functional object. After *rara* (preparing strips of fiber to make a native mat), the maker interweaves one strip with another, alternately unifying each strip to form a specific bond or meeting point until a final product is formed. This composite of all the strips emerges as a single coherent unit, as seen in this *amakan* (native mat):

FIGURE 38. Amakan of the Panay Bukidnon.
I link the idea of sync-points to Panay Bukidnon's construction of amakan. Amakan is sometimes used as flooring for dancing. Here, we can see in detail the connection of specific sync-points as well as the finished material resulting from interconnecting all sync-points. Visually, this captures the specific and general ordering pattern of síbod. In making the amakan, bamboo strips intersect. In the intersections, the maker holds the strips, with each serving as a binder to the next strip, until the whole mat section is completed. This analogy between dance and mat-weaving is similar to Kaeppler's comparison between the Tongan's dance called lakalaka (a combination of choreography, recitation, and polyphonic music) and its barkcloth design; similarities can also be noted in such connections across forms within Mohd Anis Md Nor's study of the arabesque and curving designs on fabrics of the maritime Malays and their links to Islamic dance forms.

In reference to music, I refer to the area where music and dance components meet as a sync-point. Previously, I discussed salú, which performers employ when they lose track of the dance and music synchronization. The remedy comes through listening to the music and the accented beats; musicians articulate mnemonics through the latter. Dancers then initiate accented steps in time so as to reconnect with the dance sequence. Similarly, these accented beats serve as an index to a sync-point, the location where santú happens.

How do Panay Bukidnons perceive santú through sync-points in binanog music? This perception develops through a gradual process involving the self, as well as the participation of co-performers, the audience, and the community.

Santú with self, or synchronizing with one's self, initiates this process. With *gina-isip nga limog,* or thought of words, a performer processes sound and movement within one's self. He or she warms up with a *pasibudon,* the process where a musician works on sound in a music instrument using his/ her hands. It can also be the dancer internalizing proper movements through his/her body. The process helps dancers build a sense of oneness with sound and movement. To then express this sense of unity, the musician or dancer develops motor and reflex skills according to culturally accepted forms, e.g., using li-ad among dancers; proper use of damping for drum-playing by musicians.

Pasibudon can include any act directed towards síbod. The warm-up produces the conditions that help make síbod work. Pasibudon extends beyond the binanog. In the process of making an *amakan* (native mat), pasibudon includes the interweaving of bamboo strips. This can be likened to other handcrafting activities like rara, *haból* (weaving), and so on. In sugidanon, pasibudon is described as *"palikoliko-on ang istorya asta mag-síbod"* (let the story go round and round until it becomes síbod). Chanters extend an epic's event by using synonyms or related word-associations. A master chanter uses a rich vernacular vocabulary to creatively present fresh lines at every performance that refer to an event, act, or person. For example "Humadapnon who is about to ride in his boat" is expressed in multiple ways:

> *Makalanda sa biday* (Will approach the boat)
> *Masaka sa barangay* (Will go up the boat)
> *Si Buyung Humadapnun* (The hero Humadapnun)
> *Ginuung Harangdun* (Gentle respectable person)
> *Datung Parangkutun* (A leader, an advisor).

This kind of representation goes on and on, or round and round, until the whole epic narrative is finished. In this way, síbod is realized.

In playing the *tulali* (bamboo flute), pasibudon is to let the produced sound answer back to one's *ginhawa* (breathing).[1] The air blown into the flute must respond to one's breathing. When this happens, a good flow of sound comes into being, and with it, síbod. These examples show the multiplicity of forms in which síbod is evoked and experienced in the community and how interplay, interaction, and misdirection figure into evoking and realizing síbod.

Returning to the ways in which an individual synchronizes with his/her self in preparing to make music or dance, pasibudon also means *gina-tono* (tuning-in). This does not mean pitch-tuning, but something more fundamental: adjusting the instrument to the player's body. S/he orients his/her physical and emotional rhythm to make a mnemonic work. Such music/dance acts, of course, involves santú with a mnemonic.

An agung player executing *patik* at the beginning of the binanog is an example of the santú with self. This introductory material makes use of a series of single strokes without any accent or sense of strong/weak beat differences. This is a form of pasibudon, of warming up with the instrument and with the player's self using the beginning syllable of the mnemonic, the "pa" (*) of *patakdanga*. The single strokes prepare the player for the rhythmic pattern such as in the example given below:

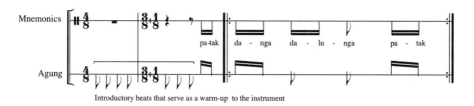

Introductory beats that serve as a warm-up to the instrument

FIGURE 39. Pasibudon.

The single strokes set the foundation for Dalunga, forming an introductory statement. Performers and dancers pick out the mode from this introduction. Once detected, instruments enter in turn. Usually, a tambur or an agung player plays the *kadul* following the patik. Either the tambur or the agung player plays using single strokes on the downbeat. This player sets the time.

There are times when a rhythmic mode has been agreed upon. In the example below, the instrumentalists agreed that they would be playing the giriling Linda mode, which has the mnemonic words: *giriling giriling giriling Linda*. All the instrumentalists begin playing together:

FIGURE 40. Playing together once mode is set.

Dancers go through pasibudon, particularly through the 'santú with self' process, when they execute the *bayhunan*. Note than in both the bayhunan and the introductory musical sections, music and motions are unaccented or unstressed. Dancers do not accent footwork nor do they execute stylized arm movements. Walking instead of dancing at the binanog's very beginning is their way of attuning their bodies to the music, adapting to the dance space, and establishing a connection with the other dancer.

A repeated pattern comprises the binanog music's base. In the example below, the main mnemonics comes after the instrumental introduction. Since this example is in *dalunga*, the syllables 'pa-tak-da-nga da-lu-nga' serve as mnemonics that form the underlying rhythmic pattern. When repeated, the pattern forms a cycle throughout the music as seen here:

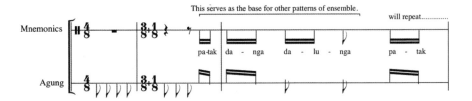

FIGURE 41. The Base.

The second phase of achieving síbod extends 'self santú' to include co-players. Here, pasibudon moves from the self to an awareness of group work. In Figure 42, the tambur player gives introductory beats, then plays the rhythmic pattern in the last measure together with the patik and kadul. Santú with co-players means that a musician plays with, and not against, the rhythm of others. The kahuy interjects on a two-beat figure every measure. This joins the sound of the patik's first two strong beats. Later, the *kahuy* shifts this figure to its second beat, and it sounds with the patik's second and third strong beats. This pattern is repeated throughout the whole piece.

Subsequently, the kadul on agung enters on the third beat and later during the measure's first beat. It simultaneously plays with the patik's last two beats and in three measures, gives a three-beat introduction, and then proceeds with the mnemonic pattern. When all parts have played their respective introductions, they synchronize their patterns with each other based on the mnemonics.

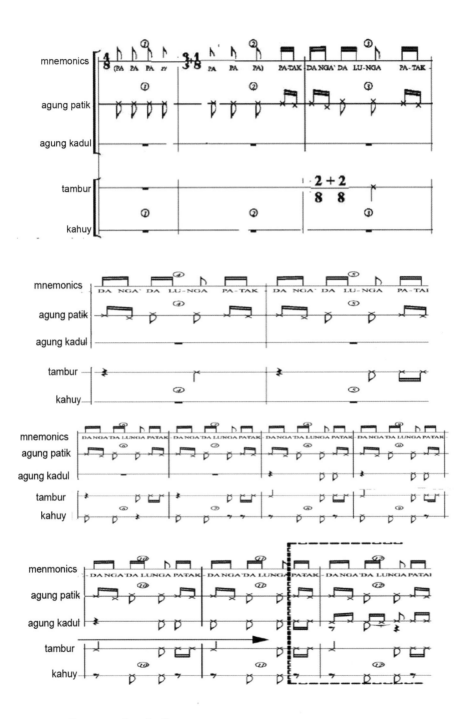

FIGURE 42. Group synchronization.

Dancers santú with musicians and vice-versa. Previously, I showed footwork details alongside sound units translating the gina-isip nga limog. Though it is the dancers who normally adjust to the music, there are cases when the musicians and audience must try to synchronize with the dancers. In the heightened sadsad, music functions as a motivator in case dancers do not rise to the climactic energy that this dance section calls for. To motivate the dancers, musicians intentionally intensify their accents and play louder, while audience participants excitedly verbalize their tàtà.

Some dancers verbalize the gina-isip nga limog in order to santú with the music. They do not just use the mnemonics as a mental guide; they sound them out. Note that in doing so, they use both sound *and* sensation to guide their steps. As a child, Miningkol would go to the river near her family's house to train her body to dance in time to a mnemonic. Her internal and physical time-keeper was her repeatedly muttered tàtà, done while executing the dance steps. She would say "*tata tata tatata tata*" or "*takda takda takdanga Da(lu)nga*," thus mimicking the kadul player's variation of segmentation on the mnemonic *patakdanga Dalunga*.

Her play and dance moves based on the mnemonic are examples of creative expressions. Instrumentalists likewise create music from mnemonic variations. In the example below, every individual has his/her own way of playing the Giriling Linda mode. They have meeting points, marked by accents or resultant high pitches brought about by stressed articulation. These points vary. I denote these variations, which I consider perceived minor and major sync-points, by marking them with short and long arrows, respectively. These sync-points are in the "Lin" and the "da" of the mnemonic giriling giriling giriling Linda. In the transcription in Figure 43, the reader can see these sync-points in the upbeat of the third strong beat followed by the fourth strong beat or the "1" in the meter 3+1.

A sync-point functions as a post, or rhythmic pillar for the cohesive support of the binanog music and dance from beginning to end.[2] Just like the native mat (see Figure 38), this support system melds music and dance materials that crisscross one another to form the unified event.

FIGURE 43. Sync-Points.

While vertical synchronization takes place, a corresponding linear motion occurs in the horizontal plane. This happens as each player concentrates on his/her part, playing in a cyclical repetition of the rhythmic pattern based on the mnemonic. Although vertical and horizontal alignments serve to manifest the synchronizations' process, what one hears is a volume of collective sound containing various clusters of strong and weak beats that is pulsing. To conceive of these elements more completely, the reader may think of them as circular motions rather than vertical or back-and-forth linear movements. Including a notion of linearity helps connect sync-points. After all, in the example of the mat, the underlying structures are linear. An underlying structural unification of all the instruments' sounds emerges from accent marking even as each one performs distinct rhythmic versions of the patterns and their underlying mnemonics.

FIGURE 44. Directional Santú.

There are relative perspectives to determining a sync-point. I do not claim that there is only one way to determine a given sync-point, nor is there an absolute means for determining synchronizations in time.[3] I present my observations based on how they were used in the actual music and dance performances during my immersion in the Panay Bukidnon community.

SANTÚ OF MOVEMENTS AND SOUND

Hanna (1992, 318) notes that "the use of time merges dance and music." A binanog dancer aligns his/her boses to music by synchronizing them with the music's beat units, time components originally found in mnemonics. From the music played on instruments, a dancer selects from a spectrum or range of strong and weak beats and enacts movements on these. Time's treatment depends on the binanog's dance phases. The adjustment to the mnemonic's beat units unfolds gradually. In the bayhunan, the dancers' walking could be natural or stylized, or sometimes their movements can border on strutting. This opening provides dancers an opportunity to sense the rhythm by tapping on strong beats.

After dancing a few rhythmic cycles, each dancer walks forward to opposing corners of the dance space. They proceed to the next dance phase, the *repasu*. Dancers now pay attention to accented and unaccented beats as well as to the affect that goes with the mnemonic. The aspect of feel, or affect, is implied in the mnemonic's myriad sound properties, the latter of which has contrasting gradations of strong and weak beats. Such gradations form a contour, which participants perceive as sound and sight. Musicians and audience members make sounds while dancers move through space in specific stylized ways.

In some parts of the binanog, particularly the repasu, dancers have a tendency to move their bodies in the same contour repeatedly. This is because they move one foot forward, then backward (or sometimes sideways), and back to the front. This is done while thinking of the mnemonic patakdanga Dalunga, which spells out both phrasing and accents. In this footwork pattern, a dancer's forward step translates the *patak*, the backward or side step is the *danga,* and the *dalu* returns the foot to its first forward position, often stamping on the *nga*. Similarly, different arm positions *angay* (match) the underscore. The dancer can move an arm in front of his/her body as one of his/ her feet steps forward. This is but one example, for there are many ways of doing the angay. This basic, balanced back-and-forth contour drives the dancers' motion within the space. Other contours arise in the course of dancing, but the front-back-front (or front-side-front) structure serves as the foundational movement.

Imas, 105 years old, demonstrated a dance movement corollary to a rhythmic mode he heard in his mind. As his arms lifted to show me his dance, he uttered: "*Angay kadya.*" (Like this). Panay Bukidnons demonstrate certain ideas by acting while matching it with words. Meanwhile, musicians observe and constantly match their music with the dancers' movements. Similarly, dancers execute their dance steps in corollary to the music. When the two match—or become identical and unified—angay becomes manifest, and to Imas, this is síbod.

Angay is not synonymous with santú. Panay Bukidnons use it to refer specifically to matching their arm and foot movements. On the contrary, santú has a wider scope. It consists of how parts of the body are involved with each other, with the music, as well as with the dance.

Feliza Castor strongly opined that one should make an individual effort to harness his/her qualities and potentials so as to effectively work with or complement the activities of others. Pointing to her different body parts, she noted that each and all take part in music-making and dancing. She learned how to beat the drum by tapping the top of her head with her fingers. She matched the rhythm she tapped out on her head with the rhythm she employed on musical instruments and in dancing. Her arms would respond to what her feet did, and vice-versa. In her examples, she showed that an individual recognizes the capacity of his/her different body parts to form a network of actions and responses responsible for the (re)production of a creative act.

SANTÙ AMONG PEOPLE

Santù makes for a useful lens through which to see relationships in the community. From music and dance, we move on to analyze the mechanics of interactions and the human factor behind the production of sound and movement events, such as binanog dancing.

Amang Baoy told me:

"... ang saot ... may limitasyon;   "... in dance ... there is a limit;
anad na ikaw nga bayi sa sa-ut,   you woman, you are used
anad na ikaw nga laki sa sa-ut.   to this dance (the binanog),
Indi mo pagbayaan ang pares   you man, you are used to this
mo nga indi mag-síbod ang sa-   dance. You do not abandon
ut. Kay may limitasyon mu. Kun   your partner whose dance does
indi pa mag-síbod, indi mo pag   not síbod ... because it would
bayaan kay alang-alang."   be untimely or half-baked."

He addressed a male and female dancer by saying "you woman" and "you man," as if directly talking to them. If both dancers are skilled and are familiar with one another, then they should help each other, particularly if they have not yet reached síbod. For Amang Baoy, falling short of síbod is not a justification for giving up on one's partner or the dance event. Each one should recommit to working with one another, particularly with tiniglalaki.

Note the central role of síbod and working to realize síbod. Achieving síbod is the goal; doing so implies fullness in action. Falling short of this aim implies that a sense of fullness has not been achieved. This is why leaving the activity would be untimely or half-baked. As a community elder, Amang Baoy advises most young performers, particularly those who are not yet steeped in the do's and don'ts of the binanog performance. He is a parangkutan as well as a *magdumala ka kultura* (culture-bearer).

While many know Feld's research on *dulugu ganalan* and ceremonial dance, he also did significant work on the Kaluli singing tradition. According to Feld, Kaluli's singing can be perceived as being both in unison and yet out-of-phase. Being in-synchrony conjures feelings of togetherness even as the vocal parts drift out-of-phase, creating a hypothetical unison (1988, 82). I noted something similar in how Panay Bukidnons focus their attention: they operate in-synchrony when referring to music and dance sync-points.

However, Panay Bukidnons play off of sync-points and set accents and phrases as a form of creative play.

Amang Baoy explained how to use one's dance step knowledge to finally reach a synchronized point: *". . . mag-abot nga daw maubos tana ang inug-aksyon, nagsíbod na tanan ang sa-ut . . ."* (". . . when the time comes that all the actions have run out, the dance has finally reached a point of síbod"). Reaching síbod requires trying out different dance steps. To run out of actions does not mean being out of ideas. Rather, after trying out ideas, one finally hits on an action that connects with co-performers.

According to Amang Baoy, this process of play and exploration is part of síbod. This emphasis on trying ideas links back to his point: that even binanog performers who have their differences eventually find their way to síbod.

As part of this process, a dancer will santù with co-players by coordinating his/her boses to those of his/her fellow dancers. The female dancer traditionally decides on the shift from one dance phase to another. Hence, a male dancer usually makes more effort to adjust to the female. In the bayhunan, the leisure walk begins and each dancer moves to and fro, crossing to opposite sides of the dance space. While dancing, the male watches the female. When she shifts from bayhunan to repasu, he would do the same. Note that in the repasu, the dancers execute a mnemonic's rhythmic pattern.

Smoothly moving together from one binanog phase to the next requires accomplishing pasibudon. Warming up the body connects each dancer to the music, the dance partner, the orientation with the dance space, and the specific dance phase. By becoming more fully attuned to each, a higher level of attentiveness and connection takes hold of the dancers. This allows for greater responsiveness and adjustment to changes in rhythm, movement, and feeling.

Synchronization among performers requires the melding of one's creative expressions with another's. A man *kaykays* (follows the steps of his partner) but does not duplicate her steps so much as combine his steps with hers in a syncretic fashion.[4] Synchronizing in this way fuses some elements of movement and style common to both male and female dance, even though both dancers maintain individual and gendered characteristics. In sadsad, both dancers accentuate the two strong beats of the mnemonic: the "tal" and "da" of the *patakdanga Talda*. By sounding simultaneously, these accents demonstrate that the dancers are truly together, moving harmoniously in-sync or in síbod. One can differentiate a male dancer's individual style from the woman's. This is in the way he moves and executes hampang, among other creative interpretations. The same holds for the female dancer, who expresses an individual and feminine style even as she dances in the same accent pattern as the male.

SANTÙ IN AFFECT

Síbod, aside from its reference to sync-points' technical aspect, which supports synchronization's presence, also involves performers' affect. Saying síbod invokes emotions that are integrated with the process and act of pasibudon. Affect can be motivated by factors of sound and motion. When a dancer shifts to the dance's next phase (e.g., repasu to sadsad), musicians put more energy into the music. The kahuy, in particular, becomes much more prominent emphasizing two heavy accents, which mirrors the dancers' accented footwork. Simultaneously the musicians work to increase the music's overall volume and dynamic range. The crowd also gets louder, eventually becoming the loudest musical grouping as they cheer and annunciate vocables in time with the music. The crowd not only adds sonic power, but also uses its power, presence, and accent placement to motivate musicians and dancers to an ecstatic performance level.

Affect in binanog is both aesthetic and stylistic. When dancers feel the music's effect on their bodies, they show it with kidò-kidò. With musicians, this is a helpful device in contrasting high and low tones and weak-versus-strong accents. Lising Jimenez of Barangay Siya did the kidò-kidò when she played the agung to express her pleasure in hearing and feeling the music. Doing so helped her play more effectively because of the musical feel's reinforcement, sensation in manifesting the rhythm, and getting a feel for the music. Similarly, dancers could readily tell where to accentuate their steps as she clearly played low and high tones. Being a dancer, she could relate the importance of showing emotions through the body and apply this to instrument-playing as a way of bringing out contrasting sounds.

SYNCHRONIZING SPACE

Space, according to de Certeau (1988, 117), is "a practiced place produced by the operations that orient it, situate it, temporalize it, and make it function in a unity of programs and proximities . . . in space, there are interphases of mobile elements and considered vectors of direction, velocities and time variables." De Certeau differentiates place from space: the former does not have the mobility associated with space. Rather, stability is implicated, as place is ordered according to the elements' distribution in coexisting relationships. This has to do with properly placing elements in distinct locations, or positioning them in relative positions in reference to one another.

The binanog traditionally happens in the receiving area, or the *tambi* (balcony), of a house. The area must be able to accommodate family members, performers, neighbors, and guests. Secondly, the place should have a bamboo floor. This contributes to sound amplification and a specific timbre when dancers stamp their feet in time to the music. Some recently constructed houses have concrete floors that do not síbod. Putting a bamboo covering over concrete may make such floors usable in performances.

The receiving area provides a perimeter that fits most small neighborhood gatherings. In cases when more guests attend, whether from the barangay or not, the binanog can be moved to the tambi. The tambi has a partially open shelter that allows people to watch from inside and outside of the house. Ventilation is good, as air easily flows in and out of the shed. This is a relief for dancers, who sweat from the rigors of dancing, and for the crowd, who can move freely in and out of doors.

Most tambis have a roof to protect performers from direct sunlight and rain. The crowd is not spared when a storm comes during a binanog. Strong winds and rain affect everybody, often discontinuing a binanog activity.

The binanog is sometimes held outside of the house. I have witnessed a binanog festival initiated, organized, and funded by national agencies during the first week of November in 2003.[5] These agencies initiated and funded this festival to encourage the Panay Bukidnon to celebrate and share their music-dance tradition. Activities were held outdoors. The funders even simulated the place where the Panay Bukidnon customarily render the binanog. They set up a makeshift bamboo floor so that the dancers could stamp their feet and musicians could beat the wood percussion on the floor. Thus, they could perform as well as they do on the bamboo floors included in most Panay Bukidnon houses.

If a place such as a house determines the performance and viewing area's perimeter, the performers and audience dictate the dance space. Space is defined as a binanog event's temporal locus, that which can be compressed or expanded by performers/audience at will. This flexibility allows hampang to come into the process. Performers operate more consciously and actively in the space than the audience, which plays more of an observer role in the binanog's earlier stages. Note that the audience engages in hampang as well: viewers move about as more persons join in the action and crowd around the space. People at the back of the crowd usually push forward to see the event. Inversely, when the event is uninteresting, the space loosens as viewers move in and out of position, with many leaving the space, leaving behind individuals who adjust to reconstruct the available space around the performers.

To concretely delineate the dancers' space from that of the audience, an amakan is laid on the floor. However, this only serves as a guide when the activity starts. Dancers sometimes forget this boundary of space, and a large enough and especially energetic crowd will move into and reorganize the space in fluid fashion.

How do performers play on and play in the space? When the binanog begins, the dancers move across opposite ends of the space (aerial perspective: man facing south, woman facing north):

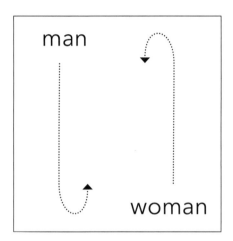

FIGURE 45. Initial Position.

The binanog starts with the bayhunan, where each dancer *bayhun* (walks) to the space's opposite end, turns around, and goes back to the starting position. Bayhunan is done up to three times. This is followed by repasu, wherein the use of footwork directly improvises on either the mnemonic or the rhythmic pattern introduced by musicians. The dancers start using their arms to simulate the banog's various flight and wing motions. Each dancer wears an uninvolved expression, projecting an air of distance from the other dancer. They carry on in a seemingly individualistic fashion, casting brief glances at each other, quickly observing each other's movements. These projections of distancing and observation serve the dancers as they sense one another and gradually get to know each other, just like strangers when first introduced. Yvonne Torres, a dancer-choreographer who did fieldwork with me to notate the dances, called this orientation. She noted that this dance section's blocking is symmetrical: as the woman moves to the dance space's right, the man moves to the dance section's left.

The music intensifies when dancers shift from repasu to sadsad. The kahuy sounds louder and more frequently. In this section, the dancer accents these two syllables of the mnemonic, e.g., *pa-tak-dang-a* <u>Dâlu</u> – <u>ngâ</u>.

As sadsad progresses in time, each dancer moves back and forth along the dance space's opposite sides by stepping forward, to the side, or backwards:

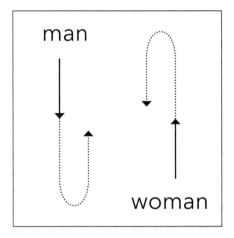

FIGURE 46. Forward and Backward.

Sometimes, dancers move to the other end of the dance space. They encroach on the partner's area before returning to the same pattern of moving forward then back. Even as this happens, symmetry between the two dancers prevails in the space. A face-to-face encounter rarely occurs:

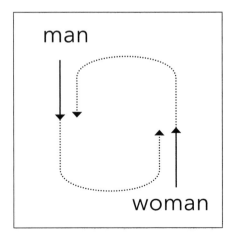

FIGURE 47. Different Directions.

After the sadsad, dancers shift to simbalud.[6] Then, they proceed to the pinanyo. Each dancer holds the *panyo* tightly on both sides as they gradually gravitate towards the center. This center locates the dance's intimate points:

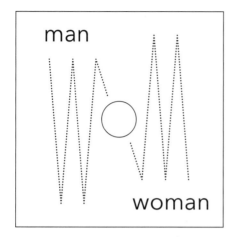

FIGURE 48. The Center.

Miningkol says the center is where the bingkit happens. Customarily, when the man gets so close that he establishes skin-to-skin contact with the woman, he pays a fine. Carlos Parle recalled that a man from Bato-Bato was penalized about 100 pesos for this infraction. This was due to intentionally manipulating the space around his female partner so that part of his body touched hers. Locals regarded this as a malicious act meant to devalue the woman's body. The penalties do not apply to women, as the community does not consider them offenders. Instead, they see women as victims of men's opportunistic tendencies.[7]

In the *pinanyo*, a bingkit is executed as the woman is challenged to discreetly get the man's handkerchief using her shawl. She employs various means to get the man's handkerchief with finesse rather than force. The man finds ways to stop her from acquiring his handkerchief. As the man's avoidance and the woman's pursuit of the panyo progress, their bodies come closer together. Dancing can be in any direction around the intimate area (see Figure 49).

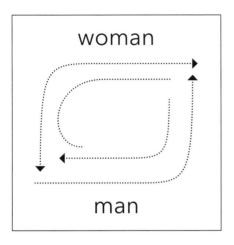

FIGURE 49. Intimate Point.

Within an imagined space, Panay Bukidnons structure another framework. This space-within-a-space comes into being when dancers move centripetally to the middle of the dance space. At the same time, the dancers gravitate toward one another. This process contrasts to the centrifugal motion in the dance's earlier sections where the dancers move along the periphery of the space, away from the center. Centripetal motion brings the dancers into greater intimacy, often ending with this proximity.

In the next chapter about *Buhok ka Adlaw* (Hair of the Sun), I discuss the direction of a certain embroidery design that I perceive as going inside, or centripetally. In Tagalog, centripetal is paloob (going inside). I link this to the analysis of movement toward closeness approaching a center point. Although the topic on movement is not my focus here, I would like to factor in the pertinence of emotions and the psyche as part of what goes on as dancers move in space.[8] When dancers hampang and arrive at the center with their bodies close to one another, something develops: a build-up and focusing of emotions that are integrated by the act of closing in on each other. This is especially relevant for those who dance the binanog to find a mate or to know someone better. Developing a certain sense of intimacy helps to move courtship forward.[9]

Armstrong (1971) writes that the affecting presence in a homogeneous culture manifests in time and space, or through their combination, in a spatio-temporal axis. Space and time respond to one unit of master affective set or principle. As a set, this is expressed in time and similarly, the same set is channeled into space. The use of one set to time and the same set to space makes both space and time connected. In relation to binanog, music and dance are both affective motions in time and space. As music-and-dance progresses, the dancers' affect similarly develops. It is intensified. Thus in the Panay Bukidnon epistemology, space and time are equivalences as much as the presence of affect, working altogether in simultaneous or synchronized ascendancy toward a heightened experience. Armstrong's theory is of course more complex than my brief explication here, but what I want to underscore is Armstrong's perspective that a culture's acts or works are part of its metaphoric base that speaks through its affective life, its ethos, or communal spirit, touching its activities (e.g., dancing, music-making, or cloth embroidery) and interpersonal relations (65).

With his statement halting on social affectations, I would like to add that the continuum of time/space/affect continues into the personal. In the binanog, the inward timing/spacing/affecting are all part of síbod. This is created as part of an effect when dancers close in on a central space.

Dancers gauge their space from one another without touching. This closeness stands in stark contrast to the distance maintained during the earlier dance sections of bayhunan, repasu and sadsad. By the dance's climax, the female dancer has to strategically position herself near the man. At this point, the alignment of space and proximity is not so much negotiated as it is dynamically implicated through a playful pursuit.

This act of making santú happen at the center of a dance space is the binanog at its most intense. The audience expresses elation as they watch the game happening in the chase and possible capture of the panyo. The music reaches its peak after the sadsad's build-up; and the audience participants become more fervent in sounding out their tàtà. Most of all, the dancers compete with each other, dancing with more agility and vitality. As síbod comes to realization, the excitement becomes cathartic.

The dancers' proximity to one another affects each personally. This directs them, quite naturally, into an intimate space and frame of mind, either initializing or actualizing the courtship ritual. Closeness in space is mirrored in personal closeness. The personal connection fulfills a social and cultural end, wherein everyone participating becomes part of an event, an event that brings all into its fold. According to Csikszentmihalyi (1990), a person who pays attention to an interaction instead of worrying about the self obtains a paradoxical result: the person no longer feels like a separate individual, yet his/her self becomes stronger. The autotelic individual goes beyond the limits of individuality by investing psychic energy in a system in which s/he is included. Through the union of this person and the system, the self emerges at a higher level of complexity.

Space is not only relevant, but also central, in establishing the physical, emotional, and social connections within the community. Males and females seeking to pair off use the binanog to help invigorate attraction. At the same time, a whole range of community members gives energy and dynamism through expressive forms. They communicate in various ways, such as through spatial channels. This experience of space feeds the process of building relationships, from the most intimate to the most broadly social.

138

CHAPTER 7

Tayuyon: A Directed Sense of Flow

THE MASTERY OF *SUNÚ*, *HAMPANG*, *SALÚ*, AND *SANTÚ* LEADS TO *TAYUYON*. Panay Bukidnons equate this latter concept of *síbod* to a good quality of performance where music and movement flow naturally and are devoid of obstruction. When there is hesitation on the part of the musician or dancer, continuities break down. This is one instance when Panay Bukidnons say "*Wara dai-a ga-síbod!*" This state of not being in síbod refers to the players' lack of fulfilling the aforementioned concepts in action.

When there is this sense of lack, flow cannot pursue its course. The concept of flow is not about flowing freely. Panay Bukidnons used the word *diretso* or tayuyon to imply a directed sense of flow. This, to them, is síbod. There is guided motion. Therefore, music and dance performers believe they are effective in translating the meaning of their actions into motion.

DIRECTION IN TAYUYON (FLOW)

While resting in Cabatangan, one of Lambunao's barangays, a town forty-eight kilometers north of Iloilo city, I met *binanog* dancers Pacing, Noning and Mary Lopez. They explained that their ancestral lineage consisted not only of dancers, but also of healers, soothsayers, and herbalists. Their elders taught them that when they danced, their dance should síbod. They demonstrated their dance styles and the various ways their arms and feet would continuously work together in time with the music. I asked them, "What does síbod mean?" While dancing, they said, "diretso." Mary demonstrated and I noticed that she was not making literal translations of diretso (to go straight forward). Instead, the movements were a combination of backward, sideways, and forward fluid motions following the music's contour. According to the community's respected elders, diretso is tayuyon: letting something continue, flow, and not to distract. I asked what causes this continuity, to which Mary Lopez answered, "When something is just right, it can continue." I thought about their definition of síbod as diretso and how being right fits into a line of thought and action, which they were establishing as they explained and demonstrated the dance. This line of thought initially established tayuyon as flow, then flow as having continuity, and that continuity happens when things are going well. This line of thought actually brings us back to the concept of sunù that provides the structural foundations of music-making/dancing and to that part of realizing sunú is found in the creative maneuverings of hampang.

I always thought that diretso was solely linear, a matter of direction in a straight-line manner. But what they said was revealing of how cyclical the idea of diretso is in relation to síbod. Even the process of meaning construction also goes through this sense of flow as it circuits to the primary and elemental phase of initiating the binanog through sunú. Thus, tayuyon is a directed flow. It is continuous because it is circular; what comes up must come back down.

Mary, Noning, and Pacing provided another perspective to tayuyon when they explained that the binanog turns out right when it is in harmony with everything around it. If one is not in harmony, distraction can happen. Aside from being dancers, Mary, Noning and Pacing are healers. They know the deeper repercussions of imbalance in the way of things. For them, music, dance, and healing are all connected to bringing harmony to the world. When people in their community get sick, these three aspects would interplay to bring the person's state of being back to his or her normal flow. Aside from the aesthetics of the binanog music and dance, there is the medico-spiritual value that translates the activities and their flow into a form of energy.

Feld (1990, 14) noted that ". . . we see that ultimately ecology—birds, waterfalls, forest presences—is the domain of the natural that Kaluli culturalize, while dance, song, costume, and poetics are domains of the cultural that Kaluli naturalize." This homology sees two types of enunciations—one from the natural environment and another from cultural expressions—but these enunciations are actually integrated in the formal patterns of a music/dance performance. Panay Bukidnons see themselves located in the wholeness of their *kalibutan*. The natural environment is part of the cultural expression in the binanog as they dance to link the structural levels of the upper, middle and lower parts of their kalibutan in axial relation to and/or from their bodies. In this context, an axis refers to the longitudinal and vertical directions determined in relation to the self. Amang Baoy explained the Panay Bukid-non's use of these axial relations in relation to the kalibutan, particularly through their physical and spiritual linkage with the different entities:

> *May dyan nga dya, may nagatangla sa ibabaw, nan . . . kung sa aton pa, ang focus tana ka isip, daw sa kahawaan bala, sa ibabaw nga bahin. Ti makita mo ang engganyo ka alima sa tunga-tunga, kun sa aton pa, dutan-on na ang hampang. Ti kun mag sadsad, kun sa aton pa, daw natandug bala ang balatyagon ka iba tungod nagatay-og ang imo nga pagsadsad . . . sa idalumnon abi nga pag-aksyon.*
>
> There are those who look up to the sky, there (pointing up) . . . in our understanding, their mind is focused on the upper space, in the portion of the above. Then you can see the motions of the hands in the middle (of the space), which means, it's an earthly play. Then if rendering the sadsad, it is as if the emotions of others have been touched (pointing to the lower dimension) . . . to the depths with such actions.

When I was taught by Miningkol to dance, one of those things she reiterated for me to do was *tulok sa ibabaw* (look up). This had to be done with an accompanying *li-ad*. She did not explain what these actuations meant, as during that time, she was concerned with teaching me the movements' mechanics. Later when she personally demonstrated the tulok sa ibabaw and li-ad, things became gradually clearer: her body and facial expression were making a connection with the space above her. This was contrary to what I was doing; my tulok sa ibabaw was without reason and so I felt like I was acting rather than enacting a purpose. In acting, there is pretense, but in enacting, something is fulfilled.

Circumscribed within the dance and music synchronizations is the Panay Bukidnons' deeper motivation to be in sync with forces from different realms. As described above, different body parts are involved in these acts of linking. First are the eyes; most community elders danced with their eyes looking up. As they looked up, they tilted their arms a bit higher than the usual shoulder-level position; this implied the motion of their wings surging up to the sky. Among the elders I observed doing this: Lising Jimenez of Siya, Suping Gilba-liga of Nayawan, and Rodolfo Diaz of Tacayan. Some young adults (between 24 to 35) trained in the *antigo* also exhibited this trait of looking up.

FIGURE 50. Antigo style.

Amang Baoy also refers to the use of the arms, extending them at the shoulder-level position and slowly, gracefully flapping them like wings. Dancers in this position imply an earthly play, a kind of connection to earth spirits, particularly the *dutan-on* and the *tubignon*. Dutan-on occupy trees, flowers and other life forms that grow from the earth. Tubignon occupy rivers, lakes, waterfalls, and other bodies of water. Dancers using this shoulder-level position flap their arms and follow the movements of the male and female *banog* during their mating season. Dancers do the *tirik-tirik*, or excitedly 'going around and around' each other, in reference to the season when the banog soars above a waterfall or above trees together while flying in circles and landing on a tree. Dancers are conscious of the earth and aware of its breadth and space as they move around their dance space, and eventually, around their partners as their dance builds to a climactic point.

Amang Baoy pointed out that Panay Bukidnons *tandug* (touch) the underground spirits in their execution of the *sadsad*. As specified, the sound created by sadsad is heavy, referring to a feeling of weight because the dancers thump their feet on the bamboo floor, intentionally creating a resonant thumping sound. The thumping is rendered twice, one foot at a time, either right or left. It is believed to shake and awaken the underground spirits, or the *idalmunon*.

FIGURE 51. Touching the underground spirits.

Sound can touch the underground spirits. It is not just a sound, but a kind of energy or force brought by a foot thumped on the ground. How can this touch the underground spirits? It is because heavy sound, according to Amang Baoy, can shake and wake the spirits' emotions. If the upper-realm spirits are believed to be reached by sight (via the dancers' eyes), those from the depths of the earth are to be touched by sound. On this note, I deliberate on the presence of sight and sound as forms of vibratory energy.

The previous section defined síbod as tayuyon. This is relevant to understand how síbod makes the performers establish a linkage with the spirits. When síbod happens in the binanog, the whole atmosphere is charged with positive and ecstatic energies. What may be seen is only the encompassing space occupied by performers and the surrounding audience. Binanog performers know that as they dance and play instruments, they go beyond this encompassed space. Moreover, with these acts, they involve the unseen spirits. The involvement happens when the act of performing music and dance produces an energy that circulates and touches the upper, middle, and lower dimensions of life connecting the dancers to each and all. Amang Baoy previously noted this touching imagery: *kun sa aton pa, daw natandug bala ang balatyagon ka iba* (it is as if the emotions/sentiments of others have been touched). This image of touching is related to the previous discussion of the sync-point in síbod as an evidence of alignment and synchronization between music and dance, music-dance and audience participants, and in this section, between the binanog and the cosmos. Touching does not necessarily mean a direct tactile connection. As explained earlier, the binanog dancers use their eyes and they look up to link with the upper world. At the same time, their arms are tilted up, resembling a banog bird flying upward.

I pondered on the word *iba* (others) used by Amang Baoy to refer to beings other than humans and assessed how this linked to the question: "Why do Panay Bukidnons, through the binanog, establish síbod with beings from different realms?" And: "What's the essence of these beings in the Panay Bukidnon's perceived reality?" Looking for answers, I thought of Menchie Diaz, a *dalungdungan* of Tacayan, and her *sugid*:

> In the olden times, when human beings had not yet inhabited the earth, a creature named Pagsandan toured the world, which was located between the sky and the land. He had planned this tour since he was a child. Before he left, he planted *tanglad* (lemon grass) on the ground to mark the spot where he was supposed to return. When he got back, he met a beautiful woman named Ginharunan who was sifting through rice grains called *lampunaya*. Pagsandan ate the grains and he fell in love with Ginharunan. He wanted to marry her but she said he had to pass the test that her father Bunturami gave to all her suitors. Bunturami was a huge creature with a seven-foot chest; and when Bunturami knew about Pagsandan and his intention to pursue Ginharunan, Bunturami challenged his strength and physical power. Pagsandan possesses supernatural powers like Bunturami and Ginharunan; in the end, he passed all the almost-impossible feats. Impressed by Pagsandan's strength and determination, Bunturami allowed the relationship between Pagsandan and Ginharunan to prosper.

> *Pagsandan today is a spirit who helps healers cure the sick. He is also a mediator between humans and the other unseen forces of the world.*

> *(Translation from interview notes, April 2004)*

In this sugid, Menchie provided information about an old kalibutan. This is a world where creatures used to occupy the land and the air or space between the sky and the land. Creatures in this sugid can walk on land and on air (or perhaps fly). This made me think of a possible parallelism between these capacities and the binanog dancers' doing the bayhunan followed by other dance steps that insinuate flying. The binanog unfolds on two levels: the land and the air. Filipino cultural historian Zeus Salazar (2006, 27) also relates a story from a Philippine myth:

> "... galing ang lupa (mga pulo't kapuluan) sa langit na inihagis nito sa dagat nang inudyok ng lawin na magalit ito (dagat) at makipag-away sa kalangitan."

> "... land [archipelago and islands] came from the heavens thrown into the sea when the eagle provoked the sea to have a row with the heavens.

Based on this narrative, Salazar notes that *"iisa ang langit at lupa"* (the heavens and land are one). I thought of Menchie's narrative and how in the passing of time, Panay Bukidnons would commemorate through the binanog what perhaps has been lost in the present world. To dance and look up, the binanog dancer establishes a reconnection with his/her kalibutan, momentarily commemorating and unifying a sundered world.

According to Menchie, Pagsandan became a powerful spirit who would aid the sick by occupying the healers' bodies. She attested that Pagsandan is one of seven spirits that possess her when she heals. Like other healers, she would conjure him from the *ispirituhanon* (spiritual realm/upper space). One of the binanog music and dance's functions is healing, especially when a *babaylan* offers food to call for the spirits' aid via the *ginalaglag*. Each hand holds a platter of food as feet dance the binanog. In the discussion of spiritual linkage, we see that síbod as a diretso or flow becomes a vehicle to transport or link the Panay Bukidnon's offering of the binanog music and dance to various forms of existence.

In the binanog, reaching out to other beings is made possible by these acts of substantiation. Substantiation (giving value) is carried out in acts such as music-playing and dancing. I've seen players beat the tambur while looking up. Men and women dancers, too, gazed up while dancing. What musicians and dancers do validates a deeper meaning beyond the recognition of the physical and material world.

Just as the kalibutan is believed to comprise various levels, síbod also operates on several levels of performance. There is síbod when musicians and dancers have synchronized their sounds and actions with one another. They also bring their music and dance in síbod with the unseen forces of the kalibutan. However, it is not unidirectional. This spirit and human interaction established through music and dance is, in a sense, social. Filipino ethnomusicologist Jose Buenconsejo (2002, 211) addresses the function of the Manobo's ritual speech like so:

> ". . . the significance of ritual speech cannot exist in and of itself. It is contingent upon and wholly relevant to the immediate social interpersonal relationships that bring people together in a humanly communicative performance. In other words, *speech is about sociability.*" [emphasis mine]

Sociability is about spirit and human interrelations established by form(s) of communication such as speech, or in the case of Panay Bukidnons, through music and dance. Buenconsejo designates the particular speech uttered by a medium and his/her ritual audience as spirit-human conversations. The players involved in a sociable conversation would be the spirits via the body of the medium, and the people or audience. Binanog performers are involved in a sociable conversation with the spirits as well. The spirits are known to, but not in the form of direct speech but rather via a medium as in the Manobo ritual. That is, the presence of spirits is felt as a form of energy. Participants feel this as they make their music and dance síbod continuously; it is the attraction or gravity between prospective marriage partners; it serves as an empowerment to the performer's sense of self; and it is that which moves the audience to excitedly participate and further a working activity.

As Amaong Baoy said earlier, it is through sound that the spirits are awakened. They are perceived as listening or watching spirits. In the binanog, when performers establish síbod with them through eye-contact, feet-stamping, and flapping of arms, the spirits listen; in fact, they make their presence and response felt via the energy of síbod. Scholar of Visayan Studies Eliod Dimzon called this experience *dawatan* (possession).[1] She did not exactly refer to a spiritual possession of a medium's body that would go on during a trance, but rather a possession of communal energy experienced by those wholly engaged in an event.

All these concepts—flow, energy, alignment, touching, and synchroniza-tion—are embodiments of síbod and, inversely, of that which síbod embodies in the binanog performance. These concepts are forms of linkages that are substantiated through the dancers' physical, acoustic and affective manifesta-tions in order to: 1) awaken or make the spirits aware of their ongoing social relationships with humans; 2) call on spirits to mediate the attraction between possible couples as they play a role in the community and maintenance of cul-ture; 3) bring the spirits to one's physicality so that dancing and making music could be more enriched; and 4) create balance and harmony in the kalibutan.

FLOWING IN MUSIC

In basal (playing an instrument), a rhythmic pattern that is repeated contin-uously assumes a movement that flows, or is in tayuyon. I asked Mansueto Parle, a tambur player, what his drumming meant to him. He said "*Ginapa-síbod ko ya pagbasal ko* (I make my playing get into a state of síbod)." When I asked him to further explain, he pointed to his head and told me that he first started to think of a *gina-isip nga limog* (thought-of sound), referring to his use of a mnemonic. Based on it, he played the tambur, using at first, the regular or repeated patterns of a rhythmic mode, and then eventually, as his hands and other expressive systems grew accustomed to the habit of repeating that pattern, moving to a more creative, personal demonstration of a mnemonic.

Mansueto's playing seemed so natural and effortless that his rhythm flowed. According to Csikszentmihalyi (1990), flow happens when one con-centrates on an activity that requires all of one's relevant skills. A skill cannot be complete with just technical skill. The input of emotions and expression plus creativity can make the music more interesting. Hampang performs a significant role in making performers go deep into their inner selves as they hampang around repetitive patterns just as Mansueto did. Aside from the binanog's musicians and dancers, the audience also becomes part of hampang as they participate by cheering and voicing a loud tàtà. I remember when Mehoran taught me to play the tambur. Her husband, Tuohan, observed me and advised: "*Pasibuda imo basal* (Establish síbod in your beating of the instrument)." I could not understand what he was trying to say. When he said this, I was only playing a simple one mnemonic syllable-to-one beat pattern (see Figure 19). According to Mehoran (Lucia Caballero), this was just sunú. When Mehoran took the tambur from me and played it, her use of the term *pasibuda* was meant to demonstrate that she was in the process of achieving síbod: she played the sunú, or rhythmic structure; varied the patterns, which was a form of hampang. Because she did it fluently and fluidly, her playing and sound were perceived as flowing. What Mehoran meant when she advised pasibuda was to warm up, play around the mnemonics, and flow with it. In effect, flowing is closer to musical contour as there was shape in the resulting sound of her playing as well as shape in the physical movements she projected while playing the musical instrument. Síbod in this case was flowing by following the sunú and rendering hampang in order to hear a musical contour.

Tao Te Ching (Redfield, Murphy, Timbers 2002), which incorporates the philosophy of *Tao* and shamanism,[2] is exemplified, among other acts, in calligraphy. Here, a student, in rendering a brushstroke, should trust his/her hand's intuitive flow, thus following an uninterrupted line. Panay Bukidnons' concept of tayuyon or flow is akin to the image of an uninterrupted line, where there is a continuity of music and dance from the binanog's beginning to wherever it is led at the end.

Csikszentmihalyi (1990) notes that people in flow situations described themselves as being so focused on the activity that they do not notice time. Their whole selves are involved in pursuing excellence so that when they reach that level, they go into an altered state of consciousness and euphoria. On a related note, Brink (2007, F11) says that some researchers such as Walter Freeman (neurobiologist, UC Berkeley) believes that the oxytocin hormone is released whenever people share enjoyable artistic activities. This hormone is responsible for increasing bonding and memory of people in these experiences. Moreover, ". . . our emotions are synchronized . . . everyone is on the same emotional page" (Brink on Huron 2007, F11) which explains why in a successful binanog, people unite, cutting through boundaries of age, authority, and status. Young and old, barangay leaders and rank-and-file members, visiting politicians, tourists and native tour guides—the differences do not matter. Those who attend and enjoy watching even if they do not dance or play instruments just feel the same so that they have successfully attained síbod and are charged by a high energy level. This energy level is responsible for Brink's notion that there are health benefits involved in music-making and dancing, as these are forms of energy that can boost one's immune system. Similarly in a Philippine dance called subli, Mirano (1989) notices that energy, or some kind of irresistible force, seems to take over the dancers who feel the pleasure of moving their bodies (particularly the hips) in response to the music. She believes that *laro*, or play in subli motivates dancers to move into another level of existence.

TO FLOW IS TO BE EFFICIENT

What happens to a binanog performance that has not attained síbod? Panay Bukidnon musicians and dancers are embarrassed when they do not make síbod work. They take time, work hard, exert effort and dedicate themselves to honing musical and dancing skills but know this is not enough. The challenge of public performance puts their knowledge and skills to a test as they risk being ridiculed. A continuum of developments happens in every binanog performance—learning/developing capabilities, synchronizing with co-players, projecting these capabilities with audience participants, disseminating positive energy or a sense of efficiency with members of the community, among others. This continuum is a síbod that brings one effective action into another. The failure to connect with co-musicians/dancers focuses individual performers to review their capabilities, redevelop their skills, and in the event of participating again, to reconstruct a fresher public image, rebuilding their social network of friends and connections.

Efficiency is tantamount to an effective use of physical resources, bringing these to a high level of communality where "culturally specific rhythms and forms of movement are not merely semiotic expressions of community and identity; rather, they become their actual realization" (Waxer in Turino 2002, 235). An effective binanog should be composed of competent and efficient performers. Brinner (1995) views competence as achievable when human beings in an ensemble interact with co-members or with people who can match their skill and potential. He remarks that competence is sometimes viewed as stocks of knowledge or checklists of things to learn and know.[3] His concept of competence refers not only to talent but also largely to the responsiveness and social relations between performers that connect their actions to a collective whole. I see the relevance of this analogy and add that there is a goal to every person's or group's exercise of competence. An intention fuels the interactivity between performers. This may be mediated by cultural, spiritual and other factors; or perhaps by just the very idea of becoming competent. When one develops skills and demonstrates competence, there is an intention to be efficient, to be conscious of producing an effect.

Competence is vital to the quality of the ensemble's performance; it is with efficiency that one's action is directed to a goal. Hence, a meaning is fulfilled;

a value is validated and evaluated. Having both competency and efficiency makes for a high quality of performance. One may be competent but irresponsible in performance. One may come ill-prepared, drunk, or without musical instruments or traditional attire. Therefore, one becomes inefficient. With efficiency, performers establish strong rapport among themselves and with the audience. That is why síbod occupies that space between competence and efficiency. A performer is competent if s/he achieves síbod and efficiently contributes síbod's value to the maintenance of tradition and family life, fostering a sense of community with co-members and with other societies. Most importantly, to reiterate Turino's note, one helps in the effort to form a realized community, not just having a sense of it.

Not only social relationships are affected in an efficient performance of the binanog. There are also economic repercussions. Musicians who do not perform well may lose part of their public image. As the community members often choose an antigo to represent them on public occasions, a performer who cannot prove his/her worth in producing síbod in the binanog can miss opportunities to earn money at cultural festivals. S/he may not be invited to represent the culture in other various institutional settings such as in university events, government projects, and tourism programs where talent honoraria provide players with extra income.

The failure of síbod sometimes lessens a performer's political power. The late Ronaldo Castor was Barangay Siya's barangay captain. He participated in numerous binanog events.[4] He was careful not to make mistakes or cause the group to fail to gain síbod as he knew he might likely lose his standing in the community. He was also aware that there would be a rippling effect of such a failure. If he would lose public admiration, he would also lose socio-political connections, friends, and support for his community projects. Even if politics and economics could be seen as unrelated to music and dance, these are forms of capability. All of these compose an individual's total personhood. In the Panay Bukidnon community, the more skills a person has, the better a person he is. In this light, not being able to bring síbod in dancing could result in failure in social, political, and economic aspects of community life. A failure of síbod is thus a disruption of diretso in the formation of one's personhood.

A binanog performance that has gained síbod translates to an achievement of maintaining traditions, particularly in the area of courtship as it is crucial to the succeeding phases of the people's life-cycle: marriage, birth of children, initiation of children, rites of spiritual offerings, and death, among other phases. After courtship, the couple gains *pangabuhi* (life), a term synonymous with family. In conversations with Panay Bukidnons, the terms marriage and family do not surface as references to union as much as pangabuhi. The question commonly asked of a visitor would be, "*May pangabuhi ka na?*" (Do you have a life?) However, what is really meant is: "Are you married? Do you have a family?" For them, to have a family is to have life. If a person from the lowlands would ask a Panay Bukidnon: "Are you married?"—a Panay Bukidnon's understanding would be whether or not s/he went through the church marriage rites. For him/her, that question has no bearing on the idea of bonding to have life/family. Thus, s/he would reply: "No, I am not married" although actually, s/he is traditionally married through punsyon.[5]

There are consequences to the conveyance of personal messages in the binanog. Because there is a sense of discomfort with the public display of affection among the Panay Bukidnon community, some men and women participate in the binanog so they can publicly express their attraction for each other. Even as it is taken as a communal activity for music-making and dancing, binanog is an acceptable avenue for self and public expression. It is also a potent force to communicate an individual's choice of life partner or to indicate agreement with the choice of one's parents. Because it is non-verbal, although one's emotions can be made conspicuous through physical manifestation, codes are employed to relay messages of a very personal nature.[6] Specific to the conveyance of a code is utilizing the *panyo.* Not only does this serve as an aesthetic accoutrement in the *pinanyo* section of the binanog dance, it is also a strategic device for communication. Dancers come closer to each other in this section. If a series of binanog events brings similar partners into a certain personal romantic relationship, it is possible that they can codify their message and relay ideas to one another. "Close proximity between human beings establishes a connection; in such a connection, messages are shared, agreed/disagreed upon and become a basis for response" (DePriest 2003). Often enough, dancers come up with creative means to encode messages unknown to the audience. However, some of these means have become conventional and easily decoded. There are other forms of readable manifestations, such as facial expressions and obvious affectations. Because the binanog has become a venue for many intentions, including personal matters, marital fights may also be revealed in the dance. Clandestine rendezvous have been planned while dancing and some extra-marital affairs have developed in this intimacy-motivating dance. Thus, as the binanog makes and maintains traditions, so too does it break them.

The binanog is an ephemeral reality. Performers succeed or fail within the event, but couples confront another reality afterwards. A young betrothed couple in Barangay Daan Sur experienced these realities. Their parents arranged a marriage for them, so as part of the process of knowing each other, they were made to dance the binanog. The man and the woman synchronized their steps well with each other and they danced in time with the music. The community agreed there was síbod happening between them. Pleased with each other's synchronization, they developed an attraction for each other. The parents made plans for their marriage. After the traditional wedding ritual and a period of being together, the woman realized that the man was a sadist as she experienced spousal abuse at his hands. Eventually, they had to separate. In some sense, this is a disconnection of cause and effect. The community expected the couple to have a working relationship because they were compatible in the dance, but this did not translate into another reality after the binanog.

Even with real-life situations, one realizes that there are many variables that arise while analyzing consequences from actions made in the binanog. A successful binanog may or may not lead to a good relationship; neither would a poorly performed binanog abort plans.

Aside from the formal function of the binanog for courtship and healing, some dancers merely dance for leisure and entertainment. For them, the function of a performance that has síbod would be the fun of performance or the challenge to one's abilities despite the consequence of such a performance on everyday life (e.g., the initiation of an illicit courtship). With the youth or teens, peer pressure is sometimes stronger than parental influence. The young would rather arouse the admiration of friends with a show of talent; they defy parental choices by dancing with other prospective mates than those suggested by parents. Socialization is important in this stage of their lives; the binanog provides them the social atmosphere to meet different people. Meanwhile, the Panay Bukidnon community's elders (60 years old and above) would perform to prove that they still possess the talent, grace and enduring stamina to undertake physically taxing activities. The effects may vary. In some events, people from the audience praised the old people's strength, nudging each other as they pointed out: "See, that's the way to really do it, the dinumaan style." The dinumaan, sometimes called the antigo, is emblematic of an aesthetically excellent way of dancing. Some young audience members do not think the same way: "*Dumaan dai-a! Ka buhay ka hurag ka boses na; mas mayad among bagsik nga boses*" (That is old style! Their actions are too slow; ours are much better as our movements are fast and vibrant)." Children between three to nine years of age try different dance steps, experimenting here and there in light and playful ways, causing mixtures of síbod and non-síbod in their performance. The audience does not take them seriously, accepting their play: "*Bata man lang na!* (S/he is just a child)." Community elders may scold them to be serious, and emphasize that the next time they perform, their music should síbod with dance, or vice-versa.

Síbod also bears an impact on young people's lives. Jory Gilmer, a boy I met in Barangay Sinunod, was ten years old when he danced with a girl his age. He was quick and witty, giving the girl a hard time during the pinanyo. She failed to capture his panyo. For some girls, a boy with movements like his would be challenging. Instead, the girl got weary of his handcloth tactics and called him names, uttered bad words, and insulted his dancing. This experience traumatized him. From that day forward, he no longer danced the binanog.

In wanting to achieve mastery in music and dance, Panay Bukidnons experience aspects of the many processual rites of living (e.g., adulthood, courtship, marriage, child-bearing, family and community task assignation, old age, death). Considering human choices, reflexivity and decisions based on intent, the consequence of achieving síbod is determined by the factor of agency. That is, binanog performers, audience members, and those involved in this event make their own choices. Aside from the instances mentioned here that explain consequences and non-consequences of actions brought about by síbod, there are other aspects beyond our comprehension that may appear to us as ambiguous and therefore may require further explanation.

Now and then, married couples test their music and dancing capabilities through the binanog; it may rejuvenate their attraction for each other. After the binanog, they figuratively dance and make music in each act of their married lives, reconnecting and constantly aiming for or achieving síbod in the process. This goes on for the rest of their lives.

The binanog is an opportune moment for one to gather many people in the community. Since houses are far apart from each other, gathering everyone consumes time and effort. People are drawn to gather and follow an agung's sound, which signals the binanog's beginning. An agung's sound resonates far and wide, reaching one's ears even across mountain ranges. I myself have been drawn to an agung's music that was played across the mountain ranges of Panay.

Síbod in the binanog also unifies people who are in disagreement with one another. I have witnessed community members alternately dancing and meeting with their elders in a truce in Barangay Siya. Siya's barangay captain, Rodolfo Castor, lined up his agenda for a meeting on March 19, 2004. It included, among other cases, settling a marital problem and a socio-political conflict between families. That day, I saw Rodolfo standing with the crowd waiting for the binanog to reach a point when everyone would agree that the dancing and the music had achieved síbod. He was particular about waiting for the binanog to reach its final phase, the pinanyo. This was the cue that he could finally get the people who gathered there to satisfyingly converge and discuss what to do in a case of social injustice. The performers and audience would not stop the binanog and convene for a community meeting until they felt more satisfied with what they saw and heard. This satisfaction was based on a quality-approved performance where everything else was in síbod. Rodolfo at this particular time had drawn his meeting constituents from the binanog attendees. Consensual decisions needed the majority of the populace as well as valid voices represented by the community's elders who would not miss the binanog. Rodolfo knew he had to wait for this moment so that he could administer his function as a leader of the community.

This particular case, of gathering a socio-political assembly, and waiting for the music and dance to síbod in the binanog, recalls the concept of diretso. Aside from the performers maintaining the ongoing tayuyon, people in power, such as the Barangay Kapitan, would heed the people's observance of tayuyon by not disrupting the event. It is a concept kept in mind by the community power-holders and the binanog action-holders.

I return to the topic of santú, particularly when performers are synchronized in music-making and dancing, and have gained their collective tayuyon. When there is santú, there is meaning in the togetherness of sounds and motions, as pointed out by Amang Baoy:

Kay indi pwede nga waay ga-
síbod imo sadsad ikumpara sa
tunog ka agung. Nan. Isa lang
sanda mo. Kay tama ka balikwa-
ut nga lain ang tunog ka agung,
lain man tunog ka imo sadsad.

Because it is not possible that
your sadsad does not síbod
compared with the sound of the
agung. There. All is "one," you see
(referring to dance and music). It
would be very awkward that the
sound of the agung is different; this
connectedness is also the sound of
your feet dancing.

Amang Baoy pointed out what constitutes their ideal world of collaboration: "It is not possible that your sadsad does not. . . ." In síbod, there is the
expected homophony between the instruments' sound and the sound of feet
dancing. Sadsad is important because it is a type of movement where the foot
is intentionally stamped in order to a produce sound, which should sound
the same rhythmically as the musical instruments do. As Amang Baoy said,
"See"—this time, directing his explanation to the visual evidence of coherence
between dancers' and musicians' motions. As a consequence of coherence, he
saw the unity of 'dance and music,' and 'sound and sight' having the kind of
oneness required in síbod.

The opposite of diretso/tayuyon is *sambud*. Sambud is a state of disorder,
as in the case of thread strips being entangled with one another, a visual imagery that runs contrary to síbod:

> Unlike síbod, sambud is to be out of sync with the
> whole tapestry that is being woven. This is having the
> knots in the wrong places or tying with the wrong
> strips in the wrong directions. (Email conversation
> with Monalisa Tabernilla, a Kinaray-a speaker, April 12,
> 2007).

Entangled threads do not ease out smoothly and become useless, for instance,
as a material for *panubok*. This condition, when applied to the binanog,
implies a non-workable performance.

Thus, tayuyon happens in a true-to-life performance that serves as a
"means of generating the on-going-ness of the culture" (King 1980, 171).
We see the functional parallelism between tayuyon and on-going-ness as

both intermediary values to culture and change. This is where the question of "Why must music and dance achieve síbod?" is recalled. With síbod, the Panay Bukidnon community continues to strive for the ideal of unity and oneness even amidst individual differences, social changes, and the impingement of ideas and materials from other societies.

CHAPTER 8

Síbod as a Pragmatic Praxis

SÍBOD PROVIDES THE PANAY BUKIDNON CULTURE WITH LIFE AND DYNAMISM. The people, especially elders, see and experience changes happening in their community. They notice that their youth are imbibing a different lifestyle as they have access to outside influences through media and economic transactions. However, síbod provides a means for regulating the impact of these forces by balancing new ideas on an existing foundation of values, thoughts, and behaviors. When done well—with flow and connection—the culture thrives within a dynamic framework.

In Barangay Daan Sur, the Panay Bukidnon youth introduced *pinato*, the duck-like style, in *binanog*. What influenced this new movement? Daang Sur settlers shared that pinato was influenced by dances shown on television. The youth would watch these dances when they went to the lowland, or mingled with peers in their town schools. The community's teenagers reveled in watching popular celebrities called the SexBomb Dancers. This group performed on *Eat Bulaga*, a popular noon-time television show in the Philippines. Back in 2003, their song "Spaghetti sa Pasko" was a big hit. Its accompanying dance, "Ispageti," involved shaking the hips while moving the body up and down. Young Panay Bukidnons imitated this dancing style that emphasized hip work and pelvic thrusts.

It is also important to consider how change is met and appropriated into existing *sunú*. I first saw the pinato style executed by Daang Sur's young dancers in August of 2003. It was danced with fast, emphatic hip movements. Even with pinato's new hip movement, binanog's traditional accentuation was applied to the pinato footwork. Thus, dancers using the pinato style were moving in the traditionally accepted rhythm even as they executed hàmpang on the old mnemonic, or sunú.

Panay Bukidnons perceive change in two ways: 1) as an innovative addition to the persisting extant binanog dance movements and music, as in *Talda,* a rhythmic mode that is considered relatively new compared to the dalunga; and 2) as a regulated change wherein the innovation should still bear the sunú, as in the continued practice of the pùntu found in the dinumaan style.

In the binanog practice, the Panay Bukidnon manage the alterations made by their youth by recalling for them the dinumaan style, since that is the binanog's main aesthetical basis. Those who are not taught this style hear about what the dance movements should be like from the crowd's comments: "*Amu dai-a! May pùntu!*" (That's the way it should be! There is intonation/ accent!). This verbalization is a public way of regulating and controlling newly absorbed influences from mass media. This regulation of change emphasizes process rather than elements that evolve. It is still related to the directed flow concept discussed earlier, which encourages the "ongoingness" of culture through the continued practice of tradition in music and dance.

Some young adults also copied the pinato movements. This is an initiative from the adults to exercise or appropriate change. Since pinato was first danced to imitate the SexBomb dancers, such as shaking the body and hips while moving downwards and upwards, adults made their versions in accordance with the binanog's sunú. They had less body shaking and hip frenzy, focusing more on foot accentuation. According to the elders, this was to correct aesthetic disorder and continue to achieve síbod so that tradition would be maintained. To maintain tradition is to continue, to flow, and to culturally survive. Aside from the earlier discussion of survival that focused on binanog's courtship function as crucial to cultural maintenance, I add that the binanog is a metaphor and meaning that people continue to live and to live for.

Lolita Castor, who prides herself as one of the adults who can perform the dinumaan, shared that she wished to learn the pinato after seeing it per-formed by young people. This surprised me at first, as I thought the dinumaan style was the only mark of an aesthetically approved binanog. I realized that the Panay Bukidnon were also curious about their youth's innovative ideas as a springboard to the evolution of the binanog. The incorporation of new dance steps may change the inner structures of the dance or may lead into a new dance genre still based on existing norms and forms.

In relation to maintaining traditional norms, binanog's identity and value are given importance by the Philippines' national government. Agencies such as the National Commission of Indigenous Peoples (NCIP) support the identities and rights of individuals in indigenous communities and assist them in building cultural pride. Indigenous peoples' identity is incorporated into the agenda of building nationhood. In a magazine article entitled "Indigenous Peoples . . . Indigenous Filipinos," Pe Benito (2003, 9) writes that "Indigenous and non-Indigenous peoples live on the same archipelago, the same country and both deserve respect and recognition. Indigenous peoples *are* Filipinos."

The Regional Director (Region VI which includes Panay) of the NCIP, Alfonso Catolin, stressed that identity is highly significant to support, especially on the issues of the licensing and ownership of ancestral lands:

> The NCIP has a mandate to protect and promote the rights of indigenous peoples as provided in the Indigenous Peoples' Rights Act. What makes a Panay Bukidnon different from the rest of the Philippines is their culture and it gives them the identity . . . our basis in applying the provisions of the Indigenous Peoples' Rights Act, especially in recognizing the rights over ancestral domains. (Interview, July 14, 2006)

A group's indigenous identity is a ticket to an ancestral right, that is, the right to claim property such as land passed on by elders. Proof of this identity is based on the continued production of traditional material culture as well as the continued practice of oral customs and traditions. Lito Espanola, the NCIP's Community Development Officer III of Region VI, explained why the NCIP assists in organizing the Binanog Festival almost every year:

> We conceptualized the Binanog Festival so you can see the Panay Bukidnon's oral tradition, songs and dances that will help us apply for the land title for Security of Tenure . . . the ancestral domain.

The National Commission for Culture and the Arts (NCCA) is involved in planning, programming, and funding preservation efforts of various Philippine cultures. The agency was conceived in 1987. Its mandate is to formulate policies for the development of culture and the arts, coordinate and implement the overall policies and programs, develop and promote the Filipino national culture and the arts, and preserve Filipino cultural heritage, among

other actions (ncca.com). The NCCA has been involved with the Panay Bukidnon in promoting and funding their Binanog Festival since 2002. Moreover, it
helped in the initial physical construction of the *Balay Turun-an* (School for
Living Traditions, or SLTs) and continues to finance these SLTs' educational
activities. Pe Benito (2003) notes that:

> . . . the identity of pre-colonial Filipinos . . . seen in their
> costumes, modes of living, and tradition was very much
> preserved…took a great deal of their tenacity to resist
> subjugation and change, especially with the presence
> of foreign conquerors who stayed for centuries.

Although the word preservation is ambiguous in the context of realistic
change, I do not want to argue for its use as it has been imposed under the
rubrics of idealized projects: cultural image for the NCCA, ancestral land
title for the NCIP, and validation through scientific mapping and territorial
boundaries with Info Mapper—an organization that helps locate land areas
of indigenous peoples. Identity can be both static and dynamic, as seen in the
binanog's practice of sunú and hàmpang. Síbod again mediates as a *santú*,
which includes among its embodiments the negotiations between the Panay
Bukidnon, governmental agencies, and other organizations.

Maivan Clech Lam, author of *At the Edge of the State: Indigenous Peoples
and Self-Determination* (de Vera 2003, 398) claims that survival depends on
a group's ability ". . . to alternately construct and collapse boundaries within
a shared system of meaning so that a useful and tolerable tension between
itself and others, between closure and exposure, may be found, enjoyed and
re-adjusted." The concept of boundary among Panay Bukidnons is perceived
not as a permanent fixture of imagined space, but more as a collapsible mental utility serving as a framework to communicate notions of differentiation
between themselves and the non-natives.[1]

The idea of delineation hinges on what the Panay Bukidnon accept as
outside against inside. They negotiate and distinguish the contrasting terms
depending on whom they talk to: a fellow *tumandok* (native) or a visitor from
the lowland.

Ness (1992) draws from the movements of routine, or daily raw behavior,
to the patterns of dance or, collectively, any symbolic public action. According
to her, the patterning of balance, timing, cooperation, power grabbing, freedom fighting and other social processes reflect Cebu, the place where *sinulog*

(a religious festival of street dancing venerating the child Jesus) is held. Just as Ness locates the body within the city and the existing socio-cultural and political elements around it, I see the binanog performers as catalysts in the ongoing formation of the Panay highland and its environment. Performers communicate to the physical (body, mental, affect) and the metaphysical/ spiritual dimensions that are believed to be part of their very existence. Moreover, the kinemic movements of their body during dancing or music-making reflect their community's socio-economic and political confluences in rapport with government and the townspeople of Tapaz and Calinog. They all mutually affect each other.

The act of identifying boundaries frames the Panay Bukidnon's way of determining identities among those they encounter in various interchanges such as economic trading or schooling for their youth. These exchanges involve negotiating new experiences while staying grounded in accepted wisdom and values. This form of adjustment has become a way of life for them, or in the same light, a way to life. The Panay Bukidnon have recognized the advantages of dealing with people from outside of their community to answer their economic needs. They exchange their cash crops for money so that they can buy things from the lowland. When a lowlander asks where their goods come from, they do not simply reply "*Tuya sa ibabaw ka bukid*" (From up the mountains). They learned that mentioning the barangay name of the goods' origin is precise and much more clearly understood among the lowlanders. Panay Bukidnons must shift in communicating reference points to acquire living needs from the lowlanders. The shifting has become natural to them, and thus has become a way of life.

CELEBRATION IN WORKABILITY

When there is harmony, there is an enduring impact of a well-performed binanog on a greater mass of people. This massive shared experience of síbod is encapsulated in the Panay Bukidnon's term *padagyaw* (celebration).

Among Panay Bukidnons, celebration is affirmed by this verbal expression: *Ga-síbod dai-a!* People excitedly shout this when everything in the binanog is found to be flowing and working well. Celebration is also elaborated when people talk about their performance, reward the dancers with newly made costumes, or re-gather in a tubà-drinking spree to talk about a successful event. These reactions mean that síbod in the binanog had been achieved; it must also be noted that these sentiments were uttered with great excitement and exclamations. I define celebration in this context as a form of the resonance and reverberation of síbod. Síbod generates resonance or sympathetic increase in the sound's amplitude that vibrates inside a resonating body such as a violin's wood casing. A resonance can be something like parents' inner pride at seeing their children learn epic chanting and binanog dancing. Gleceria Gilbaliga of Barangay Garangan expressed this when her three-year old daughter, Jally Nae, was applauded for chanting about Labaw Donggon's *kudyapi* (two-stringed boat lute) of Labaw Donggon. Rolinda Gilbaliga, another daughter of Gleceria, also danced the binanog in the dumaan style.

Reverberation is an outward directing of sound that produces extensions or repetitions of a sound image bouncing on surfaces. One reverberating instrument is an agung which, when played, is heard across mountains and seas, lakes and rivers/bodies of water. People who recount stories, or share bits and pieces of a victory in binanog dancing, are reverberating their celebration. One such account was about Adelaida Jimenez of Barangay Siya (Tapaz, Capiz), who displayed unexpected talent as she proved herself capable of getting the panyo from the taller and swifter Raffy Laluna of Barangay Rizal Sur (Tapaz, Capiz). Her strategies of using the panyo were talked about, as well as how she embodied síbod with Raffy. This act of reverberation is seen in gatherings and regatherings of people telling of events specifically during planting, harvesting, tuba-drinking, or resting when the midday sun is at its peak. In get-togethers like this, celebration is revisited and co-celebrated with others through speech, camaraderie, and verbal exchanges. In this way "*sugid*" plays a role in reifying cultural vitality.

In her conference paper entitled "The Santa Cruz *Dotoc* Tradition: Performing Liminality and Hope" (2007), Filipino anthropologist Jazmin Llana sees two focal positions for celebration: one as a process or a vessel that would bring to fruition the community's hopes and wishes; and secondly, as a triumph of the community to survive another year. Thus, celebration carries with it positive feelings, happiness, merriment, and victory—the very meanings that constitute celebration. Furthermore, Villaruz and Obusan (1994) state that dances in traditional communities are modes of celebration; they are facts of life just as real as the baskets and crafts people make. These are more than symbols. With Panay Bukidnons, the binanog is an exciting activity that they weave together over and over again. They look forward to it at the end of a day's toil, whether in the late afternoon or in the evening.

Tina Jimenez and Joy Castor of Barangay Siya (Tapaz, Capiz) look forward to teaching the area's children how to dance the binanog. To them, it is an activity worth anticipating. The celebration reflects a fullness of life through dance and music such that "they are a dimension of life itself and life is incomplete, unintelligible, and unexciting without them" (Villaruz and Obusan 1994, 34). This is why Panay Bukidnons say "Ga-síbod dai-a!" in moments when music and dance synchronize and flow smoothly. This is the ultimate expression that affirms the celebration and the hard-earned achievement of attaining síbod.

OPEN-ENDED CONCLUSION

The challenge of this book is to bring about an intelligible articulation of síbod, an ideology expressed through the performance or observance of the binanog. Explanations are undertaken through the indigenous process of sug-id. This local ideology enlarges music and dance theory's space as it not only provides for music and dance structures and their practices, but also involves the embodiment and integration of various creative forces at play: movement, clothing, socio-political negotiations, and the assertions of innovations into various platforms of traditions and conventions.

In the preceding chapters, I have argued that even as ideologies are strongly associated with political action, they serve as practical applications to organized movements that convey a coordinated body of concepts. Secondly, an ideology brings about change, though in this case, change does not simply alter the binanog's traditional aspects. It is a realized altering of what has been changed based on awareness of underlying norms and conventions, and thus serves as a change of Change. The ideological expression that is síbod permeates people's thoughts and ways as they perform the binanog; it is also a goal achieved through action. The elders often say "*basala para dya mag-síbod*" (play for it to síbod).

Panay Bukidnons often frame their life experiences through the binanog. They observe and imitate the banog's flying motions, emulate its qualities (leadership, pride, gracefulness, and skill), and project these as links to the *kalibutan* so that order and harmony are maintained in the whole ecosystem. Their experiences are interpreted or externalized in sound and movement. References to the banog and the binanog are also found in Panay Bukidnon folklore and epic stories, such as Humadapnon and Mali's dance, and in the reiteration of lifecycle rituals and festivities.

Even as síbod provides for the integration of various elements in a group and encourages teamwork, individual style and identity are not hampered.

Group efficiency draws its power from a self synchronized with others. In a broader context, the integrated and integrating quality embodied by the Panay Bukidnon is the opposite of the compartmentalized being that Azurin (1995) claims as a legacy of Filipino colonial history.[2] The Americans governed the Filipinos from 1898 to 1946, resulting in task divisions and specialization of disciplines, particularly in academe, industry, and the arts. These have not thoroughly superseded traditional modes of living and the unified fields that interpenetrate traditional lifeways.[3] Síbod makes the specialization-integration divide work either as collaborative or as distinct acts since it appropriates the synchronized self to the binanog's more interactive operations. Aptly, there is no síbod without the mastery of a field, as síbod mediates between a prepared/skilled individual and a related group and even broader functions. No síbod could occur in any underdeveloped task. I use specialization-integration in the sense intended by Csikszentmihalyi (1990, 227–40): "integration and differentiation composes the complexity that advances the human mind to a higher form of consciousness. Differentiation has produced breakthroughs in science and technology, the ability to separate dimensions of objects and processes. Yet such evolutionary achievements become destructive if these run contrary to environmental safety and disregard the integrated connection of life forms." On a related note, systems theory argues for a more fully integrated understanding of analysis. Science is at once differentiating and reintegrating distinct elements from nature.

One can focus on a specific act while integrating another. In mastering a musical skill, it dawned on me that enacting dance and not just thinking about it was a beneficial method to integrate the tactile learning of tambur playing. While I was repeating the rhythms on the tambur, I sensed that something was missing in terms of how the rhythm coordinated with my affect. Something was wrong when I damped some tones. Dancing while drumming proved to be effective because it connected my entire body and affect with sound. This pedagogy could also be applied in reverse: dancing while thinking and enacting music is effective. This is what Miningkol did as a child when she rehearsed by the river, thinking of rhythms and muttering them in a tàtà.

In Covar's concept of kasarinlan, the self is located in, and not isolated from, its community; thus, he refers to the term, "communal self," where there is a collective context to consider. As it is deeply valued in connection with the community, the self defines the Panay Bukidnon's *pagkatao*, which is reflected in the binanog. The self is specific to santú at the primary level:

self-synchronization. Before functioning with a group, a performer integrates the self by *pasibudon*. Dancers utter the tàtà even as their bodies execute the rhythmic patterns from it. After musicians warm up to their musical instruments, and dancers move in time to the tàtà, pasibudon now works as a means to make one's actions fluid. Pressing (1988) calls this automaticity, or "a phase at which it has become possible to completely dispense with conscious monitoring of motor programmes, so that the hands appear to have a life of their own . . ." (139; on Bartlett and Welford). Laneri (1975) adds that this is a change distinct from controlled processing to automatic processing as a result of extensive skill rehearsal. In preparation for the greater challenges of synchronizing with others, a pasibudon of the self is important. When one is ready, one can accommodate the social aspect of interaction: one's sound/motion against and with that of co-performers.

It is crucial to look into people's relationships during and after performing the binanog. When síbod is achieved, performers get into a directed flow. This process may be seen as both circular and linear. Linearity is seen in the directional progress of the binanog music and dance, as these are gradually built up in amplitude and degree of intensity, from the *bayhunan* to the exciting *pinanyo*. It is also through this linearity that dynamics, affect, and a sense of continuity develops, leading to a final euphoric release. This euphoria is a consequence of the community building that has been generated at the moment of heightened activity, bringing everyone together regardless of affinity, authority, and/or age. Circularity of flow is seen in the *hampang* of cyclical patterns, always recalling sunú. Circularity is an encompassing experience as it involves one's body, sound, emotion, intellect and all the human faculties. This type of flow is instinctive and protective as it balances all types of changes that may occur among community members. It is not completely enclosing nor does it open itself freely to all types of flux brought about by cultural, social, political, and economic human interactions during the event.

The circularity in the concept of *tayuyon* encourages the Panay Bukidnon community to feed upon and regenerate its own system. This, to me, is a veritable sign of self-sustainability: the ability to draw resources and strength from within, and to inspire the people to act continuously toward revitalizing culture. It is one's initiative to coach the next generation, and producing what can be recycled and reused from the immediate environment: a kind of integration with/to the environment.

But how is socio-cultural change reconciled with the issue of cultural maintenance, as the two represent conflicting categories of stasis and dynamism? For Panay Bukidnons, change is subjected to another form of change, a patterning to what has been agreed to as the communally appropriated aesthetics. Ulan Caballero raised the importance of *pùntu* to distinguish a dinumaan against the bag-uhan. A dancer who executes the dinumaan has a marked *pùntu*, qualifying his/her identity as a good dancer. A bag-uhan, on the other hand, has no clear *pùntu* and needs to develop it through more training. Identity in this case is corollary to quality of performance characterized by one's application of sunú. Having quality also means having *pùntu*: following the mnemonic structure faithfully; sounding the footwork with mnemonic accents; and appropriately applying bodily motions like *kidò-kidò* and *li-ad*.

Síbod is a practical accommodation of change. It is a flow that does not resist change, but such change should remain faithful to sunú. Even though young Panay Bukidnons dance the binanog like a pato with emphatic hip movements, their innovation bears the sunú through stamping on the music's accents, moving in rhythm, and doing hampang with the patterns based on the mnemonic. In their introduction of the duck-like dance style, they demonstrated that a different interpretation of a rhythmic mode can be made while continuing the practice of applying *pùntu* such as that found in the dinumaan style.

In collective work, there is a sense of fullness equally related to a sense of completion where there is a working relationship among the binanog's actors and elements. When there is a sense of completion at the level of performance, the next level is sought, although this could also be done simultaneously with group synchronization. This is the level of performers linking with the different realms of the kalibutan. This linkage becomes possible by another act of pasibudon. This time, it is to align one's physical and affective faculties to the kalibutan's upper, middle and lower dimensions. Binanog performers enact this linkage in specific ways. They use their eyes to *tulok sa ibabaw*, and their bodies to li-ad in order to establish rapport with the *ibabawnon*. To make the spirits of *dutan-on* and *tubignon* feel their presence, they flap their arms like the banog's wings in the *tunga-tunga*, or the middle space from their bodies; to *tandug*, the dancers sound their feet as they render the *sadsad*. In this context, síbod can be understood not just as an ideological expression, but also intimately and perhaps more profoundly, as a life-giving stream to the community and to its surroundings.

Tayuyon is therefore a medium from which thought and actions become naturally ingrained in individual players so that they can continuously perform or flow/continue playing through an event; it is comparable to automaticity (Pressing 1988), and *dulugu ganalan* (Feld 1988). Secondly, as a motivated energy that brings the players to a heightened emotional state or even to an altered state of consciousness; it is almost a *dawatan* (Eliod Dimzon in a personal conversation, January 20, 2001) or a "celebration of the triumph of the community to survive . . ." (Ilana, personal conversation, email, April 14, 2007); and lastly, as a stream of linkage to kalibutan's different spiritual realms, in order to establish circulated order and harmony in all physical and metaphysical systems of existence.

Síbod as flow may be seen in a linear perspective following sunú's sequential concepts and applications, hampang, salú, and santú. In the circular model, it encompasses all these concepts. It fluidizes actions in every sunú, every hampang, every salú, and every santú. Síbod or flow is a micro and macro operative, connecting bits and pieces of structures to effect a whole, an integration of sounds and movements. This operative is synonymous with a connective and effective system of actions realizing the ideological-expressive ideal that is síbod. Thus, when someone says "Ga-síbod dai-a!" it means, in effect, "It works!"

Toward the end of this writing, I ruminate on the limitations of my ability to write and interpret a culture I am not permanently rooted in. To say the least, my five-year sporadic immersions and one-year intensive experiences with field participants (see Appendix 2) frame the expanse of this book. However, a bulk of this scholarship owes its merits to the active voices of the Panay Bukidnon who lived and spoke to me, taught me, and lived with me, and I with them, during the period of my research. Through this book, their words and thoughts have been channeled into the limits of the written text and graphics that come with it. Significant to this attempt of representation is the record and unraveling of their pagkatao—what they thought, what they believed, what they did, and how they lived and how they continue to do so. Their perspectives and mine are interwoven sugid that perhaps would usher in a new set of meanings, feelings, thoughts, experiences, and affects. These meanings are passages that may lead to further constructions of human creativity, to be further extended and built-up by future generations.

Like tayuyon, this book is open-ended. I síbod through the river of my thoughts as if departing from Barangay Nayawan or Tacayan, riding the *balsa* (raft) navigated by the Panay Bukidnon down the Pan-ay river toward a safer shore where I would head home.

símbol

APPENDIX 1

Language Guide

IN THE USE OF CONSONANTS, A LANGUAGE MANUAL FOR AMERICAN PEACE Corps, "Learning Kinaray-a with a Native Speaker" (n.d.), states that

> Kinaray-a has only sixteen significant and distinct consonant sounds. Except for the glottal stop, the script or written symbol also corresponds to the consonant sound. The consonant sounds are /b, k, d, g, h, l, m, n, ng, p, r, s, t, w, y, and (glottal stop)/. The /p, t, k/ sounds are not aspirated at the beginning of the words. Practically, all consonant sounds occurring at the final position of the words are pronounced without release. Especially notable for the sounds /p, t, k/ and /b, d, g/ and /m, n, ng/.

The consonants b, d, k, m, p, s, t are pronounced as in English (Kaufmann 1916, 2) and is always hard like "get, goggle, gut;" "h" is always aspirated such as "hat, hit, and ha-ha;" "k" has the same sound as the "c" in the words "cat, lick, lock, luck;" "r" is pronounced like: "racket, read, rid, wrong, rung;" "w" is identical with the English words "wag, well, will, woe, would;" however, "when closing a syllable after an "a" forms the dipthong "aw", "w" is pronounced "ou" in words like "about, loud, out, gout." The consonant "y" is also a vowel in the Visayan language (author's note: Kinaray-a is considered Visayan). It forms diphthongs with "a," e.g., "may;" with "u" like "luya;" another is with "i" as in "diya."

"Accents point out the syllable that is to be stressed" (ibid, p. 4) and their presence determines changes in meanings, e.g., *tubú* (sugar cane) and *túbu* (growth; offshoot).

The hyphen (-) is used in Filipino words to indicate that the consonant preceding the hyphen belongs to the preceding syllable and consequently a slight pause has to be made before pronouncing the syllable following the hyphen, e.g., *gal-um* (thunder).

A common Filipino spelling rule states, "*Siyang bigkas, siyang baybay*" [How a word is pronounced, so is the spelling of the word] (Santiago and Tiangco 1991). I base the spelling of most local terms I used in this study on how my research participants pronounced words.

APPENDIX 2

Research Participants

1   **FEDERICO "TUOHAN" CABALLERO**, Barangay Garangan (Calinog, Iloilo), Balay Turun-an master teacher of epics, songs. Gawad sa Manlilikha ng Bayan 2002, husay. Dates of interviews: September 8, 2001; May 4, 2002; May 20, 2002; November 18–20, 2002; October 6, 2003; May 2–8, 2004; April–May 2005.

2   **LUCIA CABALLERO**, Barangay Garangan (Calinog, Iloilo), Balay Turun-an (School of Living Tradition), teacher of music instruments; binanog. Master embroiderer. Dates of interviews: April 21, 2001; September 8, 2001; May 15–22, 2002; April 12–15, 2004; May 1, 2004; April–May 2005.

3   **ROMULO "AMANG BAOY" CABALLERO**, Barangay Garangan (Calinog, Iloilo), Balay Turun-an teacher of epics, songs, binanog; the 22nd kagawad of Masaroy; "Outstanding Indigenous Leadership;" husay. Dates of interviews: September 8, 2001; April 22, 2001; May 20, 2002; November 18–20, 2002; October 6, 2003; May 2–8, 2004; April 28–30, 2004.

4   **ROLANDO "ULAN" CABALLERO**, Barangay Garangan (Calinog, Iloilo), Assistant teacher of the Balay Turun-an. Dates of interviews: December 13, 2003; April 12, 2004; May 1, 2004.

5   **ALFREDO CASTOR**, Barangay Daan Sur (Tapaz, Capiz), student. Date of interviews: March 5–9, 2004.

6   **FELIZA "LUGPIAN" CASTOR**, epic chanter, master binanog teacher. Dates of interviews: November 19–20, 2002; March 10–13, 2004; January 2–4, 2005.

7   **AURELIO "KUNE" DAMAS**, Barangay Taganhin, Tribal Chieftain, husay. Dates of interviews: October 8–9, 2003; March 14–16, 2004; May 2–5, 2004.

8   **VIOLETA DAMAS**, Barangay Taganhin, *Dalungdungan*, a spiritual healer. Dates of interviews: March 14–16, 2004; March 7–8, 2004; January 3, 5, 2005; May 2–5, 2004.

9   CONCEPCION "MININGKOL" DIAZ, Barangay Tacayan, Tribal Chieftain of Tacayan, Balay Turun-an binanog teacher. Dates of interviews: November 18, 2002; October 8–9 2003; January 21–February 10, 2004; April 15–25, 2004; April–May 2005; April–May 2006.

10   MENCHIE DIAZ, BARANGAY TACAYAN, healer. Dates of interviews: January 21–February 10, 2004; April 15–25, 2004; April–May 2005; April–May 2006.

11   ROBERTO "BUDOL" DIAZ, Barangay Tacayan, Ex-Barangay Captain of Tacayan; fisherman; farmer. Dates of interviews: January 21–February 10, 2004.

12   MAGDALENA "MAGDING" JIMENEZ, Barangay Siya (Tapaz, Capiz), babaylan. Dates of interviews: March 17–23, 2004.

13   LISING JIMENEZ, BARANGAY SIYA (Tapaz, Capiz), musician, binanog dancer, chanter. Dates of interviews: March 17–23, 2004.

14   CONCHITA GILBALIGA, Barangay Nayawan (Tapaz, Capiz), a *hantup* (master embroiderer). Dates of interviews: March 7–8, 2004; January 3, 5, 2005.

15   ESTELLA GILBALIGA, Barangay Nayawan (Tapaz, Capiz), binanog dancer. Dates of interviews: March 8–10, 2004; January 2–5, 2005.

16   JALLY NAE GILBALIGA, Barangay Garangan (Calinog, Iloilo), Balay Turun-an student. Dates of interviews: April 20, 2006.

17   MANUEL "IMAS" GILBALIGA, Barangay Nayawan (Tapaz, Capiz), binanog dancer. Dates of interviews: March 4, 5, 12, 2004.

18   CARLOS PARLE, BARANGAY BATO-BATO (Tapaz, Capiz), binanog dancer. Dates of interviews: April 18–19, 2004.

19   MANSUETO PARLE, tambur player. Dates of interviews: May 19–22, 2004.

20   NIDA PERILLO, Barangay Nayawan (Tapaz, Capiz), binanog dancer. Dates of interviews: November 18, 2002; March 14–16, 2004.

APPENDIX 3

Pinanyo

BINANOG WOMAN DANCER POSITIONS HER PANYO LIKE THE LETTER X. THIS IS an effective strategy for obtaining the man's panyo at the center.

DANCERS:
Michael Carado
and
Honelyn Carado
of
Barangay
Agcalaga
(Calinog, Iloilo)

Binanog woman dancer positions her panyo like the letter L. This is an effective strategy for obtaining the man's panyo sideways.

DANCERS:
Michael Carado
and
Honelyn Carado
of
Barangay
Agcalaga
(Calinog, Iloilo)

Man and woman shift the use of the panyo to a *wayway* (hanging style). The woman tries to find another way of obtaining the man's panyo.

DANCERS:
Eduardo Lastrilla
and
Honelyn Carado
of
Barangay
Agcalaga
(Calinog, Iloilo)

If previous attempts are not successful, the woman resorts to *si-ud*, where the panyo is hurled around the man's neck.

DANCERS:
Michael Carado
and
Honelyn Carado
of
Barangay
Agcalaga
(Calinog, Iloilo)

APPENDIX 4

Sangkap (Costume and Accessories)

SANGKAP (COSTUME AND ACCESSORIES)

I

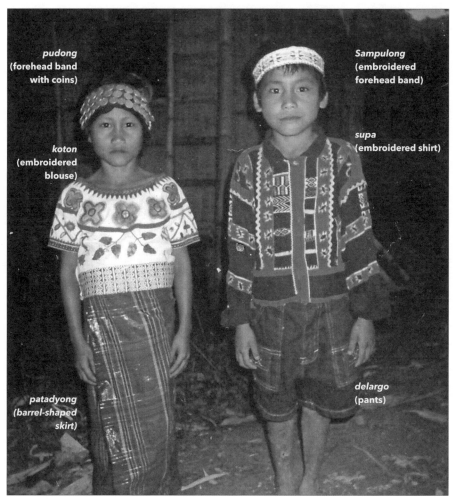

pudong
(forehead band
with coins)

Sampulong
(embroidered
forehead band)

koton
(embroidered
blouse)

supa
(embroidered shirt)

patadyong
(barrel-shaped
skirt)

delargo
(pants)

Inday and Alejandro Jimenez

II

Lucia "Mehoran" Caballero

APPENDIX 5
Bird Dance Typology in the Binanog

BIRD TYPE	DANCE STYLE	PERCEIVED BEHAVIOR(S) OF BIRDS	DESCRIPTIVE EXECUTION ON DANCE
alagit-it (cave bat)	*inalagit-it*	*gapagukguk* (looks for food; flies and produces bat sound)	*alima daw galupad-lupad; ga-huni* (hands show flying movements; any body part can make sound)
balud (spotted imperial pigeon)	*simbalud*	*gakurba pakpak* (curved wings)	*Ilibut alima pa-atras* (hands move toward back of the body)
banog (hawk-eagle)	*binanog*	*gatiririk/palakpak ang pakpak* (wings clapping)	*alima galupad-lupad; babayi kag lalaki gataririk gipalibutan ang kada isa* (hands like flying; woman and man energetically encircle each other)

dulungan (writhed-billed hornbill)	*ga-dulungan*	*Siki gakuro* (each foot or knee would curve when walking)	*gakuro daya siki sa pagbayhun-bayhun labi na gid ang laki* (foot or knee, particularly of the male dancer, curves while walking during the dance's beginning)
ilahas ga-kaykay (fowl scratching)	*kinaykay*	*gakinayay* (scratching)	*siki gakinayay* (feet scratching or brushing on ground)
manatad (common emerald dove)	*minanatad*	*gatingting sa sanga ka kahuy* (lightly walking on a tree branch)	*ikit-ikit tikang* (small steps)
pakyang*	*pinakyang*	*pakpak gina-kurba* (bird curves its wings)	*gi-kurba pakpak* (wings curve)
paki*	*pinaki*	*siki gapagilid* (feet walking in oblique direction)	*siki ga pinaki* (feet walking like the *paki* bird: slightly in oblique direction)
punay (green pigeon)	*pinunay*	*malulut; daw gapangayo turuk-un* (timid; like asking for feed)	*bayi malulut* (woman dancer should look timid)
rubi*	*sinarubi*	*galibut turuk-un* (goes around food)	*galibut sa imaw* (goes around co-dancer)
tikling (rail)	*tinikling*	*ga-tikling* (hopping)	*siki ga-tikling* (feet are hopping)

uwak (crow)	*inuwak*	*ga-apik apik; gaking-king* (beak moves forward/ backward; sits in a squatting position)	*siki gapa-sulung kag pa-atras* (feet going forward and backward)

Latest addition to the typology
(introduced by the youth of barangay Daan Sur)

pato (duck)	*pinato*	*iwad-iwad buli* (hips swaying side by side)	*buli ga-iwad-iwad* (dancers move hips side-to- side)

*   English translation not found in handbook of the
Department of Natural Resources, Region VI

APPENDIX 6
Dance Notation
NOTES ON THE BENESH BY MARIE YVONNE TORRES (DANCE NOTATOR)

IN THIS BOOK, I TRANSCRIBED THE BINANOG DANCE USING THE BENESH Movement Notation. I find this type of notation useful in representing small movements and other details that may reveal meaning and cultural symbolism. In the binanog, slightly tilting the head upward with the eyes looking up honors certain upper cosmos spirits; postures such as leaning backwards and moving the hips forward are characteristics of the antigo. These and other minute details make up a culture's distinctive character.

The Benesh Movement Notation (BMN) is defined by its inventor, Rudolf Benesh, as the aesthetic and scientific study of all forms of human movements by movement notation. It is also called choreology or dance script. During the 1940s, Benesh, with the help of his wife, Joan (a Royal Ballet dancer), created the Benesh system. They both recognized the problem of not recording the work for dance analysis and preservation, so this system was introduced. The Benesh Movement Notation has not only benefited dance education and choreography, but also has contributed to physiotherapy, anthropology, and ergonomics.

The Benesh Movement Notation provides an accurate, three-dimensional representation of movement, including precise indication of people's whereabouts and relationship to one another within the working space, the directions in which they face and their paths of travel, and the head's, limbs', hands', feet's and body's movements and positions. It also indicates precision in rhythm, quality and timing of movements. This notation works well in ballet because of the representations of techniques and calculated movements. However, do not take such precisions literally. In reality, the rendition of indigenous dances such as the binanog pays attention to myriad aspects and not merely to precision: the aesthetics of movements imitating the banog, the chase of the panyo, the courtship motive, among others do not lend themselves to any kind of notation, much less a notation geared for representing Western dance forms. The binanog dancers' movements can be fluid and less structured. Therefore, do not take the Benesh Movement Notation as the ultimate representation of the dances under consideration in this text.

HOW TO READ THE BINANOG IN THE BENESH MOVEMENT NOTATION (BMN)

The Staff

The BMN system, like the Western music notation, uses a five-line stave, read from left to right and from top to bottom. The five lines and spaces in between coincide with a certain body part in a standing position. Other positions such as sitting and lying may be recorded as well. Since the binanog is only danced standing, other explanations will not be specified. Movements are recorded in a series of frames, similar to the process of making cartoons (author's note: please see the simplified human figure shown at the bottom of this paragraph). The directional orientation is from the performer's point of view, whichever front s/he is facing. His/her right and left are left and right in the notation (author's note: as decribed, this case is for a solo dancer; for a partner dance, directional orientation . . .). Directional changes may be set below or between staves. The illustration below shows the corresponding body part for each line (shown at the left of the stave) and space (shown at the right of the stave):

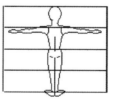

top of the head
shoulders
waist
knees
feet or floor line

head and neck
torso
hips and thighs
lower limbs

Three Basic Symbols

There are three basic and varied signs in BMN. A sign is placed in relation to the body, whether it is in level, in front, or behind. When dancing binanog, the extremities (limbs and arms) are relaxed, and a little bit bent. This kind of bending will not be notated but other movements, such as hand flexion or knee-bending, will be indicated. Below are the three signs and their bent equivalents.

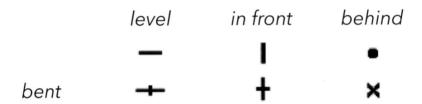

The binanog involves varied arm movements. The wrists' extension and flexion happens throughout the entire dance. The arm movements are as effortlessly natural as flapping its wings are as to the banog. The arms do this level with the body, but this motion can also be done in other directions. (Author's note: Below is a series of illustrations that show hand movements used in the binanog).

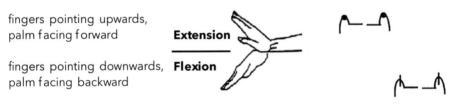

fingers pointing upwards, palm facing forward

Extension

fingers pointing downwards, palm facing backward

Flexion

Movement lines are used to trace the path the arms and legs are taking (where the movement starts and ends). They also indicate a step and jump. The step-line is written above the floor line while the jump-line is written below the floor line.

Step-lines

A- step in place
B- step forward
C- step backward

A   B   C

Jump-lines

A- jump in place
B- jump forward
C- jump backward

A   B   C

Any symbol placed along the floor line means support (author's note: support of the dancer's weight on the floor). The feet can be supported in three ways.

A- whole foot on the floor
B- heels are raised
C- tiptoe

A   B   C

When the feet are on the floor and one foot steps without transferring the entire weight on the other leg, it is called displacement.

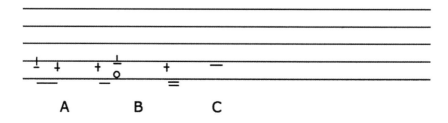

A   B   C

A   Starting with two feet on the ground, knees bent.

B   Right foot lifts a little bit to close behind the body with raised heels.

C   Without transferring all the weight on the right foot, the left foot steps in place

In binanog, both man and woman dance with a panyo. Supporting signs are used to indicate that the hand/s is/are holding a prop.

| level | front | back |

Rhythm, Quality, and Timing

There is no exact classification of timing in binanog, but for the sake of recording, the dances are written in the 2/4 time signature (written at the top left corner of the stave). The use of broken lines for bar lines, instead of solid lines, is intentional; this guides the idea of timing, but is not strictly implemented. Binanog is an improvisational dance, which leads to many variations of movement patterns. The repeated patterns are in between two symmetrical repeat signs.

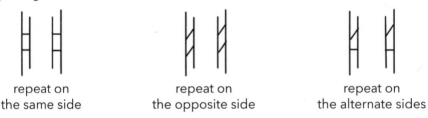

| repeat on the same side | repeat on the opposite side | repeat on the alternate sides |

Binanog footwork requires agility. There is accent (marcato) in many of the beats, but this does not necessarily pertain to sound. For women, stepping does not require too much effort compared to men. Women are more grounded, while men tend to lift their arms and legs higher.

Directions

A pin stands for a dancer or group of dancers doing the same movements. For

man   woman

two or more dancers moving differently, a sign for each dancer is needed. A pin can also show where the body is facing. The body's direction is shown by where the pinhead is pointing.

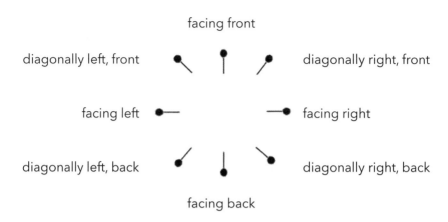

It can also indicate the degree of turn done in place or traveling.

clockwise:

| Front | 1/8 | 1/4 | 3/8 | 1/2 | 5/8 | 3/4 | 7/8 | 1 turn |

(**AUTHOR'S NOTE:** each symbol indicates a 1/8 increment in a turn)

Traveling

The traveling signs show where the body is traveling in the given space. ↑
The arrow is divided into parts to indicate traveling forward, backward and
sideways in relation to the body's direction. Remember that the direction sign
is used only when the body is moving in place, but as soon as the body moves
while traveling, there are other signs to be shown. Traveling signs work with
directional signs to specify which direction the body is facing. They are written below or in-between staves.

Traveling forward is represented by the isolated arrow-head on the right
side, traveling backward is the isolated arrow-head on the left side. Traveling
sideways to the left, in relation to the body's front, is the isolated arrow-tail on
the right side and traveling sideways to the right is the arrow-tail on the left
side. Any of these signs can be placed in different directions.

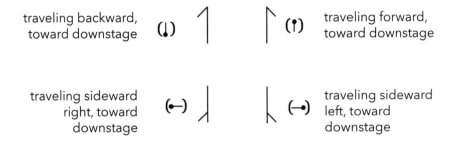

traveling backward, toward downstage **(↓)**

(↑) traveling forward, toward downstage

traveling sideward right, toward downstage **(←)**

(→) traveling sideward left, toward downstage

Traveling signs can be a straight path: ——— , a curved path: ⌒ , or a circular path: ◯ .

THE STAGE

The stage's areas are taken from the actor's point of view. If you are facing the audience, stage right will be to your right and stage left to your left. Downstage will be towards the audience, while upstage is towards the back wall (away from the audience). To locate the body's placement or travel, signs for the stage are indicated. Let us assume that the illustration below is the stage.

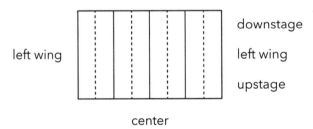

left wing

downstage

left wing

upstage

center

This is the BMN scheme.

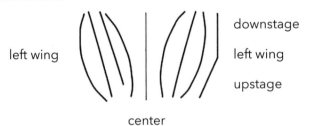

left wing

downstage

left wing

upstage

center

The slants and curves do not indicate the widening or narrowing of the stage. For the purpose of representing the stage's different areas, every line, curve, and slant is different. The centerline divides stage left and stage right. A tick,

_ , placed on the particular area of the scheme indicates the body's position. When the body is traveling, ticks are placed to limit the area of travel. Here are some examples:

| upstage wing-quarter | center | downstage right-quarter |

BENESH NOTATION OF YVONNE TORRES

Arms may be ad lib. Dancers always improvise within the given steps and body positions.
Notation shows right foot starting, but it can be with the left foot.
For woman during the repasu and sadsad phases, end of panyo can be tied
in front of waist (around the waist) or in front of chest (over the shoulders).

BAYHUNAN

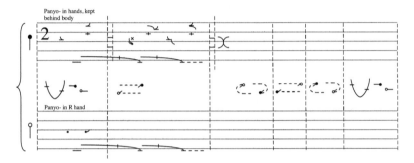

REPASU

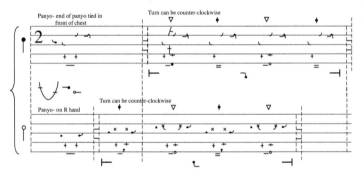

Repasu can also
be done traveling
or by exchanging places

SADSAD

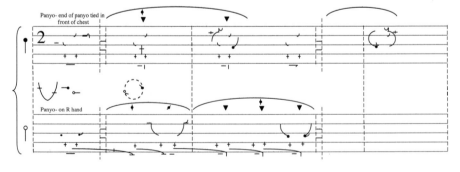

SIMBALUD

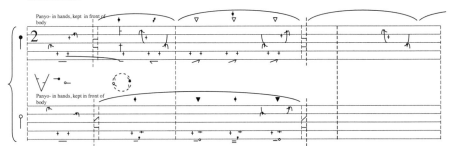

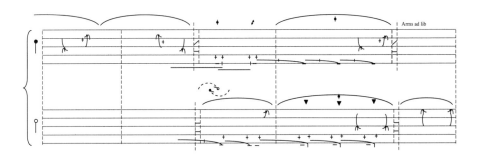

PINANYU

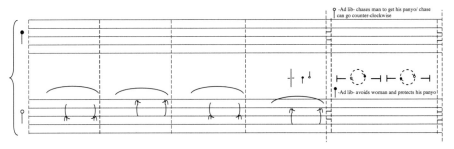

Arms may be ad lib. Dancers always improvise within the given steps and body positions.
Woman's end of panyo can be tied in front of waist (around the waist)
or in front of chest (over the shoulders).
Circular floor pattern shows clockwise, but can be counter-clockwise, and vice-versa.

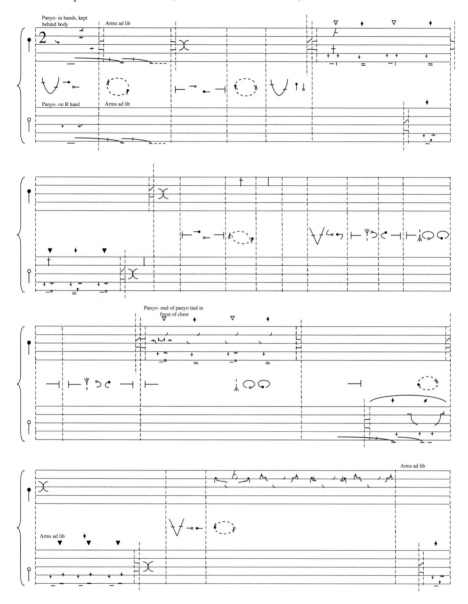

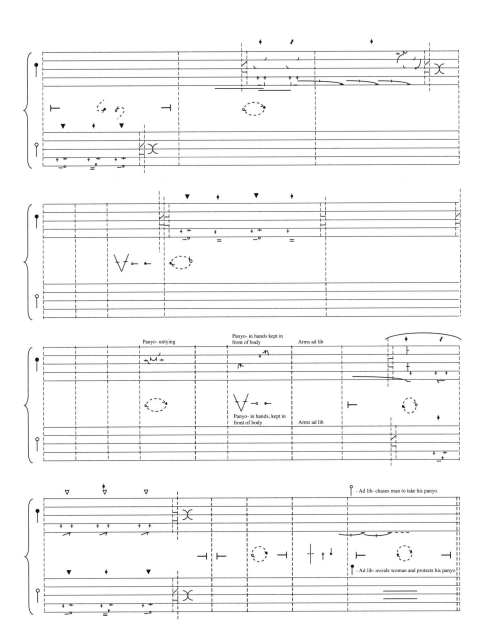

This dance was originally performed inside the house of one of the natives in Panay. The area of the stage is about 7 by 5 feet. The musicians were grouped on one side. Although the audience was scattered around the stage, the dancers somehow projected more to one side, which I consider the front.

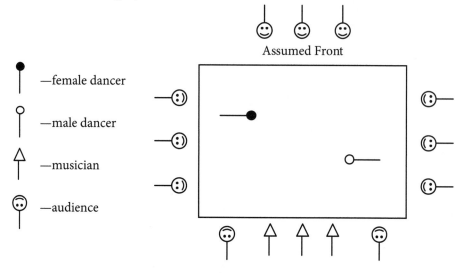

Binanog can be be performed anywhere. The circular floor pattern allows the dance to be visible from different perspectives. It can be danced inside a house, on an elevated stage made of bamboo, or even along the river.

APPENDIX 7
Rhythmic Modes

DALUNGA MODE

tarlalay Dalunga
sakbatang Dalunga
pakbagang Dalunga
padanggitang[1] Dalunga

TALDA MODE

patakdanga Talda
lanalana Talda

OTHER MODES

Six Syllabic Modes with Two Accented Endings
patakdanga dalmuk
patakdanga burtak
patakdanga dalta
patakdanga salkot
patakdanga palpal
patakdanga tangga

---

1   *Padanggitang* has four syllables like the *"patakdanga"* in *patakdanga Dalunga.*

Seven Syllabic Modes with Three Accented Endings
  bato-bato Tulindaw
  patakdanga Guribal
  patakdanga Purungut
  patakdanga Turuba

Seven Syllabic Modes with Four Accented Endings
  takdanga Kalimutang/Kalamutang
  takdanga Gurubatan

NOTE: These are all *tiniglalaki*, male rhythmic modes.
          The tinigbabayi, female rhythmic mode, has limited types
          such as the "giriling Linda."

Notes

PREFACE

1   Jocano used Sulod as a tentative term to mean Panay's mountain people. He is referring to the Panay Bukidnon.

2   In total, Magos has documented thirteen volumes: the epic entitled "Humadapnon" has four volumes, and the other nine epics are written in one volume each (email message by Magos, 28 February 2008).

3   Binanog is an idealization of the *banog* (hawk-eagle; scientific name: *Nisaetus philippensis*), a local bird found in the highlands of Panay in Western Visayas, Philippines. This bird is endowed with multifarious qualities embodied in and by the binanog dance, music, and other forms of expressivity.

4   This article was shared with me by the "Center for Western Visayas Studies" (cwvs) of the University of the Philippines in the Visayas (upv) in Iloilo City, Philippines.

5   This was "invented in England by Joan and Rudolf Benesh in the late 1940's" (Parker 1984, 81). A representation of movements, this is related to choreology defined by Rudolf Benesh as "the scientific and aesthetic study of all forms of human movement through movement notation" (ibid).

CHAPTER 1. Encountering *Síbod*

1   Boi Henwu is considered the first woman of the T'Boli, an ethnolinguistic group in southern Philippines. She represents the ideals of womanhood and wealth, as well as the link between musical instruments and birds, particularly the crimson-breasted barbet as illustrated in the T'Boli creation myth.

2   Panay Bukidnons consider winged creatures, including bats, as birds.

3   I use this in the same sense used in the Bible, which states that Yahweh is the "God of gods" or the way that Mulhall (1996, 7) does in referring to Heidegger's ruminations on the "Being of beings." I see the connection of ascendancy and transcendence among these references with the people's imaging of the banog in their expression of music and dance.

4   The Barangay is the smallest sociopolitical unit other than the family. The term
     comes from the word *balangay* (boat), the main water vehicle used by most
     early Filipinos to bring their family or group to a new place to form a settle-
     ment and/or a community.

5   Throughout the book, this information will appear in the following format:
     barangay name (township name, province name). For instance, in designating
     Barangay Tacayan, this will appear in the following way: 'Barangay Tacayan
     (Tapaz, Capiz),' which means the barangay is located in the town of Tapaz,
     which, in turn, is in the province of Capiz. For Barangay Garangan, the infor-
     mation will appear like so: 'Barangay Garangan (Calinog, Iloilo),' which means
     that this barangay exists in the town of Calinog, which is in Iloilo province.

CHAPTER 2. The Ideologue: Panay Bukidnons

1   According to Aurelio "Kune" Damas of Barangay Taganhin, the Siyaw are the
     Mexican or Spanish hired bands of armed men who frequented the Panay high-
     lands during the Spanish colonial period (1521 to the late 1800s).

2   The Panay Bukidnon refer to objects of value that a man or his family offers to
     a woman for marriage as a gift, rather than a price. Coined as a bride-gift, this
     concept is contrary to the commonly used term bride-price, which entails buy-
     ing someone in exchange for a material value. (Conversation with Alicia Magos,
     May 2012)

3   The Negrito in Iloilo and the highlands are referred to as Ati. However, the
     name would depend on the people's location. Based on my preliminary inter-
     views, the natives of Boracay, an island just north of Panay, call themselves Ata;
     they use this name particularly in their songs. The dark-skinned natives living
     in Mount Pinatubo refer to themselves as Aeta. Note that they share some cul-
     tural characteristics, such as a tradition of nomadic roaming, but are distinct in
     some ways, such as in the languages they speak.

4   Two major rivers that run through the Panay highlands are the Pan-ay and
     the Malinao. Some place names arise from an association with one of these
     rivers or their tributaries; for instance, the Akean River passes through Aklan
     Province. Other place names allude to the directional flow of a given river or
     its relative location; for example, the Halawod River is called as such because
     Halawod means the area leading to the sea.

5   According to Jocano (1968, 33), this was how the natives called their language
     as "they do not have any generally accepted term to describe it." Moreover, he
     added, "others call it Kinray-a and still others had no specific term."

6   I witnessed a *túba* event in May 2004 and my descriptions here are personal
     accounts based on this experience; some are learned from interviews. It is

interesting that the natives of Borneo also have a túba tradition and I wondered if the Panay Bukidnons learned this from them or the other way around; or if each culture discovered this fishing system on their own. Robequain (1959) describes the Bornean's method of preparing the juice of the túba plant's roots and this is quite similar to Panay Bukidnons' method. Moreover, as I noted earlier, the social bonding of community members is forged in this fishing activity. They also help one another in preparing and distributing the túba juice on the river and pursue the affected fishes later: "This is usually practiced in the smaller rivers in times of slack water, all the people of a village co-operating . . . each boat carries a supply of the tuba root, which the people bruise by pounding it with wooden clubs against stumps and rocks . . . water in all boats become milky with the juice, is poured at a given signal into the river . . . after some twenty minutes the fish begin to rise to the surface" (ibid., 139).

7   This compound naturally occurs as a breakdown product of proteins. It is used as a food flavor enhancer. A traditional ingredient in Asian cooking, it was originally obtained from seaweed but is now made from bean and cereal protein. Its chemical formula is $HOOC(CH_2)_2(NH_2)COONa$.

8   There are people in Iloilo city such as Melissa Exmundo, Joseph Albana, and Luz Camina who commission the natives to produce handmade materials like clothing embroidery, baskets, and accessories, thus encouraging the development of production skills as well as passing on skills to younger natives. There are also people, such as Eugene Jamerlan, who donate threads and textiles, which the natives then use to make embroidered dancing clothes. Nila Gonzalez, who played a pivotal role in introducing me to Panay Bukidnon culture, conducts workshops on dance involving the natives and producing shows with them.

9   Note that the generation before Estella's parents had names without surnames; surnames were introduced as part of municipal or government requirements later.

10   The kind of food to be offered is usually dictated by the spirits.

11   This refers to the Catamin family. Specific first names were withheld upon request of the family.

12   Sometimes, the parangkutan is also the husay.

13   The leader can be the Barangay Captain, or in his absence, a designated elder takes over.

14   This process comes very close to the functions of an ombudsman and/or an arbitrator in modern governance.

CHAPTER 3. Understanding *Síbod* and its Expressions

1　This is related to Clifford Geertz's (1983, 363–64) statement that "symbolic systems . . . are historically constructed, socially maintained and individually applied."

2　This photo is part of a collection that was donated to Museo Iloilo in the 1970s. However, due to fire, some records about the photos were destroyed including information about the photographer, donor, and names of the featured natives. In 2007, I volunteered to commission the restoration, printing, and reframing of the photos. This was accomplished with the technical assistance of my sister Maria Chona Muyco-Nazareno. Using digital processes, Nazareno patiently removed print blemishes caused by weathering, aging, climate, and other factors. Anthropologist Felipe Landa Jocano saw the photos and noted that these depict the Panay Bukidnon's way of life on or before the 1950s (Personal conversation, 2007). The late Museo Iloilo Foundation, Inc. trustee and historian Mr. Zafiro "Zaffy" Ledesma allowed me to use the photo, but only after I committed to do so with proper credits given to the said museum.

3　Miningkol, Barangay Tacayan's tribal chieftain, delineates each of the binanog's various dance phases. This is applicable particularly with the *tiniglalaki* and not for the *tinigbabayi*. The natives of other Panay areas, such as the Barangays of Siya, Nayawan, and Badas (Tapaz, Capiz) also contributed information regarding these dance phases during interviews.

4　Sikreto is also practiced in Siya, a barangay located in the topmost area of Panay (Tapaz, Capiz). There, I encountered a case of a man who secretly conferred with the father of a woman he wanted to marry, without her knowledge.

5　Bayaw-biit commences the guessing game rendered by the woman's family, asking the man to identify his bride from a series of cloth-covered women (usually seven of them); the cloth is used to conceal their identities from the groom.

6　This literally means to drop. In the context of the dance, it means to drop food for the spirit beings.

7　Jocano (1968) further explicates that there is a great deal of overlapping in the usage of terms to mean reciprocal labor. In addition to patabang and patawili, he also mentions *patangkuris*, "weeding the entire field and putting up fences around the rice patch" (40). On the other hand, *padagyaw* is "when the activity involved is non-agricultural, such as building a house, hauling timber, and so forth" (ibid).

8　Philippines, Republic of National Archives, the Accession Records of the National Museum of the Filipino People, on Burgos Street, Manila.

9   Here I used the spellings of place names as they appear in the Record.

10   Philippines, Republic of National Archives, the Accession Records of the National Museum of the Filipino People, in Burgos Street, Manila.

11   Some Panay Bukidnon elders noted that each *datu,* or powerful man in the Panay epic, is identified with a singular gong. In the case of Datu Humadapnon, Romulo Caballero mentioned his gong named *Libusawang.* as well as another gong name, *Magkahuwang-Huwang,* in item 6. So as not to confuse the readers, I state this difference so as to point out that sometimes, research participants may differ, if not, may share additional knowledge than the others.

12   Hungaw is a traditional joining ritual between a man and a woman. It is celebrated with food, rice wine, chanting, and dancing. Parents of the couple are engaged in an exchange of goods, animals, and other material wealth.

13   Federico "Tuohan" Caballero of Garangan, a barangay of Calinog, Iloilo, has been awarded the National Living Artist title known as the GAMABA, or the Gawad sa Manlilikha ng Bayan in 2000. The Philippine's National Commission for Culture and the Arts (NCCA) granted him this award for his tremendous ability in epic chanting. His brother is Romulo "Amang Baoy" Caballero, himself a great chanter and binanog dancer, was mentioned earlier in this book.

14   There is not much delineation between an owner or a keeper of an agung. Although an individual represents his/her family, personal ownership of an agung is not an absolute concept. Usually, owners/keepers occupy a high position in their barangay. Moreover, there is an understanding among community members that a gong is predisposed to any community's use and yet it can be passed on as an heirloom or wedding gift to the gong keeper's eldest child or sometimes the favored child. Usually, a barangay would have one agung. One factor producing this outcome is that the community does not manufacture gongs; as mentioned, Panay Bukidnons acquired the agungs mainly through trade.

15   The instruments I saw that joined *the* binanog ensemble were the *suganggang* (bamboo buzzer) and the *tikumbo* (bamboo percussion).

16   This is a traditional design patterned for most shawls done in the Panay Bukidnon community. According to Gleceria Gilbaliga, her grandmother and mother used the same design as well.

17   Armstrong (1971) refers to actualization rather than conceptualization in the context of using one's affect in artistic expressions.

CHAPTER 4. The Foundational *Súnu*

1   "Learning Kinaray-a With a Native Speaker." Unpublished manual used by the
     American Peace-Corps volunteers during the latter part of the 20th century.

2   I focus on instrument playing and dancing in this book. This chapter focuses
     on the linkage both musical performance and dancing have to language.
     Language among Panay Bukidnons is very much connected to music through
     chanting. This is one of the primary pathways linking rhythm and timing in
     language to music. Chanting also plays a role in how music sounds and how an
     instrument is played. I leave aside these linkages for the most part. Instead, I
     focus squarely on the connections between language, dance, and music-making
     via mnemonics.

3   [´] means stress in a slower or subtle manner. Orthographic conventions were
     taken from *Makabagong Balarilang Filipino*, 3rd Edition by Alfonso Santiago
     and Norma Tiangco (1991).

4   In actual courtship, the man who intends to marry a woman has to follow the
     tradition of serving the woman's family first. He assists the woman's parents in
     household and farm work. Sometimes, this servitude takes a year, followed by
     other customary ways.

CHAPTER 5. *Hàmpang* as play on Structures

1   Here, lalaki is a reiteration of the syllable *la* in *laki,* a way of playing with syl-
     lables. In Tagalog, lalaki really means man.

2   There is, however, a Binanog Festival produced by and for townsfolk in Lambu-
     nao, a municipality of Iloilo. To many, if not most persons in the towns around
     Iloilo, this is binanog practice. However, the natives of the Panay highlands who
     practice their own tradition believe that the festival still lacks the indigenous
     form in most of its street and stage performances. Lately, the local government
     of this municipality realized this lack and invited some Panay Bukidnon to con-
     duct workshops with their festival participants months before the festival.

3   I use the word language instead of dialect. In a personal conversation from
     April 12, 2005, Philippine scholar Leoncio Deriada strongly opposed the use of
     the word "dialect." He believed that "language" should equally be used for all
     types of speech/communication modes. Dialect should not be considered as a
     subset of what are considered major languages. I follow his framework here.

CHAPTER 6. Catch and Sync

1   Conchita Gilbaliga, one of the revered elders of Barangay Nayawan, provided
     this definition from her experience of playing the tulali.

2   A post signifies many things such as a place marker, a support, or a reinforcing
     material. In some sense all of these definitions come into play, since I use post
     to mean a foothold for various elements coming together and synchronizing to
     attain a sense of unity and organization.

3   There was an instance when I noticed that musicians were not consistent with
     the use of accents to translate mnemonic syllables. Each one had different
     time groupings. What the dancers did was render their own foot accentuation
     regardless of the music. This raised a question: "Where do they actually santú?"
     "With the music or with the mnemonic inside their heads" (translated earlier as
     gina-isip—a mental activity)?" This points out that sometimes there are relative
     renditions of accents that may result in different ways of synchronizing."

4   The task of following cannot be reversed since the woman traditionally does not
     follow a man's steps.

5   The following agencies organized this event: the Philippines' National Commis-
     sion for Culture and the Arts (NCCA), the National Commission on Indigenous
     Peoples (NCIP), and the University of the Philippines in the Visayas (UPV)-
     Center for Western Visayas Research.

6   Simbalud is the fourth phase of the binanog dance. In this phase, dancers por-
     tray the playfulness of male and female balud bird as they acquaint themselves
     with each other and pursue intimacy. This also represents the birds' prelude to
     mating. The representation of the balud is primarily seen in the dancers' arm
     movements. However, the act of playfulness and pursuit of intimacy is associ-
     ated with both the balud and the banog.

7   Negative sanctions for such violations of decorum have recently faded. When
     elders are not around the company of young community members doing the
     binanog, the penalty is not implemented. Even elders nowadays are not so strict
     about this observance.

8   Filipino linguists, anthropologists, and historians have extensively written about
     loob. Rey Ileto (1989) significantly positions this as an ideological poetics of
     offering and sacrifice of self over nation in Pasyon and Revolution; Teresita
     Maceda (1996) also constitutes this as a deep force among the subverted revolu-
     tionaries in Tinig Mula sa Ibaba. Albert Alejo (1990) and F. Landa Jocano (1997)
     foreground this as a significant quality of the Filipino character and values; via
     language, Prospero Covar (1995) sees various meanings in this word according
     to its changing form due to the use of syllabic affixations and attachments.

9   Those who just want to have fun have another purpose: to get close to a co-
     dancer as a means to initiate the pinanyo. Doing so is game-like and challeng-
     ing. The move to get closer is to zero in, entangle, and engage the opponent in a
     more physical and immediate range.

CHAPTER 7. Tayuyon: A Directed Sense of Flow

1   Dawatan is the term used by Eliod Dimzon, a staff member of the University
     of the Philippines in the Visayas' cwvs or Center for West Visayan Studies, in
     describing the binanog's trance-like atmosphere, which she witnessed on 25
     August 2001.

2   Tao means way, in the sense of water finding its natural course or clouds
     moving with the wind. Taoism teaches that life is dynamic (Redfield, Murphy,
     Timbers 2002). Shamanism, on the other hand, links the earthly world to the
     unseen. It has its roots in asceticism, animism and animatism. It can create
     temporarily a sacred time and space, particularly in rites that are performed to
     alleviate human suffering, or sometimes to cause suffering (Cohen 1998).

3   Brinner noted that his theory of musical competence should be taken for its
     own merits, and should not be considered along the lines of other discourses on
     competence, such as the chomskyian concept of linguistic competence and its
     offshoots. To Chomsky (1965), competence is tacit grammatical knowledge—the
     formal structure of language being abstract, idealized, and having a cognitive
     system of rules for the production and comprehension of sentences. Whereas
     musical competence deals with "the coordination and combination of simulta-
     neous 'utterances,' linguistic competence is exclusively concerned with consecu-
     tive statements" (Brinner 1995). Bauman also contrasted Chomsky's theory to
     performance; according to him, performance is natural speech, or what the
     speaker does in using language. Performance is a marked and heightened mode
     of communicative behavior instead of the usual manner of communication.

4   Castor served from early 2000 to late 2005. A political rival had him assassinated.

5   In the olden days, Panay Bukidnons practiced hungaw. Elders claim that it is
     no longer in common practice. They want to bring it back because their young
     community members are drifting away from tradition.

6   Code here is used as a constructed form of communication understood by the
     male and female binanog dancers by way of using the panyo. It is also in a way
     related to Jakobson's (1971) idea of code as conventions or rules that are socially
     mediated. Use of the panyo realizes the exclusive message of dancers to each
     other. Because some of the ways of using it have become common, people have
     access to decoding their meanings.

CHAPTER 8. Síbod as Pragmatic Praxis

1   I often heard the word "collapsible" used in reference to modern-day furniture, which could be dismantled from its constructed state and, when needed, returned to its usable former structure.

2   As Panay Bukidnons are geographically located within the periphery of the Philippines, they belong to one Malayo-Polynesian stock and are called Filipinos.

3   I point to traditional practices when I say "unified fields," as most traditions certainly include various expressions such as songs, instrument playing, dances, poetry, utensil-making, among other activities that relate to a socially shared activity and meaning, e.g., "planting/harvesting rice," which is common, for instance, among the Cordilleran groups of people in northern Philippines.

Glossary

A

agila	eagle.
agung	a bossed gong suspended/hung from a stand.
Akeanon	those who live near the Akean river. The province of Aklan derived its name from Akean.
ala-salud	a custom where people put money inside a bamboo container during a wedding feast.
alayaw	a Panay Bukidnon epic.
alyandador	serves as the mediator between individuals to help them choose their dance partners. S/he is an expert dancer and can determine whom to match during a dance gathering.
amakan	the Panay Bukidnon's native bamboo mat.
amang	grandfather.
ambahan	a traditional song used to greet a guest in a community; to welcome, or to give credence to an important person. In traditional weddings, this song form is also employed to praise the betrothed.
angay	the notion of matching.
angay kadya	like this.
antigo	an expert, usually someone old and seasoned with a certain skill.
aswang	a being of supernatural powers, but of the evil kind; typically thought to be female, she seeks to devour human bodies and/or spirits.

Ati	an ethnolinguistic group living in Panay, Philippines. They are genetically related to the Negritos of Luzon, northern Philippines. They are mostly identified as dark-skinned and have curly hair. Other than the Panay Bukidnon, these people are also indigenous to Panay islands, having traditional practices and age-old cultures. They are also known as Aeta, Ata, Agta, and other names depending on local practices.
Ati-Atihan	literally, this means "acting like the Ati." This is a festival celebrated in Kalibo, Aklan every third week of January to honour the Santo Nino, or the child Jesus. Here, people put on black soot on their faces and don costumes simulating the physical features of the Ati as this group received Catholic conversion through the symbolic image of the child Jesus. This festival celebrates this meaningful and historical event.

B

babaylan	a healer who calls a *diwata*'s presence by tinkling a ceramic bowl plate or bamboo tube.
badbad	explain.
bag-uhan	new style.
balabaw	rat.
balanak	white fish.
balangay	boat. Also *balanghay*.
balanghay	a boat used by early migrants for island hopping. This is synonymous to *balangay*.
balsa	raft.
balud	imperial pigeon.
bamphley	to cheat; to alter; to change.
bangkaw	spear.
banog	hawk-eagle; *Nisaetus philippensis*.
banwa	town.

bao-bao	turtle-like object made of silver metal. This is worn together with old coins and beads in a necklace that is used by the Panay Bukidnon while dancing.
barangay	the smallest sociopolitical unit other than the family. The term comes from the word *balangay* (boat), the main water vehicle used by most early Filipinos to bring their family or group to a new place to form a settlement and/or a community.
barangay kapitan	barangay captain.
barong	shirt.
basal	striking an instrument using a rubber-padded beater (see *kadul*).
batong-batong	tattoo.
bayaw-biit	introducing the groom to the community.
bayhun	walk.
bayhunan	a relaxed walk where dancers go to and fro across the dance floor, similar to *lisyon-lisyon*.
bayi	woman.
bi-it	token.
binabaylan	moving like the *babaylan*, or healer.
binanog	a tradition involving music, dance, and costuming based on the movements and idealized characteristics of the *banog*.
bingkit	in close distance.
biningkit	necklace.
Binukidnon	mountain language.
binukot	hidden maiden. A family's chosen daughter that is kept in a room for years. She learns the community's traditions, such as music-making, dancing, epic-chanting, and other cultural expressions. She is married off to a man who offers a suitable bride-gift to her parents.

boses	specific movements. It may have come from the word "voces," a Spanish and Italian term which refers to the voice. With the Panay Bukidnon, *boses* relates to a function of the body, not of the vocal system, although it implicitly communicates just as the voice does.
budhi	conscience.
buhok ka adlaw	hair of the sun.
bukaw	owl.
buki	people of the mountain.
bukid	mountainous areas.
bukot	kept in a room.
buladon	palm.
bulak ka labog	flower of the *labog* plant.
burtu	backward or reverse steps with pedal accentuation.
buruhisan	a medium to nature's spirits. S/he performs rituals by the river to ask the spirits for rain.
butkon	hands.
buysawang	fire and light.

C

cabanca	refers to a fellow native. The prefix *ca* means fellow and banca means boat.

D

daha	prepared meals.
dalagangan	a being known to perform unusual feats like jumping from the ground to a rooftop or chasing harmful spirits around the rooftop.
Dalunga	a male rhythmic mode. Aside from its use in courtship rituals, it is used when dancers want to demonstrate their skills or personal style in expressing the *banog*'s the graceful movements.

dalungdong	healing oil.
dalungdung	spirit guide.
dalungdungan	a healer who has a *dalungdung*. S/he is tasked to take back a stolen *dungan* from an evil spirit. S/he also uses medicinal herbs and healing oil called the *dalungdong*.
danao	container of water. Also associated with the overflow of water.
danuk	the technique of lightly bouncing a rubber-padded beater on the gong's bossed area.
dapay	a bedsheet with a bird design, usually prepared for the woman's grandfather for her wedding rites.
datu	a man of power.
dawatan	possession.
delargo	pants.
Dinagyang	a festival in Iloilo City that venerates the Santo Nino, or the child Jesus.
dinumaan	old style.
diretso	flow. See *tayuyon*.
diwata	a female spirit mythologically associated with fairies, nymphs, or muses.
dumaan nga pilak	old silver coin accessories that adorn the Panay Bukidnons' forehead band, necklace, waistband, and anklet. These are symbolic of wealth and status.
dungan	soul.
duot-panit	touching the skin.
dutan-on	creatures or spirits of land or earth.
dwende	dwarfs.

E

enkanto	the enchanted.

G

ga-banog na panit	swollen skin.
ginadu-on du-on	intensified.
gina-isip	a mental activity.
gina-isip nga limog	mnemonics, thought-of voice/sound.
gina-itib	made to face each other or sit close to each other on a pre-wedding occasion. This is required of the betrothed and their parents. They alternately drink rice wine as the bride's parents advise the groom.
ginalaglag	to drop. In a ritual, a healer holds food in his/her hands while dancing; this is a form of food offering.
ginaplang	flower-printed cotton cloth. Panay Bukidnon women sometimes substitute a plaid wraparound (see *pulus*).
gina-tono	tuning in.
ginhawa	breathing.
ginikanan	parents.
girgiti	zigzag design used in embroidery.
girong-girong	a small, round brass bell. This is part of a number of necklaces that produces a ringing sound as a Panay Bukidnon dances.
guribal	a rhythmic mode based on the mnemonics: "pa-tak-da-nga gu-ri-bal." Generally, young dancers use this mode as it is comparably faster than *purungut*.

H

haból	weaving.
Halawodnon	those who live close to the Halawod river's headwaters.
halo	water monitor lizard. This species is endemic to Panay, central Philippines.
hampang	play.
hampuro	an old name for dance, also an early form of *binanog* based on Panay epic chants' accounts. Also means "play."

hikaw	envy.
hilimuon	task.
hinampang	to play a game.
hinay-hinay	moderately slow.
hinimbis	like fish scales.
hiyaw	calls and hoots expressing excitement during a music and dance performance.
hungaw	a traditional wedding held during the punsyon.
huni	bird's chirping.
husay	A person who works out useful social arrangements, especially for parties in conflict.

I

iba	others.
ibabawnon	spirits of the upper realm.
ibid	sailfin lizard. This species is endemic to Panay, central Philippines.
idalmunon	creatures or spirits of the lower depths.
Ilawodnon	those who dwell near the Pan-ay river's delta.
inagsam	embroidery design that portrays a crocodile's pointed teeth.
ingay ingay	fingers.
iraya	a highland area where water passes through as it flows to the lower areas.
Iraynon	people who live near a river's headwaters, specifically in a mountain's interior or upland parts.
isduyong	manifests a semicircular or arc-like motion of the body when dancing.
ispirituhanon	spiritual realm/upper space.

isul	backward or reverse steps with heavy accentuation or stamping.
ituman	black beings; evil spirits.

K

kabog	Philippine giant fruit bat.
kadugo	blood relations.
kadul	striking the gong's bossed area with a rubber-padded beater.
kagawad	councilor.
kahig	feet.
kahuy	wooden percussion.
kahuy nga ginabasal/ ginabatil	wood percussion beaten on a floor or another sounding material.
kaingin	slash and burn.
kalawakaw	a neutral ground or place from which neither of the contending parties belongs.
kalayaan	freedom.
kalibutan	cosmos; world; consciousness.
kaluluwa	soul.
kamangyan	incense from the Almasiga tree.
karatung	instrument.
kasarinlan	communal self.
kasugiranon	person that one talks to.
kataw	mermaid.
katsa	cotton cloth. Before this was available in textile stores, people used flour sacks from bakeries.
kaykay	typical of brush-like footwork simulating birds that are scratching the ground. The man follows his partner's steps.

kibang	rhythmically pounding the feet on the ground.
kido-kido	moving one's shoulders up and down repeatedly as a way of expressing or responding to music.
kimona	a blouse worn inside a *saipang* or transparent and beaded shirt; sometimes it is also referred to as *kimono*.
kinamnan	an infant's double that should be retrieved from the spirit world and returned to his/her physical body.
kitenkiten	soles of the feet.
kudyapi	a two-stringed boat lute.
kulintas	necklace. Also called *biningkit*.
kurubingbing kurubawbaw	onomatopoeic sound heard from the jaw's harp.

L

labas	outside.
labog	bush sorrel/wild sour plant.
lagwas	a sheer material with lace edges, sometimes known to Filipino urbanites as a half-slip, worn under a skirt.
lakalaka	A Tongan dance, which is a combination of choreography, recitation, and polyphonic music.
lakday	traveling.
laki	man.
lalim	depth.
lamba	a huge sound like the cow's moo.
lampunaya	rice grains.
laro	Tagalog equivalent of *hampang*.
lati	moonlight.
latun-latun	a light way of dancing or playing a musical instrument.

li-ad	bending backwards. One's body is stretched back to establish rapport with the spirits of the upper realm.
libusawang	much potency.
likit	smoking.
limog	may refer to a voice or timbre. In the context of the Panay Bukidnon's musical practice, these are thought-of sounds.
lipay	female deer.
lisyon-lisyon	see *bayhunan*.
litgit	bowed two-stringed zither.
loob	inside.
lumakday	to travel.
lupon	group of leaders.

M

mabaskug	energetic dancing.
magdumala ka kultura	culture-bearer.
magkahunod-hunod	many resonances. 2. a big gong.
magkahurao	a sound that reverberates through the mountains.
magkahuwang-huwang	echoing sound.
Maka-hibong Banwa	one that can bring the whole community together.
malaing ginhawa	evil spirit.
mamà	betel nut-chewing.
maranhig	a witch or dark spirit.
matang punay	an embroidery design portraying a dove's eye.
mestizo/mestiza	fair-skinned descendants of the *Siyaw*.
Montescos	a Spanish term; people of the mountains.

O

ostinato	another form of drone; repetitive material.
oyampi	men's loincloths.

P

pabagti	an act undertaken by a man to inform a woman's parents about his serious plans to marry her. They meet and discuss the bride-gift. This usually consists of heirlooms, livestock and/or poultry.
pabayaw	to announce someone's intent publicly.
pabuyung-buyung	quickly twirling a cloth.
padagyaw	celebration.
pagbilog	a process of forming the soul in order for it to solidify. A liquefied form can be easily devoured by an *aswang*.
pagkatao	personhood.
pagkataong Pilipino	Filipino personhood.
pagkatawo	Personhood as used in *Kinaray-a* language. *See pagkatao.*
pag-sagda	a supplication for dead relatives' spirits. A white chicken is offered to fulfill certain wishes.
pahangin	backward or reverse step with stamping but with lifted arm movements forming an open arc. Sometimes the dancer bends backwards while each arm is bent back.
pahimpit	a meeting and agreement of parties representing the engaged man and woman.
pako-pako	fern.
pakpak ka aguring	bee wings.
palabor-labor	a form of embellishment or enhancement of a repeated pattern or a short improvisation based on a rhythmic pattern.
palay	rice grains.
paloob	going inside.

pamilinbinlin	reminders.
panabi-tabi	"please step aside, because I'll be passing by."
Panayanon	people living near the Pan-ay river's headwaters.
pangabuhi	life, a term synonymous with family.
pangagad	to render service. This is a practice among Panay Bukidnon men. A man has to help a woman's parents in order to win their approval. Work may include chopping firewood, pounding *palay*, and helping out with their house or farm work.
pangasi	drinking rice wine.
pangayaw	guests.
pangkat ng tagapagsunod	group of followers that has a leader and a secretary.
pangmidya	to dampen an instrument's sound to vary tone production.
panimalay	the household.
panit ka magkal	see *sobrekama*; sometimes referred to as *sudlikama*.
panubok	traditional embroidery.
panyo	a piece of hand-cloth: a handkerchief for men, a shawl for women (see *subrigo*).
parangkutan	one who is consulted about issues and problems of the community.
Pasibuda	in the process of achieving *síbod*.
pasibudon	to fluid or to make fluid one's actions. In playing musical instruments, musicians warm up to a musical instrument by repeatedly playing a rhythmic pattern until there is a sense of mastery. Thus, this term moves a learner from his/her enactment of structures to a level where playing around the structures becomes spontaneous.
Pasyon	a Filipino song genre chanted during Lent in the Philippines.
patabang	asking help from community members to perform specific tasks to prepare the land for planting. These tasks include clearing weeds and burning plants.

patadyong	barrel skirt.
patalanha	a confidential meeting that will pre-empt the actual gathering of a couple's parents and respectable community elders. Also called *sikreto*.
patangkuris	weeding the entire field and putting up fences around the rice patch.
patawili	gathering.
patik	beating the gong's rim/side using a pair of thin bamboo sticks.
pinanyo	the last phase of the *binanog* dance. This is a game where the woman tries to capture the man's handkerchief while he evades her incessant attempts.
pinato	duck-walk. Young dancers of the Panay Bukidnon community developed this as a new trend in binanog. This was influenced by television show dancers' emphasis on hip movements.
pintados	Visayan painted people, people who have skin tattoos.
pinunay	like a dove.
Poon	God.
principales	people of high position and wealth in their community.
pudong	cloth-band sewn with coins, covering the forehead and tied at the back of the head. Coins symbolize wealth and one's status in the community.
pulahan	the red spirits (see *ituman*).
pulus	a wrap-around skirt made of a deep purple cotton cloth (see *sinorkan*). This is worn on top of a long barrel skirt (see *patadyong*).
punay	dove.
punong barangay	barangay leader. This also refers specifically to a Barangay Captain.
punsyon	feast. A celebration of a good harvest when food is plenty. This feast can also be included as part of wedding ceremonies.
pùntu	intonation; the general sound of a person's speech.

purungut	a rhythmic mode based on these mnemonics: 'pa-tak-da-nga pu-ru-ngut.' Older dancers—50 years old and above—would prefer this rhythmic mode for its slower rhythm.
puruy-an	dwelling.
putian	those who are white; associated with the good spirits.

R

rara	basket-making.
ra-ra	preparing strips of fiber to make a native mat.
real de cuatro	a coin used in Spanish colonies.
repasu	a dance step that comes after the *bayhunan* in *binanog*. Dancers start to make dance steps in time with the rhythm of the music. This is also associated with dancing without foot stamping.
rondalla	ensembles of plucked/strummed string instruments.

S

sabacan	small basket for produce.
sabor	extra flavor.
sadsad	stamping; an accented footwork.
saipang	outer blouse.
sakayan nga bulawan	golden boat.
salú	catch; remedy an error.
sambud	state of disorder.
sampulong	an embroidered forehead band.
sanduko	knife; weapon. In the Panay Bukidnon tradition, this is an heirloom given to the bride's sibling.
sangguniang bayan	a group that performs specific functions implementing the mayor's directives.
sangkap	implements used during an activity such as clothes, or accessories.

Sangleys	Chinese merchants.
Santo Niño	the child Jesus.
santú	synchronization.
sapat	insects.
saragdahon	spirits that occupy a babaylan's body.
saragudun	spirit-guide; fed with offerings to aid healing.
sarapang	three-pointed spear.
sarug	bamboo floor.
serruano	a healer who cures the sick with guidance from a spirit; also offers food to appease angered elements that may have caused one's illness.
síbod	Panay Bukidnon's ideology; a body of ideas that link a musical/dance structure with play or expression, with ways to recover from error during performance, with synchronization, and sense of flow through mastering structures. It is an important local source of thought and action that leads an individual or community to achieve its objectives. It has manifold definitions extending from cultural expressions of music-making and dancing, to socio-political negotiations in the pursuit of a workable situation in the community.
sibulan	a large ceramic wine jar.
sigbong	shoulders.
siki	feet.
sikreto	a secret meeting. See *patalanha*.
simat	banana leaf plate.
simbalud	dancing like the *balud*. Arm movements simulate a bird's opened wings, steadily suspending them midway at shoulder-level in a soaring pose. A *panyo* can also be used to express these movements.
sinorkan	a deep purple cotton.

sinulóg	Another term for *binanog*. Must not be confused with the *sinúlog* of Cebu.
sinúlog	A dance form practiced in the Eastern Visayas, particularly in Cebu. A religious festival of street-dancing venerating the *Santo Niño*.
sinumbrahang itum	an embroidered black long sleeved-shirt. Also called *supa*.
sinumbrahang pula	embroidery on a red blouse.
sinumbrahang puti	embroidery on a white blouse.
sirangans	those who can see the other dimensions of beings, normally invisible to the human eye.
sitsiritsit	crickets.
si-ud	trapped. Achieved when a woman dancer hurls a *panyo* around the man's neck.
Siyaw	Spanish colonizers.
sobrekama	an embroidery design taken from bed covers. Among the Panay Bukidnon, this is connected with an image of a snake's skin. Also called *panit ka magkal*.
subing	jaw's harp.
subli	a traditional music-dance form found in Bauan, Batangas (southwestern Luzon, Philippines).
subra...tara-taririk	whirls round and round in an extreme way.
subrigo	a shawl, usually draped over a person's shoulders. Also called *panyo*.
substantiation	giving value.
suganggang	bamboo buzzer.
sugid	to tell.
sugidanon	the Panay people's epic-chanting. Comes from the word *sugid*.
Sulod	people of the mountain.
sulog	*rooster.*

sungayan	1: male deer; 2: gong with a strong, piercing sound.
sunú	structural bases and conventions of musical and dance expressions.
supa	see *sinumbrahang itum*.

T

tabungus	big baskets for palay or grain.
tagabanwa	townspeople.
Tagalog	the Philippine national language/dialect.
takurong	veil.
Talda	a rhythmic mode considered relatively new compared to the dalunga.
tamawo	enchanted beings said to look like men but without an upper lip canal.
tambi	balcony.
tambur	a cylindrical drum with two heads. Only the top head is beaten, but the lower head should resonate well with the sound coming from the upper head.
taming	shield.
tandug	to touch or affect.
tanglad	lemongrass.
tapis	a cloth used as a layer on a barrel skirt. This can be any flower-printed cotton fabric; or sometimes as a plaid wraparound.
tàtà	vocalization associated with the mouth's rhythmic movement while one dances. It typically involves a kind of tongue-click, something like the sound "tsk-tsk." It could also refer to sounds or words verbalized by a mass of people with much gusto in time with the instruments of a musical ensemble.
tawag-Linaw	clear sound.
tayok	ladle.

tayuyon	flow; physical and spiritual linkage.
tebongbong	bamboo tube used while chanting in the process of healing.
terno	a matching shirt and skirt. Among the Panay Bukidnon, this consists of *saipang* and *patadyong*.
tikling	barred rail.
tikumbo	a bamboo idiochord.
timbang	helper.
tinigbabayi	dance or music distinctly addressed to, or performed by, women.
tiniglalaki	dance or music distinctly addressed to men, but performed by a couple consisting of a man and a woman.
tinola	boiled vegetables.
tinyente	captain.
tirik-tirik	whirling in an extreme way.
túba	an event held during May, when fishes are abundant. The word "tuba" comes from a name of a tree; its bark is pounded into fine powder and mixed with water in order to produce an intoxicating liquor. Panay Bukidnons pour this into a river to cause fishes to get drunk and become unconscious within several hours.
tubá	coconut wine.
tubignon	creatures or spirits of the water.
tubu	growth.
tubu-an	body.
tubungan	lower part of the house; sometimes referring to the outdoor extension of the house.
tulali	bamboo flute.
tulok sa ibabaw	to look up.
Tultugan	bamboo drum; also refers to a festival of bamboo instruments and other bamboo-based materials in Maasin, Iloilo.

tumandok	native.
tunga-tunga	the approximate middle space from one's body.
turuba	a dance step marked by accenting one's foot thrice.
tuway-tuway	knees.

U

urang	water prawn.
uwak	large-billed crow.

V

Vagamundos	a name associated with the group's habit of changing places to escape Spanish religious conversion.
vetsin	monosodium glutamate.
voces	Spanish and Italian term for voice.

W

waluhan	giving eight days to each wife.
wayway	holding a pointed corner of the panyo as it hangs down.

Z

zarzuela	musical theatre.

Bibliography

Alcedo, P. 2007. Sacred camps. *Journal of Southeast Asian Studies* 38: 107–32.

Alejandro, R. G. 1985. Bird imagery in Philippine dance. *Dance as a cultural heritage,* edited by Betty True Jones, II: 78–82.

Alejo, A. 1990. *Tao po! Tuloy!: Isang landas ng pag-unawa sa loob ng tao.* Quezon City: Ateneo de Manila University Office of Research and Publications.

Anderson, B. 2002. *Imagined communities: Reflections on the origin and spread of nationalism.* Revised edition. Pasig City: Anvil Publishing.

Armstrong, R. P. 1971. *The affecting presence: An essay in humanistic anthropology.* Urbana: University of Illinois Press.

Aron, M. 1980. Dance and music relationships: A dance ethnologist's view. UCLA *Journal of the Association of Graduate Dance Ethnologists* 4 (Spring): 9–15.

Azurin, A. 1995. *Reinventing the Filipino: Sense of being and becoming. Critical analyses of the orthodox views in anthropology, history, folklore and letters.* Quezon City: University of the Philippines Press.

Bakan, M. 1999. *Music of death and new creation: Experiences in the world of Balinese Gamelan Beleganjur.* Chicago and London: University of Chicago Press.

Bauman, R. 1992. Performance. In *Folklore, culture of performances and pop entertainment,* 41–49. New York: Oxford University Press.

Belsey, C. 1990. *Critical practice.* London and New York: Methuen.

Benitez, K. 1983. Towards an understanding of gong-drum ensembles in Southeast Asia: A study of resultant melodies in the music of two gong ensembles from the Philippines. PhD diss., University of Michigan.

Blair, E. H., and J. A. Robertson. 1909. *History of the Philippine islands, XXXIII from their discovery by Magellan in 1521 to the beginning of XVII century,* edited and annotated by Antonio de Morga. Cleveland, Ohio: Arthur H. Clark: Kraus Reprint Co.

Blum, O. 1987. An initial investigation into Ghanian dance in order to ascertain aspects of style by the analysis and notation of the dynamic phrase. In *A Spectrum of World Dance* XVI: 52–67, edited by Lynn Ager Wallen and Joan Acocella.

Bohlman, P., and B. Nettl, eds. 1991. *Comparative musicology and anthropology of music: Essays on the history of musicology.* Chicago and London: The University of Chicago Press.

Bolinger, D. 1989. *Intonation and its uses: Melody and grammar discourse.* Stanford, CA: Stanford University Press.

Bourdieu, P. 1980. *The Logic of practice.* Cambridge: Polity Press.

———. 1985. The genesis of the concept of "Habitus and Field." *Sociocriticism* 2: 2, 11–24.

Bowman, W. 1998. *Philosophical perspectives on music.* New York and Oxford: Oxford University Press.

Brink, Susan. 2007. Sing out, sister. *Los Angeles Times*, 23 April.

Brinner, B. 1995. *Knowing music, making music: Javanese gamelan and the theory.* Chicago and London: The University of Chicago Press.

Buckland, T. J. 2001. Dance, authenticity and cultural memory: The politics of embodiment. *Yearbook for Traditional Music* 33: 1–16. International Council for Traditional Music. Canberra.

Buenconsejo, J. 2002. *Songs and gifts at the frontier: Person and exchange in the Agusan Manobo possession ritual, Philippines.* London and New York: Routledge.

Burrows, D. 1905. *Census of the Philippine Islands 1903.* Vol. 1. Washington D.C.: Bureau of Census.

Chernoff, J. M. 1981. *African rhythm and African sensibility, aesthetics and social action in African musical idioms.* Chicago and London: The University of Chicago Press.

Chomsky, N. 1965. *Aspects on the theory of syntax.* Cambridge: MIT Press.

Chun, I. P. 2002. Indian Tala and Korean Chnagdan. Paper presented at the symposium: A search in Asia for a new theory of music. Quezon City, University of the Philippines.

Cohen, S., ed. 1996. Shamanism. In *The International Encyclopedia of Dance,* 5: 576–78. NY and Oxford: Oxford University Press.

Corpuz, O. 1989. *Roots of the Filipino people.* Quezon City: Aklahi Foundation, Inc.

Covar, P. 1993. Kaalamang bayang dalumat ng pagkataong Pilipino. *Diliman Review* 41, no. 1: 5–11.

———. 1995. Unburdening Philippine society of colonialism. *Diliman Review* 43, no. 2: 15–19.

Csikszentmihalyi, M. 1990. *Flow: The psychology of optimal experience.* New York: Harper and Row.

de Certeau, M. 1988. *The practice of everyday life.* Berkeley: University of California Press.

de Coppet, D., ed. 1992. *Understanding rituals.* London and New York: Routledge.

de la Peña, L. C. 1991. Magical rituals in food: Quest among the Bukidnons of Caratagas, Calinog. PhD diss., Division of Social Science, University of the Philippines in the Visayas.

de Leon, F., Jr. 1990. The roots of people's art in indigenous psychology. In *Indigenous Psychology: A Book of Readings*, edited by Virgilio Enriquez, 311–27. Quezon City: Philippine Psychology Research and Training House.

DePriest, D. 2003. Human synchronicity theory. 11 December. Capella University. http://scholar.google.com/scholar?hl=en&lr=&q=cache:E7sduzirvsAJ: eukab.com/human_synchronicity_theory.pdf+Human+Synchronicity+Theory+dePriest.

de Saussure, F. 1960. *Course in general linguistics*, edited by Charles Bally and Albert Sechehaye in collaboration with Albert Reidlinger. Translated from the French by Wade Baskin. London: Owen.

de Vera, A. 2003. Silence of the lands: Prior consent and ancestral domain rights. *Philippine Law Journal 77*, no. 3: 398–436.

Denzin, N. K. 1996. *Interpretative ethnography*. Thousand Oaks, CA: Sage Publications.

Deriada, L. 1991. Introduction. *Ani 5*, no. 3 (December). Cultural Center of the Philippines.

Dillingham, B., and L. White. 1973. *The concept of culture*. Minneapolis: Burgess Publishing Company.

Donegan, P. 1993. Rhythm and vocalic drift in Munda and Mon-Khmer. *Linguistics of the Tibeto-Burman area* 16.1: 1–43.

Dorn, P. 1991. *Ala Turka/Ala Franka. Cultural ideology, musical change.* Cahiers d' etude sur la mediterrance orientale et le monde turco-iranien. No. 11 (January–June). http://www.ceri-sciencespo.com/publica/cemoti/textes11/dorn.pdf.

Doromal, G. 1993. The weaving tradition of Iloilo: Focus on the patadyong. *Proceedings of the 2nd Conference on History and Culture*, 4–6.

Ealdama, E., A. V. H. Hartendorp, ed. The Monteses of Panay. *Philippine Magazine*, no. 1 (357) (Jan. 1938): 24–25, 50; no. 2 (358) (Feb. 1938): 95–97, 107; no. 3 (359) (Mar. 1938): 138, 149–50; no. 5 (361) (May 1938): 236–42; no. 6 (362) (June 1938): 286–87; no. 9 (365) (Sept. 1938): 424–25, 487–90; no. 10 (Oct. 1938): 468–69, 487–90.

———. 1958. Two folktales of the Monteses of Panay (Visayan Islands, Philippines). *Folklore Studies* 17: 226–28. Asian Folklore Studies, Nanzan University.

———. 1984. Sound structure as social structure. *Journal of the Society for Ethnomusicology* 28, no. 3 (September): 383–409.

Ellingson, T. 1992a. Notation. In *The Norton/Grove handbooks in music: Ethnomusicology; An introduction*, 153–64. New York and London: W.W. Norton and Company Oxford.

———. 1992b. Transcription. In *The Norton/Grove Handbooks in Music. Ethnomusicology; An Introduction,* 110–52. New York and London: W.W. Norton and Company Oxford.

Enriquez, V., ed. 1990. *Indigenous psychology: A book of readings.* Quezon City: Philippine Psychology Research and Training House.

Errington, S. 1998. *The death of primitive art and other tales of progress.* Berkeley, Los Angeles, London: University of California Press.

Eugenio, D. 1990. *Philippine folk literature: Folk songs 7.* Quezon City: U. Folklorists.

Feld, S. 1974. Linguistic models in ethnomusicology. *Journal of the Society for Ethnomusicology* 18, no. 2 (May): 197–217.

———. 1978–1979. Aesthetics and synesthesia in Kaluli ceremonial dance. UCLA *Journal of the Association of Graduate Dance Ethnologists* 2 (Fall-Winter).

———. 1984. Sound structure as social structure. *Journal of the Society for Ethnomusicology* 28, no. 3 (September): 383–409.

———. 1986. Sound as a symbolic system. In *Explorations in ethnomusicology: Essays in honor of David McAllester,* edited by Charlotte J. Frisbie, 147–58. Detroit: Information Coordinators.

———. 1988. Aesthetics as iconicity of style, or "Lift-up-over sounding": Getting into the Kaluli groove. *Yearbook for Traditional Music* 20: 74–113.

———. 1990. *Sound and sentiment: Birds, weeping, poetics, and song in Kaluli expression.* 2nd ed. Philadelphia: University of Pennsylvania Press.

Foster, S. 1998. Choreographies of gender. *Signs* 24, no. 1 (Autumn).

Frenay, R. 2006. *Pulse: The coming age of systems and machines inspired by living things.* First edition. New York: Farrar, Strauss and Giroux.

Garfias, R. 1985. Social context as a determinant of style and structure in Asian dance. In *Dance as a Cultural Heritage* II, edited by Betty True Jones, 52. Dance Research U.S.A.: CORD Inc. Annual XV.

Geertz, C. 1983. *Local knowledge: Further essays in interpretive anthropology.* New York: Basic Books.

Giurchescu, A. 2001. The power of dance and its social and political uses. *Yearbook for traditional music* 33: 109–121. International Council for Traditional Music. Canberra.

Gourlay, K. A. 1980. Alienation and ethnomusicology. In *The ethnography of musical performance,* edited by Norma McLeod and Marcia Herndon, 123–46. Norwood Editions.

Gove, P. B. and Merriam Webster editorial staff. 1968. *Webster third new international dictionary of the English language, unabridged.* Massachusetts: G. & C. Merriam Company, Publishers Springfield.

Hanna, J. L. 1988. *Dance, sex and gender: Signs of identity, dominance, defiance, and desire.* Chicago and London: The University of Chicago Press.

———. 1992. Theory and method: Dance. In *The Norton/Grove handbooks in music: Ethnomusicology; An introduction,* 110–52. New York and London: W.W. Norton and Company Oxford.

Hornsby, J. 2004. Agency and actions. *Royal Institute of Philosophy Supplement,* edited by John Hyman and Helen Steward, 55: 1–23. Cambridge University Press.

Hose, C., and W. McDougall. 1912. *The pagan tribes of Borneo.* London: McMillan and Co.

Hosillos, L.V. 1984. *Originality as vengeance in Philippine literature.* Quezon City: New Day Publishers.

———. 1992. *Hiligaynon and literature.* Quezon City: Aqualand Enterprises.

Hyman, L. 1978. Tone and/or accent. In *Elements of tone, stress, and intonation,* edited by D.J. Napoli. Washington, DC: Georgetown University Press.

Ileto, R. C. 1989. *Pasyon and revolution: Popular movements in the Philippines, 1840–1910.* Quezon City: Ateneo de Manila University Press.

Jakobson, R. 1971. Language in relation to other communication systems. In *Selected writings,* 2: 570–79. Mouton: The Hague.

Jameson, F. 1983. Postmodernism and consumer society. In *Postmodernism and its discontents, theories, practices.* London, New York: Verso.

Jocano, F. L. 1968. *Sulod society: A study in the kinship system and social organization of a mountain people of Central Panay.* Quezon City: University of the Philippines Press.

———. 1984. Labaw Donggon: Epikong Sulod. In *Antolohiya ng mga panitikang ASEAN,* 115–94. Quezon City: APO Production Unit, Inc.

———. 1997. Filipino value system: A cultural definition. In *Anthropology of the Filipino people,* vol. 4. Quezon City: PUNLAD Research House.

———. 1998. *Filipino social organization: Traditional kinship and family organization.* Manila: Punlad Research House.

———. 2001. *Filipino worldview.* Quezon City: PUNLAD Research House, Inc.

Jose, V. 1979. Ideological trends in folk literature. *Philippine Social Sciences and Humanities Review* XLIII, nos. 1–4 (January–December): 185–249.

Jourdain, R. 2002. *Music, the brain, and ecstasy.* Reprinted. Quill.

Kaeppler, A. L. 1993. *Poetry in motion: Studies of Tongan dance.* First edition. Nuku'alofa, Tonga: Vava'u Press.

———. 2001. Dance and the concept of style. *Yearbook for Traditional Music*, 33: 49–63. International Council for Traditional Music. Canberra.

———. 2003. An introduction to dance aesthetics. *Yearbook for Traditional Music* 35: 153–62. International Council for Traditional Music. Canberra.

Kartomi, M. 1992. *On concepts and classifications of musical instruments.* Chicago: The University of Chicago Press.

Kaufmann, J. 1916. *Principles of Visayan grammar.* Manila: Catholic Trade School.

Keil, C. 1979. *Tiv song: The sociology of art in a classless society.* Chicago: The University of Chicago Press.

Kim, U., ed. 1993. *Indigenous psychologies.* California: Sage Publishers.

King, A. 1980. Innovation, creativity, and performance. In *The ethnography of musical performance,* edited by Norma McLeod and Marcia Herndon, 167–212. Norwood, PA: Norwood Editions.

Kobak, Cantius, OFM, and L. O. Gutierrez, trans. 2002. *History of the Bisayas islands, by Ignacio Ferdinand Alcina.* Manila: University of Santo Tomas Press.

Kondo, D. 1990. *Crafting selves.* Chicago: The University of Chicago Press.

Lagos, Ramon, Sr. 1968. The history of Simsiman. Unpublished manuscript.

Lal, D. 1997. *Unintended consequences: The impact of factor endowments, culture and politics on long-run economic performance.* Oxford University Press.

Laneri, R. 1975. The natural dimension of music. PhD diss., University of California, San Diego.

Learning Kinaray-a with a native speaker: A manual of Peace Corps volunteers. n.d.

Levman, B. 1992. The genesis of music and language. *Ethnomusicology* (Illinois) 36, no. 2 (Spring/Summer): 147–70.

Li, G. 2001. Onomatopeia and beyond: A study of the Iuogu Jing of the Beijing opera. PhD diss., University of California, Los Angeles.

Lu, M.-Z. 2004. The ethics of reading critical ethnography. In *Ethnography unbound,* edited by Stephen Gilbert Brown and Sidney I Dobrin, 285–97. Albany, NY: SUNY Press.

Maceda, J. 1963. The music of the Maguindanao in the Philippines. PhD diss., University of California, Los Angeles, California.

———. 1998. *Gongs and bamboos.* In *A panorama of Philippine music instruments.* Quezon City: University of the Philippines Press.

Maceda, T. 1996. *Mga tinig mula sa ibaba: Kasaysayan ng partido komunista ng Pilipinas at partido sosialista ng Pilipinas sa awit, 1930–1955.* Quezon City: University of the Philippines Press.

Magos, A. 1992. *The enduring Ma-aram tradition: An ethnograpgy of a Kinaray-a village in Antique.* Quezon City: New Day Publishers.

———. 1995. The Binukot [well-kept maiden] in a changing socio-political perspective, ca. 1850–1994. *Edukasyon—UP-ERP Monograph Series* 1, no. 4 (October-December): 61–77.

———. 1996. The Sugidanon of Central Panay. *Edukasyon--UP-ERP* Monograph Series 2, nos. 1 & 2 (January to June): 117–23.

———. 1999. Sea episodes in the Sugidanon (Epic) and the boat-building tradition in Central Panay, Philippines. *Danyag* 4, no. 1: 5–29.

Manuel, E. A. 1963. A survey of Philippine folk epics. *Asian Folklore Studies* 17: 1–76. Asian Folklore Studies, Nanzan University.

———. 1975. Glimpses of Manuvu culture. In *Tuwaang attends a wedding: The second song of the Manuvu's ethnoepic Tuwaang.* Quezon City: Ateneo de Manila University Press.

Map Quest. 2006. *Philippines* (map). http://www.mapquest.com/maps/maadp?latlongtype=decimal&latitude=11.2167&longitude=122.4.

Marchland, M. H., and J. L. Partpart. 1999. *Feminism Postmodernism.* London and New York: Routledge, Reprint.

McLeod, N., and M. Herndon. 1980. *The ethnography of musical performance.* Norwood, PA: Norwood Editions.

Mendoza, S. L. 2002. *Between the homeland and the diaspora: The politics of theorizing Filipino and Filipino American identities.* London: Routledge.

Miller, T. E., and S. Williams, eds. 1998. Southeast Asia. In *The Garland encyclopedia of world music.* Vol. 4. New York and London: Garland Publishing, Inc.

Mirano, E. R. 1989. *Subli: Isang sayaw sa apat na tinig; One dance in four voices.* Manila: Excel Printing Services.

———. 1997. *Ang mga tradisyunal na musikang pantinig sa lumang Bauan Batangas.* Manila: Aria Edition.

Monson, I. 1996. *Saying something: Jazz improvisation and interaction.* Chicago: University of Chicago Press.

Mora, M. 1987. The sounding pantheon of nature: T'Boli instrumental music in the making of an ancestral symbol. *Acta Musicologica* 59, Fasc. 2 (May-August): 187–212.

Morga, A. 1598. *Sucesos de las Islas Filipinas con anotaciones del Dr. Jose Rizal* [microfiche]. R. Martinez, puerto de la Habana . . . [microfilm].

———. 1609. *Sucesos de las Filipinas.* Mexico: Cornelio Adrian Cesar, Blair and Robertson. The Philippines Islands, vol. XV. Cleveland: Clark, 1903–1909.

————. 1868. *The Philippine islands, Moluccas, Siam, Cambodia, Japan and China at the close of the sixteenth century*. Translated from the Spanish with notes and a preface and a letter from Luis Vaez de Toress by Hon. Henry E. J. Stanley. London, Hakluyt Society, xxiv.

Mulato, S. A. 1991a. Hiniraya: Kagamutgamutan Kang Hiligaynon. *Ani* 5, no. 3: 25–36.

————. 1991b. Hiniraya: Ancestral root of Hiligaynon, Deriada, Leoncio (trans.). *Ani* 5, no. 3: 37–48.

Mulhall, Stephen. 1996. *Heidegger and Being and Time*. UK: Routledge.

Murphy, J. S. 2000. Lessons as dance history. In *Dancing bodies, living histories: New writings about dance and culture*, edited by Lisa Doolittle and Anne Flynn, 130–69. Canada: The Banff Centre Press.

Myers, H. 1992. Fieldwork. In *The Norton/Grove handbooks in music. Ethnomusicology: An introduction*, 165–218. New York and London: W.W. Norton & Company.

Nattiez, J. 1990. *Music and discourse: Toward a semiology of music* [*Musicologie générale et sémiologue*, 1987]. Translated by Carolyn Abbate. New Jersey: Princeton University Press.

Ness, S. A. 1992. *Body, movement, and culture: Kinesthetic and visual symbolism in a Philippine community*. Philadelphia: University of Pennsylvania Press.

Nida, E. A., and C. R. Taber. 1969. *The theory and practice of translation*. Leiden: Brill.

Nketia, J. H. K. 1990. Contextual strategies of inquiry and systematization. *Journal of the Society for Ethnomusicology* 34, no. 1 (Winter): 75–95.

Novack, C. 1990. *Sharing the dance: Contact improvisation and American culture*. Madison, WI: University of Wisconsin Press.

Parker, M. 1984. Benesh movement notation. In *Dance notation for beginners*, edited by Ann Kipling Brown and Monica Parker, 79–168. London: Dance Books Ltd.

Pe Benito, M. R. 2003. Indigenous peoples, indigenous Filipinos! In *Info mapper. A Publication on surveys, mapping, and resource information technology*, vol. X.

Pertierra, R. 1995. *Philippine localities and global perspectives: Essays on society and culture*. Quezon City: Ateneo de Manila University Press.

————. 2002. *The work of culture*. Manila: De La Salle University Press.

Pfeiffer, W. 1976. *Indigenous, folk, modern Filipino music*. Dumaguete City: Silliman Music Foundation, Inc.

Pressing, J. 1988. *Improvisation: Methods and models in generative processes in music*, edited by John Sloboda. Oxford: Clarendon.

Qureshi, R. B. 1986. *Sufi music of India and Pakistan: Sound, context and meaning in Qawwali*. Cambridge: Cambridge University Press.

Railton, P. 2005. Ideology. *The Oxford companion to Philosophy*. Oxford University Press. *Oxford Reference Online*. 18 January 2007. http://www.oxfordreference.com/views/ENTRY.html?subview=Main &entry=t116.e1176.

Redfield, J., M. Murphy, and S. Timbers. 2002. *God and the evolving universe*. New York: Jeremy Tarcher/Putnam.

Reid, L. 2003. The range and diversity of vocalic systems in Asian languages. A paper presented to the Symposium: A search in Asia for a new theory of music. University of the Philippines.

Reyes-Aquino, F. 1946. *Philippine national dances*. New York: Silver Burdett Co.

———. 1953. *Philippine folk dances I-VI*. Manila: Francisca Reyes-Aquino.

Rice, T. 1987. Toward the remodeling of ethnomusicology. *Ethnomusicology* (Illinois) 31, no. 3 (Autumn): 469–88.

Riviere, H. 1993. On rhythmical marking in music. *Ethnomusicology* (Illinois) 37, no. 2 (Spring/Summer): 243–50.

Robequain, C. 1959. *Malaya, Indonesia, Borneo, and the Philippines*, translated by E. Laborde. 3rd ed. London: Longmans.

Rosaldo, R. 1989. Introduction: Grief and a headhunter's rage. In *Culture and truth: The remaking of social analysis*, 1–21. Boston: Beacon Press.

Salazar, Z. 2004. *Liktao at epiko: Ang takip ng tapayang libingan ng Libmanan, Camarines Sur*. Quezon City: Palimbagan ng Lahi.

———. 2006. *Ang Pilipinong Banua/Banwa sa mundong Melano-Polynesiano*. Quezon City: Bagong Kasaysayan.

Sam, Sam Ang. 1990. *The pin peat ensemble: Its history, music and context*. Wesleyan University, 1988. UMI (University Microfilm International) dissertation Information Service.

Santiago, A., and N. Tiangco. 1991. *Makabagong balarilang Filipino*. 3rd ed. Manila: Rex Bookstore.

Seeger, A. 1980. Sing for your sister: The structure and performance of Suya Akia. In *The Ethnography of musical performance*, edited by Norma McLeod and Marcia Herndon, 7–42. Norwood, PA: Norwood Editions.

———. 1987. *Why Suya sing: A musical anthropology of an Amazonian people*. Cambridge: Cambridge University Press.

Shepherd, J. 1993. Difference and power in music. In *Musicology and difference: Gender and sexuality in music scholarship*, edited by Ruth Solie, 46–65. Berkeley: University of California Press.

Shore, B. 1991. Twice-Born, Once conceived: Meaning construction and cultural cognition. *American anthropologist*, new series 93, no. 1: 9–27.

Stokes, M. 1997. *Ethnicity, identity and music: The musical construction of place*. New York: Berg Publishers.

Tenzer, M. 2000. *Gamelan gong Kebyar: The art of twentieth-century Balinese music*. Chicago and London: The University of Chicago Press.

———, ed. 2006. *Analytical studies in world music*. New York: Oxford University Press.

Tolentino, H. 2005. Binanog dance: Glimpses of transformation. *Palayag: Proceedings of the 14th Conference of West Visayan History and Culture*, 41–63.

Tope, L. R. 1998. Appropriating language: Language and nationalism in Southeast Asia. *Diliman Review 46*, nos. 3–4: 25–40.

Trimillos, R. 1972. Expanding music experience to fit today's world. *Music Educators Journal 59*, no. 2: 90–94.

———. 1999. Gender in dance performance: Constructions and paradigms from the Asia-Pacific region. *1998 Philippine International Dance Conference: Dance in Revolution, Revolution in Dance*, 145–54, edited by Basilio Esteban Villaruz. Manila: World Dance Alliance-Philippines.

Turino, T. 1990. Structure, context and strategy in musical ethnography. *Ethnomusicology* (Illinois) 34, no. 3 (Fall): 399–412.

Turner, V. 1986. *The anthropology of performance*. New York: Performing Art Journal Publications.

Villaruz, B. E. 1995. Philippines. In *The dances of ASEAN*, edited by Zainal Abbidin Tinggal. Quezon City: ASEAN Commitee on Culture and Information.

Villaruz, B. E., and R. Obusan. 1994. The ethnic tradition. *The CCP encyclopedia of Philippine art*, vol. 5. Manila: Cultural Center of the Philippines.

Wacquant, L. 2011. Habitus as topic and tool: Reflections on becoming a prizefighter. *Qualitative Research in Psychology* (London) 8: 81–92.

Wade, Bonnie. 2004. *Thinking musically: Experiencing music, experiencing culture*. New York City: Oxford University Press.

Waxer, L. 2002. *The city of musical memory: Salsa, record, grooves, and popular culture in Cali, Columbia*. Middletown, Connecticut: Wesleyan University Press

Williams, D. 1976–1977. An exercise in applied personal anthropology. *Dance Research Journal* IX, no. 1 (Fall/Winter): 16–30.

———. 1983. A new paradigm in movement research. UCLA *Journal of the Association of Graduate Dance Ethnologists*, vol. 7 (Spring).

———. 1991. *Ten lectures on theories of the dance*. Metuchen, N.J., & London: The Scarecrow Press, Inc.

———. 1999. The Roots of semasiology. *Journal for the Anthropological Study of Human movement* (New York University) Special issue 10, no. 3: 109–80.

Yepes, V. 1996. *Historia natural de las Islas Bisayas del padre Alzina/Victoria Yepes: Alcina, Francisco Ignacio, 1610–1674.* Madrid: Consejo Superior de Investigaciones Cientificas.

———. 1998. *Historia sobrenatural de las Islas Bisayas: Segunda parte de la historia de las islas e indios Bisayas, del Padre Alzina, Manila, 1668–1670.* Madrid: Consejo Superior de Investigaciones Cientificas.

Zizek, S. 1992. *The sublime object of ideology.* London and New York: Verso.

Index